Man Hunter in Indian Country
George Redman Tucker

by Norman Wayne Brown

EAKIN PRESS ⅴ🔼P Fort Worth, Texas
www.EakinPress.com

Dedication

To my wife Bettie for her support. To authors Bill Neal, Bill O'Ne-al, Chuck and Pat Parsons, and Mike Tower, friends always. To my fellow Disabled American Veterans and to the memory of my son Jason Wayne Brown.

Contents

Foreword

I have known Norman Wayne Brown for a number of years and collaborated with him on several projects. He is an exceptional historical researcher, following clues wherever they may lead, letting them decide the truth. In doing so, he often is as surprised as his readers when myths are separated from reality. *Man Hunter in Indian Country* is a work wherein Brown, try as he might, simply could not make his protagonist, nor anyone who he associated with, a shiny paragon of virtue. It's a problem people have been having with those occupying Indian Territory law enforcement for years.

For instance, in the opinion of Indian Territory pioneer D. C. Pendergrass, from an interview preserved in the Indian and Pioneer Files Archives and Manuscripts Division of the Oklahoma State Historical Society: "There were two kinds of marshals: brave ones who tried to do, and did, their part to enforce the laws; and cowardly ones who turned crooked because they were afraid to enforce the laws."

Early Indian Territory newspaper editor Tom C. Fields was of like mind. In Field's estimation, all the territory's deputy U. S. marshals were bullies who used alias whiskey warrants to fatten their pocketbooks by arresting men who were not criminals. And, while there was some veracity to the charge, the allegation did not apply to every officer or incident. However, that truth did not stop Fields from using a January 1894 complaint filed against U. S. Deputy Marshal H. H. (Hilly) Lindsey. Briefly described on the front page of the *Purcell Register*, dated January 5, 1894, the facts of the incident are Deputy Lindsey, fully empowered to inspect any luggage he found suspicious, took possession of a traveling salesman's valise after the man refused to unlock it. Then, Lindsay cut it open. On hearing of the episode and that Lindsey had failed to find any contraband, Fields wrote a hateful editorial condemning not only Lindsey, but all federal deputies.

In the late 1880s, Indian Territory was a sewer of criminality. Lawlessness was so bad the combined budgets of the Fort Smith based Western District Court of Arkansas, which had jurisdiction over the territory, dominated nearly one third of the federal budget. A beleaguered Congress decided the way to relieve the budget was to place the services of a district court closer to the outlaws infesting the territory. To this end, in March 1889, President Benjamin Harrison signed acts creating the Federal District Court of Indian Territory at Muskogee, Indian Territory and the Eastern District Court of Texas at Paris, Texas. Both courts were opened within weeks.

At Paris, incumbent Marshal Richard B. Reagan sent out a call for men who could ride, shoot, and make responsible decisions independently. One of the first to answer Reagan's call was George Redman Tucker, a constable at the Red River border town of Spanish Fort, Texas, who was neither saint nor sinner, but a sufficient mixture of both to survive his times. It was Tucker who Brown first determined to glorify. Then, reality got in the way.

Normally, finding a character's written memoirs is the best thing that can happen to an author attempting to present a man's life story. However, in Tucker's case, the first thing Brown discovered was that Tucker was not one to let truth get in the way of a good tale. And, the more Brown checked Tucker's version against secondary sources, the more apparent it became the man often minimized or omitted key details or enlarged his part in an event. Worse, Tucker did so randomly, for reasons known only to himself.

What Brown finally recognized is that, while large sections of the found manuscript were accurate and verifiable, other, smaller sections were not and had to be explained. The careful research undertaken to handle this treatment of misinformation led to the discovery of new facts, particularly in Wyoming's Johnson County Range War.

It was in the Johnson County Range War episode of Tucker's life that Brown first came across the names of a core group of men associated with the Eastern District of Texas and later Indian Territory district courts to which Tucker was a member. Those men were: Tom Smith, Jeff Mynatt, Dave Booker, Bill Little, and Buck Garrett. Although many of their adventures were alone or with other deputies, these six men were as inseparable as cousins and each influenced Tucker's life as surely as a hammer affects the nature of a nail. So much of their life and times is found amid these pages too.

I could go on and attempt to justify Tucker and his code of ethics. And, maybe, in the process even turn him into a sympathetic character. But, such an exercise is not important or appropriate. George Tucker was what he was. He made no apologies, nor did he feel it was necessary for later generations to understand his actions. Even if Tucker had a problem with truth, Norman Wayne Brown, with *Man Hunter in Indian Territory*, has pieced together a biography which gives us an accurate glimpse of this long ago man and his time. So, sit back a little deeper in your chair and get ready to enjoy a word picture of how George Redman Tucker and crew believed the Old West really was and how it ended.

— Mike Tower
historian and award winning author

Acknowledgments

My sincere thanks to Mike Tower for sharing his extensive knowledge of Indian Territory as well as both sides of the law. Mike spent countless hours of research and provided insight as to how things were back before Indian Territory became part of Oklahoma. Also thanks to Chuck Parsons for his help in various aspects of this project. Thanks to Kurt House for his information on the death of Deputy U.S. Marshal Jeff Mynatt and photo of Mynatt's pistol. Thanks to Tommy Tucker, a grandson of Marshal Tucker, who visited him a few years before his death. And thanks to Justin Barnes for photographs of a pistol handed down to him from George Tucker. Thanks also to Bill O'Neal for his recommendation. There are countless others who provided assistance and you have me sincerest appreciation.

Introduction

Deputy U.S. Marshal George Redman Tucker was a well-known lawman in his heyday and was only one of many deputy marshals who worked against the criminal element in the wild and unsettled Oklahoma Indian Territory. Therefore, this work is extended to include the "law game" played by many of the fearless deputy marshals who were friends and associates of Tucker and who helped tame the lawlessness in Oklahoma's Indian Country.

Those early deputy marshals drew no salary prior to July 1st of 1896. They were paid a small fee for serving a warrant and received additional pay for travel. Sometimes they collected a reward posted by the railroad, local, or state government. If a federal reward was posted the deputy was not allowed to file a claim. To add insult to injury, the deputy's boss, the U. S. marshal, deducted twenty-five percent from their travel pay. But, they went ahead and put themselves in harm's way on a daily basis for reasons known only to those who served. Perhaps it was "Just trying to make a living."

Deputy George Tucker and fired deputies Tom Smith, Jeff Mynatt, Dave Booker, and Bill Little, along with future deputy Buck Garrett, a posseman at the time, were hired by Tom Smith to travel to Wyoming in early 1892 to dole out frontier justice to rustlers and outlaws. They were referred to as regulators, invaders, assassins, hired killers, or hired gunmen. Amazingly, Tucker claimed he went to Wyoming as a hired gun still wearing his deputy U. S. Marshal badge. The other deputies had allegedly been fired prior to being hired for the Wyoming trip.

There are a number of other deputies who served in addition to the "Wyoming Five." They were deputies Joe Letherman, Los Hart, Sam Williams, Jim Chancelor, W. W. "Bill" McCall, George Stewart, Selden Lindsey, and a host of others.

An interview conducted on February 17, 1937, by federal field worker Jennie Selfridge, assisted greatly in establishing a time-line for formidable lawman tucker. That interview was published in the *Indian Pioneer Papers* as part of the Indian Pioneer History project for Oklahoma and was indexed as Interview #4126. In addition to the *Indian Pioneer* papers was a manuscript written by Tucker and listed in the John Alley Collection: Box M-8: Folder 7-15, Western History Library at the University of Oklahoma, at Norman. Those pages had been edited, with pen and ink corrections and notations by Mr. John Alley. In comparing the two documents it was noted the interview with Selfridge was identical to some of George Tucker's manuscript. However, the Selfridge interview was cut short with nothing mentioned of the regulators involved in the Wyoming Cattleman's War of 1892.

In addition, many Tucker gunfights, such as the accidental killing of an innocent boy or the unpleasantness of hogs unearthing a baby's murdered body were not mentioned in the Selfridge interview. She omitted well over one-half of Tucker's manuscript. Moreover, the omission of Selfridge piqued my curiosity. Was the difference the result of trying not to offend? Or was it political correctness? Or was the exclusion of data simply the popular thing to do at the time the document was re-written?

In 1936 historians were looking for the up-beat, the pioneer spirit. They wanted history to show folks overcoming long odds on very little so as to boost state morale. The interviewers were given a preset list of questions designed to gather specific data. This was a popular time in Oklahoma for naming outlaws and lawmen because very little had been collected previous to the Indian and Pioneer interviews.

Because most of those questioned were of advanced age, historians saw the process as a last chance to talk to the founders of the state about what conditions were really like. But specific crimes were avoided as being too risky in terms of liability; with slander bringing lawsuits. And, too, as to participation in the Wyoming War, one has to remember Frank Canton, who died in 1927, had been very influential in "Okie" politics and he didn't want any but his own version of the Johnson County War and state leaders did not want to see anything which would reflect badly on admired men. Another example is Fred Waite who participated in the Lincoln County, New Mexico War. In the entirety of the Indian and Pioneer collection there is but a single reference, with no details to his involvement.

I know revisionist history is not popular with some, but it is instances such as these which require a fresh and unvarnished look.

I say let the old men tell it like it was; not as we want it to be.

George Redman Tucker wrote his autobiography around 1934 when he was seventy-nine-years-old. His death certificate lists his date of birth as August 19, 1855. The Indian Pioneer Project profile gave his place of birth as Franklin County, Ark., which is correct. However, his father, William's, place of birth was Kentucky and not Tennessee as reported. He did reside in Tennessee before removing his family to Arkansas.

The profile also reported his mother Cathleen as being born in Texas, but she was actually born in Tennessee and died in Texas. A possible reason for the erroneous information was that the field workers received their data from the interviewee or if senile, their spokesperson. Tucker was at least eighty-three-years-old when the field worker conducted the interview. However, it is highly likely that she used his autobiography without actually conducting a face to face interview with him.

During the research phase of this project, a number of lessons learned about these early pioneering adventurers included their ability to recall events and people. But their recall should be taken with a grain of salt. Again, just because it was said and just because it was written, does not, in itself, make it factual. It is very likely these salty old pioneer lawmen would not let truth stand in the way of a good story. While we seek the truth, it is not always as one thinks it is or should be when we visit the ghosts of these almost forgotten trail blazers.

Moreover, just because they were lawmen does not make them shining stars. Many played both sides of the law and justified their actions with just trying to make a living. The shining star was sometimes a tarnished badge. With that in mind, the following chapters will endeavor to tell the true story of some of those pioneer lawmen. Broad consideration was given to federal census records, federal court records, news articles, various books, family information, interviews with experts on the Indian Territory, Judge Parker's western division of Arkansas, and the United States Marshal Service, as well as the breaking up of Parker's vast jurisdiction of the entire Indian country.

There are many misconceptions about life on the western frontier, local law enforcement, and the United States Marshal Service. The western fiction writers and western movie makers often betray the United States Marshal as a gun toting, hard riding gunslinger who gets his man. This could not be further from the truth. The marshal's position was a political appointment and his deputies were solely responsible for serving warrants, and transporting prisoners. The marshal had administrative duties and few were active in the field.

George Redman Tucker left his unpublished autobiography as a firsthand account of his life as a man hunter behind a badge. His story has been compared to archived records, new articles, and other sources in an attempt to support his claims. At least one incident Tucker wrote about lays self-claim of doing the unthinkable and that was turning arrested prisoners over to a lynch mob without any resistance what-so-ever. The research trail led to an interesting conclusion. Some information was almost unbelievable based on what really happened concerning the Paris gunmen who went to Wyoming as regulators for the Cattlemen's Association.

Is there truth in reading our western history? Some say that history thus far recorded is flawed and somewhat false. The retelling of stories become altered and distorted. That makes the research part of any written history extremely important. But getting the correct story told is what really counts.

Chapter One

The Early Years in Arkansas

The ground was frozen so the women dug one grave for two murdered men.

The mountainous area north of the Arkansas River in Franklin County, Arkansas, has always provided a breathtaking view, especially in the springtime. The Tucker family could sit on the front porch and view the Boston Mountains rising into the eastern sky. Daylight would be all around before the sun rose over the nearby mountain peaks. It was here, near the Mulberry River that William M. Tucker and his wife Catherine settled down to raise a family and make a living raising crops and livestock.[1]

Life was good and crops grew well in this region. An abundance of native grasslands, plentiful rainfall and numerous streams helped fatten the livestock as they multiplied. The area

The Boston Mountains, shown here are where George Tucker was born and raised.
Photo from author's collection.

was at peace when their seventh child was born on August 29, 1855. After William and Catherine agreed on this son's name, George Redman Tucker was written in the family Bible. The boy was part Cherokee, part French, and part Irish. George was four years younger than his brother, William H. "Bill" Tucker, and later in life they would remain very close and ride the river together.[2]

Growing up near the towering mountains in western Arkansas, George Tucker and his brothers, like most mountain men, became proficient with firearms in an effort to keep food, that being wild game, on the table. Powder and shot were not something one wasted in those days as

George Redman Tucker played the law game for half a century. In the 1920s, he was described as old, wearing a three-piece suit, gray Stetson, carrying a large pocket watch and cane, and wearing a gun belt with a large Colt pistol with notches on the handle. His was a bad man, not evil but tough. *Photo courtesy of Dickerson Research Center, National Cowboy & Western Heritage Museum, Oklahoma City, Oklahoma.*

money was always in short supply and few trading posts or mercantile stores existed nearby. But, all was about to change as the calendar on the wall was flipped to the year 1861. That's when the war between these United States came, like a hoard of locust on northwestern Arkansas.

The United States had split almost down the middle over slavery and state rights. The Tuckers, like many, did not own slaves nor did they believe it right to put anyone into bondage. But many in the south did own slaves and had they not, it is likely the war between the states would not have taken place. On the other hand, most southern folks did not believe the government had a right to tell people what they could and could not do with their property and lives. After all, those who did own slaves were usually wealthy and they saw slaves as property. Many would proclaim,

"If Lincoln wanted them freed there should be compensation."

The William Tucker family did not choose sides and none of his sons were willing to pick up arms against the Union. Nor were they inclined to support the Union to take up arms against kinfolks and southern neighbors.

Other Tucker relatives living in the area did take up arms on both sides of the conflict. William's brother, Doctor P. Tucker, who lived in the same county of Franklin, Arkansas, joined the Confederate infantry. Just to the north was Madison County and they were unionists. George and Doctor's cousins, John and Robert Tucker, joined on the Union side and served in the Missouri cavalry. But bushwhackers roamed in that neck of the woods and those renegades did not discriminate between causes. They picked on anyone they came across, especially those who were weaker and fewer in numbers.[3]

John A. Tucker was one of George Tucker's uncles and a brother to his father William. It was believed that he was the victim of not only a double murder but also a double burying. In other words, two men were said to be buried in the same grave and were named Burk and Tucker.

Mrs. Sibyl Carter and Alva Burk solicited funds to erect a headstone for the two men without knowing what their first names were or when they were killed and buried. In 1975, they did erect a headstone at the Bollinger Cemetery, located ten miles south of

Two men, William Burk and John A. Tucker were buried in the same grave after being murdered by unknown assailants and buried in Bolinger Cemetery, Madison County, Arkansas. *Photo courtesy of J. D. Little.*

Kingston in Madison County, Arkansas.[4]

What were the facts known about these two men? What led to their demise? The what, where, when, and how came to mind over this little mystery.

The commonly accepted story is Burk and Tucker were shot and killed by a group of renegades as they watered their herd of horses on the King's River in Madison County. That was in the winter of 1864. Most of the grown men were off to war so the women had to bury them. The ground was frozen so they dug one hole and planted both Burk and Tucker in the same grave.

A number of versions are floating around in that country. The most likely of these stories to be a factual account was the fact that William Joseph Burk and John Abraham Tucker, being killed by bushwhackers and buried in the same grave, came from sworn testimony. A daughter of John A. Tucker, Lucinda Tucker Casey and John's widow, Sarah Tucker, made an affidavit stating they saw rebels shoot and kill Joseph Burk and testified that he was wearing a uniform. Widow Sarah, on her pension application, stated "Joseph Burk was in the cavalry of the Southern Army."

However, no archived records support her claim. Actually, he was a member of a Captain Blevins' "Home Guard," an independent unit. The federal pension of the Widow Burk was denied. The two women further testified that Burk and Tucker were killed on September 6, 1864. This date, placing the shooting in the fall, would discount the frozen ground story. It seems the truth of the matter was the women just were not up to digging two graves.[5]

Due to the unsettled nature of life in northwestern Arkansas during the Civil War, one can see why many families feared for their safety and had to constantly be looking over their shoulder, not knowing if or when a hot ball from a rifle or pistol would kill them and send them to an early reward in the Promised Land. The William Tucker family decided to seek sanctuary away from the hot bed of violence in northern Arkansas and Texas was the place they believed to be a sanctuary location.

Chapter Two

Wagon Train to Texas

On the south side of the crossing, there were six dead men, lying as they had fallen in fighting.

Franklin County, Arkansas, is one of those counties with two courthouses. Even to this day they remain separated. The main center of government is a two-story courthouse on the north side of the Arkansas River in the town of Ozark and the secondary center is south of the river in the little town of Charleston.

Crossing the Arkansas River was not an easy task in the early days and most business was conducted on one side or the other. If one resided south of the river, he bought his groceries there, conducted courthouse business there, died there, and was buried in a cemetery on the south side and *vice versa* for the north side. This

When the Tucker Wagon train made the difficult crossing of the Arkansas River at Ozark, there was no bridge and a ferry was not used until a few years later. The ferry was named "The Twin City." *Photo from author's collection.*

5

was logical for if one crossed the river it had to be by boat, floating the wagons, or swimming, as no ferries operated in the vicinity. If one went by foot, they either walked to the Charleston courthouse or knew where to borrow a horse. The county of Franklin is about thirty miles east of Van Buren and Fort Smith, where Hanging Judge Isaac Parker's court was located.[1]

George Redman Tucker and his family lived north of the river, dividing Franklin County almost in the center. They lived at Beech Grove, about ten miles north of the county seat of Ozark. His father William and his brothers had brought their families from Tennessee and there were many other settlers in the country who also hailed from the Volunteer State.

However, William was not originally from Tennessee. He was born in Kentucky. Moreover, he had also been to Texas even before it became a Republic. In fact, it was there; probably in the Red River country, that he married his first wife Catherine. Their oldest son John R. Tucker was born there in 1841. Records also indicate Catherine was a native of Texas or possibly Tennessee. At any rate, by the time the Civil War began, the Tuckers were Arkansawyers.[2]

George had no more education than the average pioneer child in those days. He attended a one-room log cabin, called "Beech Grove School" and was taught by Mr. B. J. Weldon. Actually, George was probably referring to Bartly J. Welton.[3] There were twenty-five or thirty students in attendance at the school and that was the only school ever attended by George. He never forgot Mr. Welton and it is probable that this teacher instilled a sense of pride and self-worthiness within George and made him the product of his own curiosity. The reason was that George believed himself to be well-equipped in self education and personal experience, after being exposed to the harsher aspects of life.[4]

When the Civil War broke out, George was too young to serve or realize its importance or to know the reasons behind the sad state of affairs, where brother fought against brother, families split apart and where those who refused to fight were branded traitors, or deserters. But, he, like many, was a product of that tragedy. The aftermath brought forth a breed of mankind that was lawless and put little value on human life.[5]

The county was split in its allegiance to the North and South during the Civil War. To the north, around the Madison County country was the Union section of Arkansas, where a lot of settlers were from northern states who pledged allegiance to the Union. To the south lived those with southern sympathies. This Tucker family decided it was not their fight. As the conflict progressed, things began getting pretty hot, for the bushwhackers were operating throughout the country.

Approximately 5,000 Union troops, under the command of General Francis Herron, arrived in Madison County on January 7, 1863. The soldiers pursued bands of Confederate guerrillas operating in the area and chased bushwhackers who were roaming the countryside. In January of 1863, members of Co. G, 8th Missouri Calvary, under the command of Lieutenant Colonel Elias Briggs arrived in the mix and the war in Arkansas was on.[6]

The Tucker family must have seen the handwriting on the wall as they, along with about fifteen other families, decided it was best to leave that dangerous place in Arkansas and head for Texas. Being George's father, William, had lived in Texas, back in the late 1830s, he was probably elected to lead the party.

Forming a wagon train to travel hundreds of miles over unknown trails or roads was not an easy task to undertake. Many

The Tucker family along with an unspecified number of neighbors left Franklin County, Arkansas, by wagon trail and relocated to Red River County, Texas. *Photo from Charles and Catherine Schulze Collection, Irving Public Library, Irving, Texas.*

preparations had to be made and most had to be made far in advance of the scheduled departure time. Even though George was only eight or nine years-old at the time, he remembered the preparations being made before leaving Franklin County.

Almost the entire group consisted of farmers who, in addition to personal goods, had cows, goats, and hogs to take with them to Texas. The cows could be tied behind the wagons or trailed off to the side without fear of being lost. Hogs were another matter as, although they could be herded, they were slow and difficult to manage. The many brush-lined miles to Texas necessitated they be sold, butchered; or caged. The latter created a horrible stench around the wagons.[7]

George referred to a covered wagon used in this move as a "Nach," or a tarpaulin wagon. That is, they traveled in what was later called a wagon-cloth wagon, which means that a tarpaulin or canvas was stretched over some framework on the wagon bed, making a sort of improvised house on wheels. The wagons carried bedding, clothing, pots, pans, dishes, shot and powder, and food. Tools and other items were attached to the sides of the wagon. Food included bacon, coffee, flour, sugar, salt, corn meal, rice, and dried beans. Wooden furniture such as tables and chairs were left behind as they would make them after settling in Texas.

There were, as George recalled, between sixty and seventy-five people, counting the large number of children, who made that trip to Texas with the Tucker family.[8]

They traveled from around the Boston Township south to Ozark and crossed the wide and deep Arkansas River. They attached logs to the wagon sides and floated the wagons across as there was no ferry, bridge, or low water crossing.

They were reminded of the state of affairs brought on by the war. On the south side of the crossing they saw six dead men, lying as they had fallen in fighting. They had been dead for a time as their legs were rotted off at the knees, or just above their boots. They knew those men had been Union soldiers, for they wore boots. Confederate soldiers in Arkansas did not wear them according to George.

Evidently bushwhackers had attacked them at the crossing and no one had taken the trouble to dispose of the bodies. The image of those dead men remained with George for a long time and he remembered the scene as "indeed a squally time." George expressed it as, "Everybody was dodging. No man knew who his real friend was. Everybody, that is, the men, went armed. It was too dangerous otherwise; and was bad enough if they did."[9]

They made that bug-out trip in the spring of 1864. A trip like that was a major move and families had to prepare well in advance. Crops had to be gathered in the late summer and fall. Hogs had to be killed in the winter months to prevent the spoiling of the meat. Hams and bacon were cured and hung in the smokehouse over smoldering coals. Corn was shelled from the cob and either taken to a "grist mill" for grinding or was hand-ground. Spare corn was shelled and bagged as whole grain in sacks or baskets. Corn would not spoil but would get weevils which could be sifted out. Other seeds were stored for the trip for planting in the new land. George did not remember how long it took.

It was approximately 300 miles from Franklin County, Arkansas, to Clarksville in Red River County, Texas, the second county west of the Arkansas line and lay just below the Red River and Indian country. So, considering the roads, conveyance, and need to rest animals, the journey probably took a month or longer.

The Tucker family settled down in Red River County and all was well for a year. Then, in the last year of the war, 1865, George's mother, Catherine, died. George was only ten-years-old at the time.[10]

He moved in with his sister, Martha Ann, who was almost eighteen-years-old (born July 10, 1847) and her husband, W. A. Knox, another farmer. George had little memory of his stay with these in-laws but he did remember that shortly after being taken in, the entire family moved back to Franklin County and landed back on the old farm at Beech Grove. By that time George was age fifteen according to the 1870 federal census records.

Upon returning George noted that times were almost as dangerous as during the war and said "it was not long before the rackets began." It is unclear exactly what his meaning was about rackets. It seemed to be a bit of "Hell raising" by some unfriendly neighbors.

George wrote that at this time he went back to Texas with his brother, being said sibling was old enough to marry. He was referring to his brother William H. "Bill" Tucker and his wife, Livicia Ogden Tucker, and their two small boys. Bill and Livicia were married in Ozark, Arkansas, before leaving for Texas.

Livicia Ogden was born January 1, 1855, in Franklin County, Arkansas, and grew to womanhood there and married William "Bill" Tucker, a Tennessean by birth, on March 31, 1872.

The young couple followed the plantation way of life for a time and then when they had two small sons, Dowdy and David, they listened to the call of the west and went to Hillsboro, Hill County, Texas, along the Brazos River. Still following farming, ranching and stock raising, Bill Tucker discovered that western Hill County lacked the rainfall necessary for raising crops so he branched out a little each year and finally reached Spanish Fort, Texas, directly south of the Red River. Some years later, at Petersburg, Indian Territory, he opened a mercantile store, but it was some time before his wife could be reconciled to crossing the river and making her home in what she proclaimed as "uncivilized Indian Territory."

The move to Texas probably took place during the winter of 1876. This is based upon William's son, George David, being born in Arkansas during July of 1876. Therefore, the winter of 1876 seems to be valid for their move to Hill County, Texas. Here, George and Bill rented some cotton land and worked it, staying about a year. He remembered picking cotton there, an activity normally conducted in the fall of the year. But, it was a dry year and they made a poor crop.[11]

Chapter Three

Fleeing Texas as a Fugitive

Friends of Faulkner started after me, but I stood them off with my old cap and fuse pistol.

It was in Hill County, in the year 1877, at a place called "Gulley Rock," where young George Redman Tucker got himself into a pickle by being mislead into what he described as a "snake-pit." While gunfights were common in the old days, George called this one his first serious altercation.

Fighting with guns in the wild old West was rarely like on the silver screen in those Hollywood "B" western movies like the 1952 movie *High Noon* starring Gary Cooper. Of course, there were exceptions such as Wild Bill Hickok facing off Dave Tutt in Springfield, Missouri. Tutt missed but Hickok's bullet was true and it was one shot, one kill. It boiled down to whom was a better shot.[1]

"There was a man known only as Hill and he had a reputation as being a mean and unsavory character; a "low fellow" in the neighborhood according to George. But, George fell in with him and Hill took him to a saloon located out in the country, not far from Gulley Rock. Before they went, Hill borrowed a gun and gave it to George.

After George and Hill arrived, Hill seemed familiar with the place so he lead the way inside the little saloon. There were a number of men inside the establishment and almost immediately Hill became engaged in a heated argument with a customer named Faulkner.

After a while, the argument escalated and both Faulkner and Hill drew knives and started swinging the sharp blades at each other. Both men were holding their own and both were bleeding all over the floor. Then, Faulkner's knife slashed toward Hill's head and as it made contact, raked across his skull, making a grinding noise.

George believed Hill had gotten the worst of the fight and figured he was so badly injured that he would bleed to death. That's

11

when George figured he would be next, so he decided it was time to make a run for it. As he fled from the saloon, a group of men started running after him. They were allegedly friends of Faulkner. George saw that they were gaining on him steadily so he stopped and faced them as he removed the old "cap and fuse" pistol, probably a flintlock pistol, from his belt and they came to a halt as none were carrying firearms.

George stood them off and the pistol was primed and loaded with shot. The gun was ready to fire. All George had to do was pick a target and pull the trigger. But, for some reason he did not fire. "I do not know why I did not shoot unless it was because I was too scared," George explained.[2]

Some of the crowd inside the saloon had thrown Hill into a vacant room thinking he would bleed to death. But Hill surprised them by getting up and kicking out the glass in the window and climbing out. He came running up the road as fast as he could but, according to George, it wasn't very fast. "He was as bloody as a stuck pig and I ran out to meet him."

Hill then took the pistol from George's hand, turned and aimed it at Faulkner as he pulled the trigger. The pistol fired with a loud bang and Faulkner fell to the ground without movement, apparently dead. The pistol was loaded with lead shot and it scattered when he fired and also hit two men of Faulkner's gang, wounding them seriously.

George admitted to being scared far more seriously in this affray than anything ever before in his life. Of course, being shook up would be an understatement as this was the first time he had ever seen a man actually shot and probably killed before his own eyes and probably the first time he has been chased by a group of toughs with killing on their minds.[3]

George and Hill were on foot but they eluded the gang. They ran, even with Hill seriously injured, until they were out of sight of the saloon and the hostile crowd. As they slowed to a a walk, George told Hill they should go to his brother Bill's place, so they made their way slowly to Bill's farm. This was George Tucker's first brawl.

After questioning Hill, George learned that Hill and Faulkner had a personal feud going on between them for a number of years. They learned later that, to their surprise, Faulkner had not been killed and eventually recovered from his wounds, but they never dreamed that he would ever walk again on that day when they fled from the vicinity of that saloon near Gulley Rock.

Faulkner turned out to be James A. Faulkner, a merchant in Hill County, at the time of the fight. The gunshot did not kill him and apparently, no one ever shot him again. He didn't get thrown off a horse and break his neck and he didn't drown crossing any rivers. Nor did he die in bed with his boots off. Ironically, on July 18, 1928, on a state highway at Waco, Texas, Mr. James A. Faulkner was struck by a auto truck and all of his ribs were crushed on his left side. He died within minutes.

It is ironic that per the 1870 federal census records, James Faulkner was living next door to a George W. Tucker but, apparently a different Tucker as that George was listed as being from Alabama. Mr. Faulkner was born January 14, 1843, and came out of Georgia. He was an early pioneer of Texas and resident of Hill County for a long time. His mother was a McMichael and the McMichael and Faulkner families were early settlers in Texas.[4]

Once George Tucker and Hill arrived at brother Bill's house, Bill told George and Hill that the law may come looking for them and advised they get out of the country. He gave George a small amount of traveling money and George and Hill started traveling on foot until they reached the railroad tracks at Fort Smith. Then they started walking the ties through Fort Smith and about another forty miles eastward, reaching George Tucker's old home in Franklin County, Arkansas. That's when he and Hill parted company and George never heard "hide nor hair" of Hill after that. He figured Hill would survive, being he was a tough fellow.[5]

George did not return to his father's place in Franklin County, but went to a cousin's place, Andrew Jackson "Jack" Tucker. He was a deputy sheriff of Franklin County. Jack was older than George by six years and was living near the town of Ozark. Jack was a son of Starling Tucker and Starling was a brother to George's father, making George and Jack first cousins. Jack would take his wife and children and move to Montague County, Texas, before 1880.

Meanwhile, he took George in and was told what had happened. He advised George to stay there until things blew over a bit. George took the advice being he had no other place to run. He still had the old pistol obtained from Hill which he had carried all the way from Texas. Jack told him it would be a good idea to get rid of that gun so George did. Hill never told George from whom he had borrowed the gun so there was no point in trying to find the owner. Anyway, Hill cost someone back in Texas their gun. Being cousin Jack was a deputy sheriff of Franklin County, George was in a good position to learn if any attempt was being made to bring charges and try to locate him.[6]

After George had been hiding out with cousin and lawman Jack Tucker for a while, he decided to ride into Ozark one day. George had no horse and Jack had no extra mounts so George rode double behind Jack on his horse. They had been in town for about an hour when a local lawyer named Dick Berry approached Jack and asked if he had heard that young George Tucker had gotten into trouble down in Texas? Jack replied that he had not heard anything about it. "Well, they are after him now," said Berry.

Nothing more was said and soon Jack and George left town. They had no idea how or when attorney Jack Berry had obtained his information but it seemed to be accurate. George had been hiding out at Jack's place for three months so it was time to make preparations to flee to another hiding place.[7]

George was dead broke and had no transportation except his feet. So, what was he to do? Where could he go that would be the least likely place the law would look for him? George decided that would be right back to his brother's farm in Hill County, Texas. Right under the law dogs' noses. So George packed his kit of meager belongings and took to the road again, walking directly to Hill County, Texas, which is about fifty miles south of Fort Worth and about four hundred miles from Ozark, Arkansas. While not specified by George Tucker, it is likely he caught rides with wagon travelers and or a south bound train.

When George arrived at his brother Bill's place, he kept a low profile, working on the farm with Bill, chopping, cultivating, and picking cotton at harvest time. Things were quite and he heard no more of the attempted murder episode of which George, in reality had not harmed anyone. At best, he was an accomplice in the fight, but iffy at best. That could have played a role in the law forgetting about the incident.[8]

George remained with his brother and his family for quite a

spell and then they agreed to move to Peoria, in the western part of Hill County. They stopped at the Bragg farm where Bill obtained a renter's agreement with the owners and planted a crop of cotton. They failed to take into consideration that the further west one goes, the drier it becomes. This was a mistake, as that part of Texas hardly ever had two good growing seasons in a row. Their work for the year went for nothing as there was little rain and too dry to make anything like an average crop. Consequently, they remained at the Bragg farm for a little less than a year.[9]

*   *   *   *   *

When George Tucker wrote his autobiography, he made no mention about who he married. However, there is a record of a marriage between George Tucker and Martha Ellen Chapman which occurred on November 1, 1877, in Hill County, Texas. We do know that George's son Bert Tucker was born at Spanish Fort, Montague County, Texas, in 1880.

Discouraged, George left his brother Bill in Hill County, probably in 1878, and joined up with his cousin Jack in Montague County, Texas. Jack had moved his family from Ozark, Arkansas, and had been living there since 1877. From there he and Jack went up into Indian Territory, west of Fort Smith, Arkansas.[10]

Jack was married with a family and it is likely that George was married and had his wife along even though he never spoke of his marital status. They stopped not far from Fort Smith, where they made what George called "a pretty good crop of cotton."

It was in Indian Territory where son Bert claimed he was born in 1880. Jack, George, and families stayed in Indian Territory for about a year and then went back to Texas. This was not the first time for Jack Tucker to be in Texas. He and his wife married in 1867 in Franklin County, Arkansas, and a son was born in Texas during 1871. They returned to Franklin County around 1873 but were back in Montague County by 1877.

When they returned this time from Indian Territory, they returned to Montague County and discovered that brother Bill had come up from Hill County and was now farming in Montague County, located to the west of Cooke County, of which Gainesville is the county seat. They made a tolerably good crop there that first year which was probably 1879. It was while farming here that George entered into the profession of peace officer.

How does a farmer get himself hired as a lawman? It was a change that was least expected by George. His cousin Jack was the lawman back in Arkansas. The only experience George had was trying to run away from trouble. Lawmen were not supposed to do that. Here he was, a twenty-three-year-old married man with one son and not much of a bright future working as a laborer for his brother Bill. George was never sure when this golden egg fell into his lap but believed it came about in 1878 or 1879. Based on the events and time frames it was most likely 1879 or 1880. George was about to have visitors to come see him from Burlington.[11]

Chapter Four

First Years as a Lawman

*There will always be enough fools in the world to make the peace officer
a necessary instrument in every community.*

George Redman Tucker was working in the field one day on
his brother's farm when he spotted a group of men riding
toward him. He removed his cotton sack and walked over to the
fence. The men approached and introduced themselves but in later years George could not remember their names or exactly when
he was confronted. Did they reopen that old charge of Hill and
Tucker trying to kill James Faulkner?

Tucker was apprehensive, to say the least. The spokesperson
for the group was the mayor of Burlington. Actually, the town had
to be renamed when the township applied for a post office. There
was already a Burlington and the government would not allow
two of the same name. Therefore, the town was renamed Spanish
Fort. It was located just southeast of Red River Station where the
cattle trail up to Kansas passed through.

The cowboys came into town to drink, gamble, make purchases in the stores and saddle shop, and raise a little hell. In addition,
whiskey runners and other outlaws hiding up in Indian Territory
often came across the Red River to cause mischief in the saloons
and other businesses in Spanish Fort. Shootouts and murders were
frequent events and the town marshal job was vacated, probably
due to death by lead poisoning from the barrel of a six-gun in the
hands of an outlaw or wild cowboy.

The mayor did the talking and asked George if he would be
interested in pinning on the badge as Spanish Fort's town marshal? A town marshal in Texas was officially named constable in
those days. George Tucker did not appear to have a reputation
as a gunman or a quick draw, but may have had some impressive confrontations in Spanish Fort that caught the attention of the
town officials.

George was familiar with firearms as he, like most frontiersmen, had to provide wild game for the table on a regular basis. He was told if he took the job, the pay was five dollars per day, plus expenses. That really got George's attention, being he was working at back-breaking work on the farm for a lot less money. He accepted the mayor's offer on the spot.

He was not sure of the year he took the job but believed it was around 1878. He said he was twenty-three when offered the job. He was born in August of 1855. That would support 1878 as the year he pinned on the badge. However, based on the events that led up to his arrival in Montague County, he was in Hill County in 1877 and Indian Territory 1878 and to Montague in 1879. Nothing is known of those who wore the badge before him.[1]

• • • • •

Spanish Fort was first known as Burlington, but as that designation was already taken, the town had to come up with another name when they applied to the Government to establish a post office. Two towns of the same name hit a sour note for the government and they let the town know. It was ei-

Constable badge. A town marshal in Texas was officially pegged as constable. *Photo from author's collection.*

ther change the name of the town or do without a post office. They did and it was approved as Spanish Fort. Thinking the area had first been inhabited by Spanish soldiers and thinking the remains of an old structure was their fort, the town council decided "Spanish Fort" would be most appropriate.

Apparently the early settlers were unaware the ruins were actually the skeletal remains of an old French trading post where the French traded with a small group of Wichita Indians called Taovayas. The Wichita Indians were made up of village groups and were never organized as a tribe. Looking at Comanche or Arapaho we think in terms of large units, encompassing large territories. This was not the case with the Wichita village groups. According-

Spanish Fort Historical Marker. The town was first named Burlington and later changed to Spanish Fort. However, records indicate lawmen continued to refer to the town as Burlington. *Photo courtesy of the National Register of Historic Places.*

ly, each village was autonomous, functioning somewhat as a band under its own name. The Taovayas were such a unit.[2]

Captain Randolph Marcy led an expedition through the area in 1852 to explore the sources of the Red River. He observed that the Wichita tribes had cornfields and recommended Medicine Bluffs near the Wichita Mountains be established as a fort to control the Indian tribes of the south plains. This location would become Fort Sill, Indian Territory.

The history of the area indicates that the Taovayas tribe, flying the French flag, established a fort in the bend of the Red River where the white settlement of Burlington was established. The fort was established in 1750 to defend against Spanish incursions in the area. In 1759, the Spanish, under Colonel Diego Ortiz Parrilla, attacked the tribe's fortified position in the area, but were defeated by as many as 6,000 Indians of both the Taovayas and Comanche tribes.

When someone suggested Spanish Fort for a new name for Burlington, it was assumed that Spanish forces had built the fortification. A story exists that the French traded silver snuff boxes to the Indians for pelts. This is why many silver arrow points around Spanish Fort have been found in recent years with the use of metal detectors. An unwanted find by a treasure hunter, was a human skull in a ditch next to a wheat field. But, regardless of

A lithograph of a Wichita Village, probably located in Oklahoma between 1850-1875. The Taovaya and Wichita tribes lived in beehive shaped houses thatched with grass and surrounded by fields of maize and other crops. *Lithograph courtesy of Smithsonian Institution National Anthropological Archives.*

their ignorance, or maybe because of it, the name Spanish Fort was approved as an official postal designation.[3]

The town of Burlington, later Spanish Fort, was an untamed western frontier town where a mixture of outlaws, thieves, and murderers from the Territory congregated. Local folks, trail drivers, and cowboys added to the mix and turned the town into a war zone on a regular basis. The reason for an abundance of rambunctious cow hands was the Red River crossing of the old Chisholm Cattle Trail, just to the north of Spanish Fort near Red River Station. Both towns were popular stopping places for the cowhands making cattle drives up the Chisholm Trail to the railheads in Kansas.[4]

*   *   *   *   *

When George took the town marshal job it came with its problems. George knew it had to be a dangerous profession, especially since Spanish Fort had a reputation for being wild. There were shootings on a regular basis and picking a farm boy who apparently had not proven his abilities indicated the town leaders may have had some difficulty getting someone to replace the vacated badge holder. One hundred and fifty dollars per month was a lot of money in 1879. No one, not even George Redman Tucker, knew why the town officials went to him and offered him the job. So, George Redman Tucker became the peace officer of Spanish Fort.

Later, he also served in dual capacity as marshal and deputy sheriff of Montague County.

Time has erased Red River Station. A cemetery is located there and is the only physical reminder that the town ever existed.[5]

The old town marshal job at Spanish Fort was vacated for unknown reasons. According to George, "There had been some trouble there and the old officer had been removed."

When George agreed to take the job to keep the peace he understood its meaning. He said, "I knew what the peace was and I was not inclined to be afraid of anybody. But I could shoot well

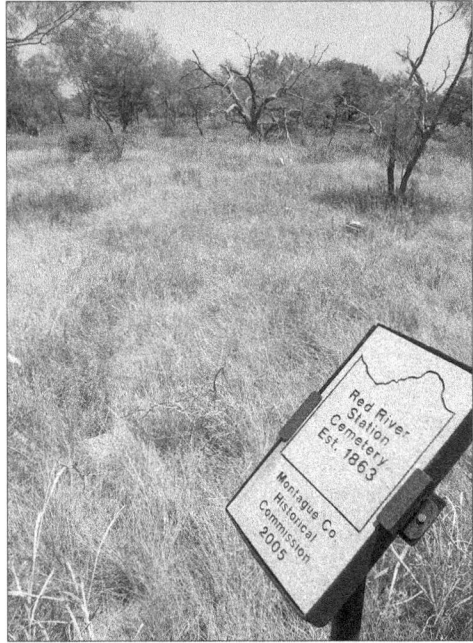

The lonely and remote Red River Station Cemetery is not maintained and while there are headstones, it could be dangerous to walk around the site, especially during the warmer months when rattlesnakes are lurking nearby. *Photo from author's collection.*

and scarcely remember when I couldn't shoot."[6]

It was a tough time and Montague County was a tough country during those early frontier days. The big thorn in the side came about, especially so, by the Indian Territory located to the north, across the Red River. The territory was a lawless country where "Gun Law" prevailed and when the thieves and gunmen came across the river into Spanish Fort, most of them were pretty salty and "not in the habit of acting like church members," according to George.

When George Redman Tucker agreed to take the law enforcement job as town marshal of Spanish Fort, he put away the tools of his farming way of life and moved his family to town. He was about to see what the fruits of his new labor would produce. George was a believer in a phrase from his Bible which stated: *Man must live by the sweat of his brow.* Other thoughts probably went through his mind like *Thou shall not kill* but, George knew that eventually the law of averages would catch up to him and he would have to kill or very possibly be killed.

He knew there was no turning back or the turning of the other cheek. He would have to strike back hard to gain the confidence of the town people. Was he going to stand up to the task of having to take another man's life? Maybe he thought about his religious upbringing and reading of Daniel, who killed the lion, or David, who slew the giant? But, the monetary offer was just too good for George to turn down.[7]

George explained it this way; "I knew that there existed the hazard of personal injury, maybe even of death. But those were conditions that people accepted in frontier communities. And besides, the salary was more than acceptable."

In those days, one did not make five dollars a day in the farming business. So, George accepted their proposition and moved to town and pinned on the lawman's badge.

But George had on his thinking cap and was coming up with an idea. He went to his brother, Bill Tucker, and cousin, Jack Tucker, and made his pitch. He suggested something he had heard about from some of the deputy marshals out of Judge Parker's court over in Fort Smith. He told them he was going to set up a group of men who had nerve and could shoot when the chips were down, and see about putting them in a "posse." He had no paid law officers to help him keep the peace in town. George was it, lock, stock, and barrel. With a posse of trusted men, he could call on one or two, or five or six well-armed men, if necessary, to assist in cases needing backup. The posse system would work very well for George in the following years.[8]

George must have handled Spanish Fort's need for law and order to most everyone's satisfaction for, about a year later, they held an election to decide if George would keep his position as town marshal, or to determine if Spanish Fort favored another candidate. George was challenged by a man named Bill Bagwell, but he never had a chance according to George.

Bill Bagwell was listed in the 1880 federal census as William H. Bagwill, age twenty-eight, born in Missouri. According to his pension record, dated December 23, 1901, Bagwill served as a volunteer during the Civil War. In the fall of 1885, a local tough named Jake Chambers was charged with assault with intent to murder

Bagwill for unknown causes. Bagwill seemed to be a good citizen and was a saddlemaker in Spanish Fort, living with his nineteen year-old-wife Angelina and infant son, Joseph. Apparently, he was a good candidate, but George won by a landslide. Even after George Tucker left Spanish Fort, Bagwill never became the town marshal. He lost his wife at a young age, and by 1900 he was a bartender in one of the Spanish Fort saloons.[9]

After the election George continued his job without a break in service to the town. George did not expect things to remain peaceful simply because he was the police officer. His philosophy was that peace officers would always be a necessary instrument in every community being there would always be enough fools in the world who would not conform to the laws of society. During his years of law enforcement, he made his share of petty arrests, serious arrests, and fights that ended in serious or mortal injury to the peace breakers.[10]

Chapter Five

The Violent Land

I was pulling iron, but he put spurs to his horse and ran like the devil.

— G. R. Tucker

Being a lawman anywhere near Indian Territory in those early days, especially Chickasaw Nation, was going against a stacked deck, loaded with jokers of unsavory and violent dregs of society. One man alone could not be expected to keep the peace and deal with the criminal element that came flowing across the Red River to steal, plunder, rape, and murder.

The territory was infested with a hotbed of lawlessness. Many wanted to become lost from the civilized, law abiding part of society, mainly to escape prosecution for their crimes. Therefore, George Tucker, like many other lawmen, needed and had assistance from his newly established posse. Records indicate that George Tucker, as the town marshal, was also a deputy sheriff of Montague County, On December 17, 1884, the Montague County Commissioners' Court authorized the payment of $2.50 to officer G. R. Tucker for expenses to journey in the inquest case of James Hill, deceased, and the clerk was ordered to issue script for the same, payable from the general fund. This alone would indicate that George was serving as a deputy sheriff of Montague County.

Possemen were locals who answered the call from a lawman when needed to confront a situation. They were usually paid a fee for their assistance. These possemen furnished their own horses, guns and ammunition when helping the lawman chase down a criminal. Bill Tucker and Buck Tucker were regular possemen for George. Bill was George's brother and Buck was a cousin. Payments were authorized and paid by the town or the county commissioners.

One of the first men George had to deal with was Jim Melton. There was nothing unusual or outstanding about Jim Melton. He was a young man of about twenty-five-years of age who lived across the Red River in the Indian Territory. According to George,

"He was a tough character, especially when he got drunk. Melton saw himself as being tougher than any peace officer who ever wore a gun."

George was on the lookout for Melton as he had an order to arrest him to appear as a witness in a trial at Gainesville. One day Melton rode across the Red River and George confronted him when he pulled into town. He pulled his pistol and told Melton he was under arrest. Melton didn't put up a fight so George disarmed him and took him into custody.[1]

While Melton was transported by Tucker to the trial, the doctor at Spanish Fort took Melton's horse, which he had put in the livery stable in town. The doctor was keeping tabs on the daily cost to Melton for stabling his horse. When Melton came back from Gainesville and learned what had been done to him about stabling his horse and presenting him with a healthy bill, he became extremely upset and became madder than a rabid dog. He went to one of the saloons and proceeded to get drunk.

It was January, with a cold north wind that possibly added to Melton's disposition. He had enough to drink and still had enough money to pay off the doctor so he went to the livery, paid him, and saddled up and rode out of the stable and stopped his horse in front of the saloon.[2]

Marshal Tucker was inside watching some men play a game of billiards. Melton hollered for Tucker to come outside but Tucker didn't hear him. Someone came over and told Marshal Tucker there was a fellow outside who wanted to see him. Tucker started out and when he got into the doorway, Melton, sitting on his horse in front of the saloon, raised his gun and pointed it at Tucker.

Tucker figured he was done for but just as Melton pulled the trigger, his horse gave a quick side-step and the bullet missed Tucker. Tucker then pulled his six-gun but Melton had already put the spurs to his horse and was riding like the devil was after him toward the river.

Tucker and his brother, Bill, one of his possemen, jumped on their horses and took out after him. They had Winchester rifles and as they rode after Melton and gained a little distance, they both started shooting at him. They chased after him and continued the chase across the river into Indian Territory. Finally, after chasing him for at least a mile and after firing a number of shots,

This was the crossing near Red River Station and Spanish Fort. The river crossing was hazardous before, during, or after flooding. *Photo from author's collection.*

Melton suddenly tumbled from his saddle. He did not move after hitting the ground.

When they reached Melton, they dismounted and approached him cautiously. He was still breathing, but appeared to be dying. He had been hit with a rifle bullet right through the neck, a mortal wound. Tucker wasn't sure if it was his bullet or his brother, Bill's, bullet that scored the hit.

"In a sense, it was a shame to see such a nice looking fellow killed because he insisted upon being tough." wrote Tucker. He went on to say, "He was a big fellow with as nice a physique as I've nearly ever seen. I surely hated to see him killed, but there wasn't anything else to do about it."

After all, Melton had tried to kill the marshal and a frontier lawman in Tucker's place couldn't afford to get soft with tough men on the shoot. That ended George Tucker's first killing episode.[3]

This was probably Marshal Tucker's first involvement in a serious incident, excluding the Faulkner incident at Gulley Rock, and surely, according to him, ended in his first killing episode. There would be many more to follow. It is unknown exactly how many people George Redman Tucker killed or wounded during

A drawing depicting Marshal Tucker and brother, Bill, giving chase and killing young Jim Melton in Indian Territory. *Drawing from author's collection.*

his many years as a man hunter. He never gave a complete accounting. He did say however, "I have hunted men, killed men, both good and bad, some innocent, and some who could instruct the Devil in the ways of crime."[4]

*   *   *   *   *

The George Tucker law enforcement records are from his unpublished autobiography, newspaper accounts, and the notches on his gun. Some western history buffs believe that only "tinhorns" notched their guns. While a grandson said he had seen George Tucker wearing a pistol with notches on the handle. It was reported that the last known colt revolver owned by George was sold at auction in Oklahoma City, to an unknown buyer, not so many years ago.

As a child, a living descendant recalled seeing George for the first time and said "He scared the hell out of me. He was dark headed, had a mustache, chewed tobacco and wore a big gun with notches on the handle."

Another living descendant, a Mr. Barnes, reported that his father gave him a pistol that belonged to George Tucker along with a copy of the book *Banditti of the Plains*. The pistol has no notches on the handle. Apparently George had interest in the book as he was one of the characters therein. The descendant remains in ownership of both items.[5]

The incident involving Jim Melton most likely resulted in Tucker being seen in a positive light with the voters of Spanish Fort after the election of 1880, as he was elected by popular vote and kept his position as constable of the town. As a young man of only twenty-five-years of age, George Redman Tucker was gaining a big reputation as a man with the "Bark" on and one not to be trifled with.[6]

The good Lord put the coyote on earth for a purpose; the four-legged kind anyway. The two-legged variety was a different story. This one served no valuable service to man or beast. The vast majority of western people recognized this trait and dealt a swift blow to those unsavory characters. Today, many who would have died in a shootout or hanged from a cottonwood limb are warehoused in state prisons throughout the land. A big majority will commit new crimes upon release back into society. Only a few will face the death penalty and only after years of legal maneuvers under the guise of constitutional rights of due process. Times change, views change, but misfits usually do not! And, most locations are no safer from the coyotes today as back then.[7]

Old Man Dayton

George considered a story about "Old Man Dayton" to be interesting enough to tell in his autobiography and the incident happened not long after the Jim Melton killing. It was the second case that stuck in Tucker's memory as he wrote about it many years later.

"It wasn't quite so pitiful as the Melton case," said Tucker. There was an older man, tough-acting character who came to Spanish Fort from across the Red River, up in Indian Territory. He was known only as "Old Man" or "Old Man Dayton." He would come over and buy a few things and then go to a saloon and get pretty drunk. It would be difficult to say how old he was according to George who said, "He might have been forty or he might have been fifty-five. But, he had the typical appearance of a mean fellow."

On an occasion, without breaking his routine, Old Man Dayton crossed the Red River and went down to Spanish Fort and visited one of the mercantile stores where he made his few purchases.

Then, as expected, he went to the saloon where he commenced to drinking whiskey. He got himself a bit drunker than usual on that day. Suddenly, Old Man Dayton became taller and stronger than ever before. Being he was now feeling ten-feet tall and as strong as a grizzly bear, he decided it would be a good idea to give the bartender a thrashing. Therefore, he commenced to go after him. He decided his best move would be to tackle the bartender and once he had him on the floor he could do some serious kicking and put some boot leather to the man's head and ribs.

Best laid plans do not always turn out the way planned however. The scene, for some cloudy reason, did not turn out the way Old Man Dayton had it pictured in his mind. The first phase of his plan did succeed. He did tackle the bartender. Phase one was accomplished. Now, all Old Man Dayton had to do was implement phase two, kicking in the bartender's ribs and head.

Here was a bartender, tackled and on the floor. But, to Dayton's surprise, the bartender was no weakling. He got to his feet rather quickly, reached down and scooped drunkard Dayton up and raised him overhead. He then ran with Dayton, who was screaming and waving his arms wildly, through the swinging saloon doors, and threw the old codger into the street. He sailed through the air for quite a spell until he crashed to the dusty street among the dirty and stinking horse droppings.

The old fellow was skinned up a bit in the squabble, but his temper was highly bruised, much worse than his body. He mounted his horse that was hitched to the rail in front of the saloon and rode off toward his home turf. Everyone thought that was the end of it and Old Man Dayton would sleep it off and forget about the incident. That was not to be the case.[8]

After a short time, Dayton was spotted on horseback as he came roaring hell-bent for destruction back across the Red River. He had gone home and retrieved his weapons. He was carrying a Winchester and a six-gun. He galloped on into town and brought his lathered horse to a stop in front of the same saloon from which he had been given aerial flight. He was hell-bent on revenge for being thrown out into the street and he began to make trouble right away.

Marshal George Tucker, along with his brother, Bill, and cousin, Jack Tucker, acting possemen, approached Dayton in front of the saloon while Dayton was still mounted and Marshal Tucker yelled, "drop your weapons Dayton, you're under arrest."

Dayton did exactly what the lawmen figured he would do. He wanted a gunfight. Dayton pulled his six-gun from the holster, raised the gun, pulled back the hammer and fired. The hot lead hit Bill Tucker in the arm as he, George, and Jack pulled iron and started blasting away at Dayton.[9]

Dayton took numerous hits after getting off only one shot that wounded Bill. Dayton's six-gun dropped from his hand as he was thrown backwards off of his horse as a hail of bullets continued to puncture his body. After leaving the saddle, he landed in the dirt on the other side of his horse and did not move. Marshal Tucker approached him as he lay in a puddle of blood. Tucker knelt down and felt for a pulse. There was none. Old Man Dayton was dead. Tucker and his possemen had killed him.

"There was nothing else we could do," said Marshal Tucker. "He had gone plumb loco." This was the second recorded incident of George Redman Tucker sending another man to his grave. However, it is not proven exactly who's bullet, or bullets, killed Dayton. It is likely all three made killing hits on Dayton.

No additional knowledge is known of Dayton or his family. He may have lived alone or may have left a wife and children. No newspaper reports were found concerning this incident and no federal census was taken in 1870 or 1880 north of the Red River, in the territory. In 1900 and 1910 a few with the surname Dayton started to appear in the area and could be offspring. He will have to remain "Old Man Dayton," the "Loco Coyote."

The Watson Gang

Marshal Tucker considered the Watson Gang to be one of the most notorious of all outlaw gangs. They had a hideout in the southern part of Indian Territory. They actually lived in and around Courtney Flat [now Courtney]. The gang was named after its leader and Watson was said to be the shrewdest member.

"There was a policy of intimidation and sometimes of robbery," wrote Tucker. "To a man, they were tough and proud of it. Of course, all went armed and were careless with their guns, too careless for the peaceable, law-abiding citizens of the more-or-less, civilized communities. When the Watson gang came to town, they didn't come for a friendly visit, but came to raise cane and take over. They announced their intentions openly and the people took to their houses or other places of shelter."[10]

Members of the gang were William Watson, the leader; William. R. Watkins, somewhat of a merchant; J. M. Poe, George Carrolton, Henry Glasson, J. L. Trowbridge, Charles Heimer, Lee Pemberton, and a few others. The lawlessness of the gang was extensive.[11]

On the last day of October 1879, gang leader, William Watson ,and partner in crime, Peter Malone, stole 1,000 pounds of cotton seed from an undisclosed location in Indian Territory. They drove the ill gotten seed by wagon southward and crossed the Red River into Texas near Spanish Fort. They were delivering the stolen seed nearby to cohort Wyatt Williams.

The theft was reported to the federal authorities at Fort Smith and a federal warrant was issued from Fort Smith on December 4, 1879. A deputy U.S. marshal served the warrant on Watson the 26th of that month at Courtney Flat, near W. R. Watkins' store and residence. Of course, Wyatt Williams denied being involved at the examination trial.

On March 15, 1881, William Watson and Roscoe Turner stole eight hogs from Arch McGehee. That turned into quite an event after Watson was arrested. He tried to bribe the deputy marshal who served the warrant and the possemen who took him back to stand trial in Fort Smith. Of course he claimed innocence, saying he "killed the hogs by mistake."

On the first day of October 1882, William Watson shot and killed John Phelps. For some unknown reason, a murder warrant was not issued on this case until February 17, 1887. One of the "Three Guardsmen," Deputy Marshal Heck Thomas would serve the warrant.

If a man would steal hogs, he would surely steal horses and that's exactly what William Watson did. The official charge was larceny which sounds a little better that hog or horse thief. Watson allegedly stole a horse from D. Smith. The disposition of that case is unknown.

On March 28, 1885, the *Fort Worth Daily Gazette,* Fort Worth, Texas, reported that William Watson was involved in a double killing that occurred on the 25th, involving William Watson and another man at Bitter Creek, in Indian Territory. The newspaper report

erroneously stated that William Watson and another party drew
Winchesters and standing only three feet apart shot each other to
death. Actually, the Watson man was named Frank and he was
involved in a gunfight with Frances Copeland. One report stated
that Watson killed Copeland and Copeland's brother pulled his
pistol and shot Watson through the heart, finishing him off.

Another newspaper report claimed William Watson was there
also and had entered his horse, Silver Tail, in a race against Tom
Fletcher's brown mare that took place on March 21. A dispute
sprang up between Frank Watson, not William Watson, formerly
a cattle inspector for Texas firms at Anadarko.

The *Cheyenne Transporter* reported that Frank Watson was
killed instantly and Copeland was carried off mortally wounded. The report stated that William Watson was a brother-in-law
of Wyatt Williams, a well-known cattle owner. According to this
report, no third party had anything to do with the gunfight.[12]

So, as all things must come to pass in due course of time, the
Watson Gang came to Spanish Fort late one night in January 1886.
It was on a Tuesday night, an hour after midnight when nine outlaws of the Watson Gang crossed the Red River from Indian Territory. Their intent was to paint the town red like old times and once
again put fear into the hearts of the residents; just what bullies
love to do.

William "Bill" Watson, Bill Weems, Jack Harrison, Bud Starr,
Lute Jackson, Lee Pemberton, and three others, whose names
were unknown, rode into town on that late night, with Watson
as their ring leader. After parading through the town, carrying
Winchesters, they let it be known that they wanted to "court the
marshal." They took over the town of Spanish Fort, frequently
referred to by its original name of Burlington. All the businesses
were closed so they proceeded to the home of saloon owner, J. B.
Marsh. They woke him and told him they were out of whiskey
and wanted more. He went with them down to his saloon and
opened up. They started drinking again and then drew their guns
and started shooting up the place.

Marshal Tucker claimed he was allowed to hire one badge tot-
ter on the police force, a prior stonemason, officer Charley Cook,
who was regularly employed in that capacity, and on duty that
night. According to Tucker, Charley Cook was a tough man and

a good peace officer for such a wild town as Spanish Fort. When Cook confronted the gang they all pulled guns and opened fire. Bullets began to fly, thicker than hailstones as Cook took cover. He knew when to duck and back off as he was highly out-gunned. But, according to Tucker, he could always be depended upon when things got a little tight.[13]

While this battle was taking place Marshal Tucker was sound asleep in his quarters. At four o'clock in the morning, he was awakened by the shooting. He got up and dressed and went out into the street. He spotted Cook coming up to his house.

"The toughs are taking over the town," Charley told George.

"What toughs?" George asked.

"The Watson Gang," said Cook. He told Tucker what had transpired and talking it over they decided to go after the gang. They were both armed with six-guns but decided that shotguns were also needed and would be more effective for close-up work as well as better weapons during darkness. Tucker's logic was the scatter guns would give them a good spread of shot and deal plenty of misery to anyone on the receiving end, especially in a group or crowd. One good shot would put one or more men down if it hit in the right spot.[14]

So, Tucker and Cook took a pair of shotguns from Tucker's house and started calling for assistance from dependable men. They recruited John Inman, a forty-six-year-old family man who came to Texas from Illinois and a transplanted Missourian named L. Phillips, both regular possemen.

With George in the lead, followed by three reliable men, they started walking side by side for the center of town. The gang members were scattered about town, shooting their guns and having what they considered to be a good time. Tucker told Cook and the two possemen that he had decided it would be best to wait until the toughs came back together and formed one group. Slowly, but surely, the outlaws began to come in by twos and threes, all joining up in the saloon. Then, they started their hell raising inside. One of the drunken misfits decided, just for fun, to ride his horse into the saloon. When Tucker figured they, plus the horse, were all inside, he and his men would be ready to call the tune.[15]

"Don't shoot unless they start it," George told his men. He, Cook, Inman, and Phillips took their selected positions, ready to splatter the toughs with scatterguns. George put them on hold while he called out to the wild visitors to surrender. The answer he received was short and sour as they yelled "Go to Hell!" It was emphatic.

The gang started the dance by opening fire and the lawmen raised their shotguns and started blasting away. They were not quite close enough to do a great deal of damage with the shotguns and as the battle continued everything became confused for a moment. Tucker and his men hit one man, then another, then a third, and one horse, possibly the one in the saloon, was hit and killed. Four other horses on the street, belonging to the gang, were wounded. The gang fought their way outside and worked their way to the other horses, some riding double, and fled across the Red River into Indian Territory.

Notwithstanding the brave efforts of the officers to effect their arrest, the gang got away but did leave blood on the field of battle The officers were unhurt. As for the gang, it was later learned, three bullets took Lute Jackson, one in the small of his back, one in his thigh and one in his ankle. His poor horse received a full-load of buckshot. Bill Weems was shot in the thigh, Bill Watson in the left ear, and Jack Carroll was hit twice, once in the left arm and once in the ankle. The wounds were serious, but not fatal.

The lawmen made no attempt to follow them, for they were greatly outnumbered and at a distance, shotguns were ineffective. Only Winchester rifles would have been the weapon of choice. The confrontation must have done some good. The Watson Gang remembered the reception that was given in town and they gave Spanish Fort a wide berth thereafter.

But, it wasn't over by a long shot. Tucker and a host of other lawmen were destined to have future difficulty with the Watson Gang. The difficulty would be a lot more than Tucker could have imagined. But for now, three men were wounded in this affray and one or more may have died from their wounds. The citizens of Spanish Fort were outraged by the lawless actions of the Watson Gang. They applauded the acts of Marshal Tucker and his posse in dealing with the lawless drunken rioters.[16]

After the first encounter with the Watson Gang, one might say this unsavory group of misfit criminals was to be placed on Tucker's list of "those I want to get." Tucker did not add any kills to his list and it stood at two with the killing of Melton and Dayton. The Watson Gang was a thorn in his side with their evil doings. They had tried to tree his town and it had not worked. The Watson Gang seemed to be more irritating than a heat rash.[17]

Not long after the gang's raid on Spanish Fort, these lawmen would clash again with the Watson Gang. One of Spanish Fort's merchants, Tillman H. LeForce, gave a man named William Watkins, dry goods to take to his store in Courtney Flat, Indian Territory. LeForce was selling goods illegally in Indian Territory. The reason was LeForce did not have a license or permit from the Indian agent to engage in trading with the Chickasaw tribe or any other Indian tribe.

The Chickasaw tribe did not believe Watkins had purchased the goods but was an agent for LeForce. The Indian agent and tribal officials believed Watkins and Watson had a fraud going whereby Watkins was allowing the LeForce goods to be sold through his store and they were splitting the profits. Watkins being an intermarried Chickasaw could have a store on his place if he wanted.[18]

Robert Murray was also a United States Indian policemen and could arrest anyone he wanted to in Indian Territory, whether they were Indian or not. Those officers are not to be confused with those of the various tribes. In the Chickasaw Nation, there were four counties, each with an elected sheriff and two constables. Some were also U.S. Indian policemen; some were not.

Some of the U.S. Indian police were also deputy U.S. marshals, most were not. Tucker referred to Robert Murray as Frank in error. In Murray's case, he was a commissioned constable of the U.S. Indian police and his boss was Captain Sam Sixkiller. Sixkiller was the first captain of the Indian police and also served as a deputy U.S. marshal. He was murdered in 1886.

They both worked for Robert Latham Owen, Indian agent of the Five Civilized Tribes headquartered at Muskogee, in the Creek Nation. Owen was part Cherokee Indian and Indian agent from 1886 to 1890. He would go on to become one of the two first U.S. senators to represent Oklahoma. Murray had an order to put LeForce and his goods out of the Chickasaw Nation because he was not a licensed or permitted trader. Although Watkins could run a store without a permit, it appeared to the lawmen and probably to Robert Owen, that LeForce was trying to put one over on the tribe and the federal government by entering into a trading deal with Watkins.[19]

Murray's first act was when he came to Spanish Fort and confronted LeForce and asked him to go over to Courtney Flat and bring his goods back to his own store in Texas. LeForce agreed with Murray's instructions and took a wagon and driver for the goods. Of course LeForce went alone and later returned empty handed. He explained to Watkins that he had come to get the goods as requested by Indian policeman Murray but said the Watson Gang stood him off under the threat of death, forcing him to return empty handed.[20]

The Indian police and the tribal officers could, by treaty, put undesirable non-citizens, bag and baggage, out of the Indian Nations at any time, even if they had a tribal permit.[21] All Murray had was an order from Agent Owen to evict William Watson and Campbell Leforce but that's all he needed; that and a sufficient force to accomplish the task.

Murray knew Sheriff McLain wanted Watson because McLain had sent copies of his warrants and a governor's requisition to the Chickasaw governor, who in turn had sent it to Agent Owen and Owen found the documents supported eviction and arrest. Therefore, Murray had all the authority he needed to arrest Watson and turn him over to McLain.

McLain recognized he was out of his jurisdiction and could see the potential for a number-one train wreck. He made it perfectly clear to Murray that he would help take Watson but flatly refused to be used in enforcing any confiscation of goods. For their part, Watson and Watkins knew Murray was a federal officer with full authority to take Watson into custody. Watkins, however, thought he could bluff his way into keeping the LeForce goods.[22]

Robert Murray at the time of this incident was one of the richest men in the Chickasaw Nation. He was also a member of the Chickasaw legislature. Moreover, there was bad blood between Murray and Watkins. During 1884-1885, Murray had been in a partnership with rancher Wyatt Williams and Jim Fitzpatrick, wherein Wyatt Williams had been running a herd of cattle on Chickasaw grass controlled by Murray and Fitzpatrick.

Gang members, Watson and Watkins, were thick as thieves with Wyatt Williams and involved in all kinds of chicanery which is verified in testimony found in Watson's criminal history. Anyway, in the summer of 1885, Wyatt Williams took a herd of cattle to the Kansas market, sold the entire herd, and returned to Texas without paying his partners their share. Then, Williams sold some equipment and the remaining animals to another party. Problem was he did not own what he sold.

The man he sold to tried to take possession but Murray refused to allow it until Williams settled with his partners. The man went back to Texas, confronted Williams and demanded his money back. Williams, embarrassed at being found out, sent gunman Bob Woods and his band of outlaws up to take the stuff back that Williams had tried to sell. Woods and outfit thought they could make a frontal attack, so they rode into the Fitzpatrick range yard headquarters with six guns blazing. As they rode in firing their guns at anything that moved they suddenly ran into a hail of lead from men hidden behind log walls. The men behind those walls were wielding Winchesters and literally shot the gang to pieces. Therefore, Murray had no reason to be a fan of either Watkins or Watson, chums of Wyatt Williams.[23]

But when it came down to the facts about the raid by the lawmen on Courtney Flat, Tucker said, "I never learned the true facts of the case. It might well be that the merchant really didn't want to get possession of the goods. However, Bob Murray, the Indian police officer, was intent upon his mission and he never rested until he had permission to take the goods by force."[24]

Accordingly, Murray telephoned[25] Indian agent Robert L. Owen, asking for warrants for the arrest of members of the Watson Gang. Owen telephoned back immediately that the warrants were on their way by mail. Murray came across the Red River to Spanish Fort on February 21, 1886, and related this information to Marshal Tucker. The United States Indian policeman now had the authority and approval to arrest the gang. He and Tucker contacted Montague County Sheriff L. L. McLain by telephone and a posse was formed to go across the Red River.

To retrieve the goods, wagons and wagon drivers would be needed, along with deputies and possemen. Tucker was a deputy sheriff of Montague County while serving as the constable of Spanish Fort. Tucker believed the warrants pending arrival were valid and later believed he should have waited but did not. However, Tucker apparently never understood the situation fully. They all wanted a good crack at the Watson Gang anyway, and were eager for the chance.[26]

Besides Murray, the party included L. L. McLain, sheriff of Montague County, Bill Black, a deputy; George Tucker, and possemen, Bob and Bill Nix; Bill Bagwill, George's brother, William "Bill" Tucker, and their cousin, Jack Tucker. Also there was Jim Avis, along with the following six wagons and drivers; Dan Hurst, John Orr, John Abney, Bill Mount, Wade Norton, and Sandy Horton. The team totaled sixteen men and most had prior experience as lawmen or possemen.

The party left Spanish Fort one morning at daybreak and crossed the river into Indian Territory. They arrived shortly at Courtney Flat. Tucker referred to the place as a sort of second bottom delta land and the bottom land extended some miles north to a low bluff. The top of the bluff was prairie lands that rolled away toward the Canadian River. The bottom land was rich soil, ideal for growing crops. In those days grains and fruits were the most productive. That is where the small settlement of Courtney Flat was located. It was said to be a lawless community where the Watson Gang called home.

As they approached the small clump of houses which surrounded the Watkins' store, policeman Murray rode on ahead with a shotgun across the saddle in front of him. The posse members, heavily armed were hidden behind the drivers in each of the six covered wagons. There were fifteen of them divided among the wagons. Murray had told them to stay hidden and not show themselves unless it was absolutely necessary. As Murray approached the store he was recognized by the gang members and they poured out of the houses to confront him. Those outlaws didn't seem to care much whether a man was an officer or not.

When they appeared with their guns, Tucker and the other lawmen hidden in the wagons knew the stealth approach was not working, being Murray had been identified by the gang. So, they commenced to pour out of the wagons with killing on their minds. "There wasn't much harm done in killing a man in those days and especially not if he was a member of the Watson Gang," wrote Tucker.

The posse was carrying shotguns and six-guns. Without waiting for anything or anybody, they opened up and started firing. A gang member named Trowbridge was hit and went down. Tucker figured they had killed him and it would have been a lucky day if it had been true. Or so Tucker thought. Tucker believed it would have saved him, the sheriff, possemen, and wagon drivers a great deal of future trouble.

However, wounding or killing Trowbridge did not prevent what was about to unfold. The rest of the gang took to their heels and put boot leather to good use as they scrambled to get out of gunfire range, which they quickly did. The posse members loaded the supplies in the wagons and returned to Spanish Fort. Everyone was jubilant and quite content that they had done a pretty good day's work. But they were to hear more of the episode very soon.[27]

Chapter Six

Lawmen on Trial

Being accused of attempted murder by a murdering outlaw gang was a hard pill to swallow.

One of the worst situations to be encountered by any lawman is to have members of the criminal element turn the table on them and have them charged with crimes. Lawman George Tucker and a host of lawmen and teamsters of Montague County, Texas, were about to be served with warrants of arrest after complaints had been lodged against them by the Watson Gang for attempted murder and theft of private property.

Everyone involved, and there were many, seemed to be aware that the members of the Watson Gang were outlaws and believed them to be in violation of federal law by taking dry goods to a prohibited owner in Indian Territory. Legality probably never entered the minds of the Watson Gang. Everyone involved on the side of the law seemed to be only interested in stopping the illegal activity with whatever means necessary, even gun work, to confiscate the goods. In this quest to deal a blow to the Watson Gang, these lawmen now had grief coming their way.

William Watson was the leader of the gang and while debatable, his brother, John Watson, was probably a member of the gang as well. The first known, or documented crime committed by William Watson was when he and Peter Malone stole the cotton seed in Indian Territory which took place on October 30, 1879. They took the seed across the Red River into Montague County, Texas, and they were caught at Wyatt Williams' ranch as they were in the process of delivering the seed to Williams. His ranch was near Spanish Fort.

Of course, Wyatt Williams was a partner in crime with Watson who was his brother-in-law, being he was married to Watson's sister. These two old boys were thick as fleas on a yard dog. While not mentioned, it is likely that Marshal Tucker and his posse nabbed the thieves.

The crime was committed in Indian Territory and under the control of the U. S. marshal of the Western District of Arkansas, at Fort Smith. A federal warrant was issued there on December 4, 1879, and a deputy marshal traveled from Fort Smith to Courtney Flat, twenty-five miles north of the mouth of Mud Creek, Chickasaw Nation, and served the warrant on Watson the day after Christmas 1879. The arrest took place near gang member W. R. Watkins' store, located near Watson's house. Watkins denied being involved in the theft at the examination trial. Any documentation on the disposition of the case is unknown.[1]

Then, on March 15, 1881, William Watson and Roscoe Turner entered into high crime by stealing eight hogs valued at $64, from the pens of Arch McGehee. A hog thief was listed in most lawmen's book as the lowest crime a criminal could pull.

A federal warrant was issued August 1, 1881, being the high crime was committed in Indian Territory, near Courtney Flat. Twenty-two year old Deputy Jacob T. "Jake" Ayers was called to the marshal's office and given the warrant with instructions to go after William Watson and bring him in for stealing the hogs.

The marshal allowed Ayers to take a sidekick with him for backup and Deputy Marshal Bass Reeves agreed to ride with him. This was common practice for deputies to travel in pairs, even when going after hog thieves. Reeves agreed and they rode out of Fort Smith, Arkansas, for the long ride to Courtney Flat, located down in the Chickasaw Nation just north of Spanish Fort, Texas.[2]

It was the 25th of September when they arrived just north of Courtney Flat. They stopped in the brush and made camp. Then deputies Ayers and Reeves rode into Courtney Flat and approached William Watson's house. Ayers called for Watson and found him home. He did not resist arrest and Deputy Ayers read the arrest warrant to him and then put the handcuffs on him and had him to ride double on his horse.

Later Watson tried to bribe Ayers in the presence of Bass Reeves and George Tucker's cousin, Frank Tucker, who had been hired as posseman, guard and cook for this trip. The bribe amount Watson offered was $150, later upped it to $300 and at one point Watson had Deputy Ayers write a letter to his cohort Wyatt Williams, telling him to mail plenty of money to McAllister, a town in eastern Indian Territory and on the route of travel back to Fort

The federal jail in Fort Smith was located in the basement. There was a cell for soli-
tary confinement and regular inmates slept on the floor. *Photo courtesy National Park
Service, Fort Smith, Arkansas.*

Smith. Deputy Ayers intended for his party to stop there before
going on to Fort Smith.[3]

After delivering the prisoner to the jail in the basement of the
federal courthouse in Fort Smith, Deputy Ayers, Bass Reeves, and
Frank Tucker remained nearby as they knew they would be required to testify as witnesses in the larceny and attempted bribery
charge against Watson. Frank Tucker had family nearby in Franklin County, only about forty miles to the east and it is likely he
took time to visit his relatives.[4]

When the case came to trial on September 12, 1881, and the
court declared in session, the charges were read against William
Watson. Theft of hogs and attempted bribery on the 16th day of
August, 1881, in Indian Territory, when defendant made promise
to J. T. Ayers, the sum of $300 to let him go. The plaintiff was Wil-
liam H. Clayton, U. S. attorney, and defendant, in custody of the
Marshal and by his attorney Burt Duval *Esq.* with the following
testimony from deputy U. S. Marshal Jacob T. Ayers, resident of
Fort Smith, Arkansas.

After being sworn in Deputy Ayers was instructed by prosecutor Clayton to provide the details about the bribery. Avery re-

sponded that he did arrest William Watson on the 16th day of August, near Burlington, [Spanish Fort] Texas, either in Montague or Cooke County. "I put him on my horse with me and we ended up at Kirk Williams' house. Watson wanted to stop there and make some arrangements for some money."

Watson discussed the need for money with Williams. Watson called Deputy Ayers to the side a few feet away from Bass Reeves and asked how much money it would take to let him go. Ayers reported that he turned him down flat.

Deputy Ayers and party rode out that night and after crossing the Red, stayed the remainder of the

William Henry Harrison Clayton, best known as W. H. H. Clayton was born October 13, 1840 and died December 14, 1920. He was the United States Attorney for the United States District Court for the Western District of Arkansas and the chief prosecutor in the court of "hanging judge" Isaac Parker for fourteen years. *Photo from author's collection.*

night at William R. Mathews' place. The next day they traveled to Courtney Flat and Watson offered his brother John's horse as a gift to Ayers who again turned him down.

The next day their camp was moved to Spring Creek. During the four days they remained in that camp, Watson made numerous attempts to bribe Ayer with various tactics, all without success. Then, the camp was moved to the Washita River, three miles below Cherokeetown where they remained two nights. Watson wouldn't give it up and tried again. He had upped his offer from $100 to $300. Then, he wanted Ayers to write a letter to his father-in-law, John Turner, to tell Wyatt Williams to send plenty of money to McAllister as they would be going through the town. Deputy Ayers did not know if Watson mailed the letter but when he inquired at the post office in McAllister, no reply had been sent. That ended the questioning by the prosecution.

Deputy Ayers was then crossed-examined by the defense attorney and Ayers' story was basically the same. He testified that he was justified in making the arrest of Watson as he had a warrant for his arrest issued by Stephen Wheeler and directed to the marshal of the Western District of Arkansas.

Ayers explained that the constable of Burlington, George Tucker, was with him, being he also had a warrant for Watson's arrest, issued by a justice of the peace at Burlington, Texas. Tucker's warrant was issued for larceny in Indian Territory. Ayers further testified that to his knowledge there were no charges in Texas for larceny against Watson.

Watson was arrested at Turner's house and he admitted it was Turner's house and Constable Tucker, Deputy Marshal Bass Reeves, Johnson, and another man whose name Ayers did not know was there when he made the arrest. He further stated that the defendant's brother came to the camp and he also tried to bribe him. He spoke about employing an attorney.

"He might have asked me how much it would cost him to employ an attorney to beat the case before the Commissioner." Ayers stated. "I think he did and that I told him I did not know. Then I went back across the Red to serve subpoenas."

Deputy Marshal Bass Reeves was called to testify next as he was with Deputy Marshal Jacob Ayers on that trip. "I was his posse," said Reeves.

His story was basically the same as Deputy Ayers. He did add that when Watson spoke privately to Ayers about a bribe, it wasn't really private as he had overhead the entire conversation. Deputy Reeves also testified that Watson asked him what he thought Ayers would take to release him.

"I told him Ayers could not release him, that one deputy had already gone to the penitentiary for such as that," Reeves said.

Deputy Reeves was referring to an incident back in August, 1879, when Deputy Marshal Sam Waters accepted a bribe of $125 from a man named Campbell who had committed manslaughter. Waters released him from jail and then left the country. Four years later Waters came back and turned himself in. He was then convicted and sent to federal prison.[5]

Deputy Reeves was crossed-examined by the defense and again told the same story. Then Frank Tucker was called to the stand. Frank was serving as a posseman, guard, and cook. He was with Jake Ayers on his last trip when he brought in Watson. He overhead Watson offer money on several occasions and also tried to bribe Frank into releasing him. "I told him I could not," stated Tucker.

William Watson claimed self-defense on the larceny charge saying "I killed them hogs by mistake." It surely was a mistake but not for committing the crime, only for getting caught. He was found guilty of larceny and attempted bribery. The judge told him that he was going to release him under the condition that he pay restitution for the killing of the hogs, valued at $65 and let him return to Courtney Flat.

It was ironic that this foolish, if not completely stupid outlaw was willing to offer $300 and a horse to escape when in the end it only cost him $65, travel, jail, and court time.[6]

Deputy U. S. Marshal Jacob T. Ayers was born on October 12, 1858, and he was just a young man in his early twenties in 1881. Unfortunately, this outstanding young man died of a gunshot wound the following February. He wasn't shot by any of the criminal element in the vast and dangerous Indian country he and other deputies rode to serve subpoenas, warrants, and make arrests to bring law and order to a violent land. Jacob Ayers pistol accidentally discharged and put a bullet in his leg. He died a week later with complications from the injury. He was buried in Oak Cemetery, Fort Smith. "He was a gentleman and died a brave man," proclaimed the *Fort Smith Elevator*.[7]

There was no doubt that William "Bill" Watson was nothing but an outlaw. Sam Sixkiller, captain of the U. S. Indian Police was quoted as saying, "William Watkins habitually kept a band of outlaws about him and on his place and William Watson has the reputation of a lawless desperado." On December 24, 1886, Captain Sixkiller was murdered in Muskogee by two men named Dick Vann and Alf Cunningham.[8]

A point to be considered was the roles of possemen employed by various local law enforcement and deputy U. S. marshals. Officers of the law kept a list of people's names who could be trusted to shoot straight, follow orders, had good horses, and available when called upon to help a lawman confront or chase an alleged wrong doer. These men were paid a fee for assistance, usually by the town or county if assisting a local lawman and by the federal government if assisting a deputy U. S. marshal. However, the officer usually made the payment and filed a claim with the appropriate agency for reimbursement.[9]

After the gunfight and confiscation of goods from the Watson Gang at Courtney Flat, Marshal Tucker believed gang member Trowbridge had been killed and buried up in the territory but that was not the case. Trowbridge had recovered from his wounds and went to Shannon, Texas, where he swore out warrants against every member of the posse. He had somehow obtained everyone's name.

On March 18, 1886, United States Marshal Cabell of the Fort Smith district sent Deputy Marshal Spangler down to Montague County to serve warrants for sixteen men. They were issued by the United States Commissioner's Court in Sherman, Texas, which commanded the U. S. marshal to arrest Marshal George Tucker, the Montague County sheriff, the posse members, and teamsters, for robbery and assault with intent to murder Trowbridge and Watson on February 21, 1886, in Chickasaw Nation, in the Western District of Arkansas.[10]

It just so happened that after Deputy Marshal Spangler served those warrants he went over to Sherman and arrested Tom Goodman on the 24th of March, who was leading a railroad workers' strike.[11]

Upon arrest of the Tucker party, they appeared before the court to be officially charged and all gave bond and were released until trial. Judge Rickets, a very elderly man, was the judge of that court. He set a date and they went to trial. Judge Bryant was the prosecutor and one of Tucker's best friends, but he showed no favoritism in the case according to Tucker.

They were charged with the theft of over $7,000 worth of goods. The evidence showed that the Tucker faction had warrants for the arrest of the Watson Gang members, but the warrants bore no dates. Those were the warrants Indian agent Robert Owen had sent to Murray. It appeared as though the sixteen men were really in for it, and likely would have been had it not been for a lawyer's appetite for whiskey and the resourcefulness of a man named Jameson.[12]

In George Tucker's autobiography he wrote that the charges

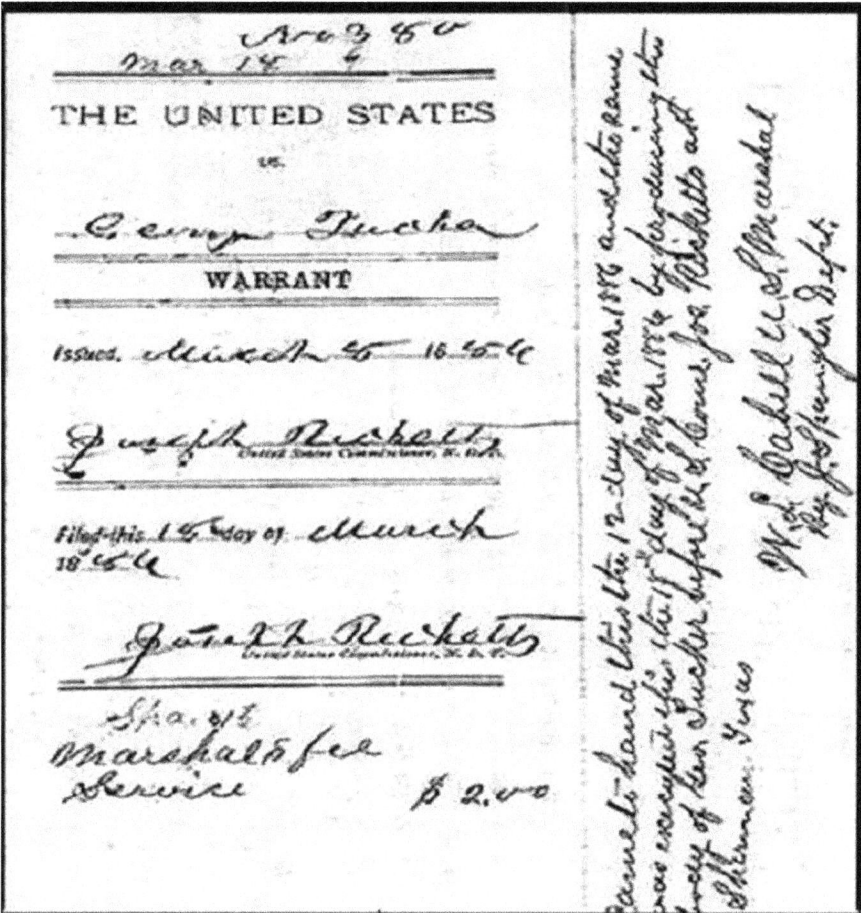

Arrest warrant for Marshal Tucker. The document reflects a fee for serving the warrant at $2. The writing on the right side states: Came to hand this, the 12th day of March, 1886, and the warrant was executed this the 18th day of March, 1886 by producing the body of Geo. Tucker before U. S. Comm. Jos. Ricketts at Sherman, Texas. Signed W. L. Cabell U. S. Marshal by J. Spangler Deputy. *Photo courtesy of Mike Tower.*

were filed in Shannon, Texas. Shannon was only a small community and never a town. Records prove the charges were filed in Sherman, Texas, with the federal authorities. The rule then was prisoners had to be taken to the nearest U. S. Commissioner for examination, sort of, but not the same as a preliminary trial, to determine if the evidence indicated advancement to trial or to be released and dismissed. If witnesses failed to appear at this examination, it did not give the accused an automatic right for either a mistrial or release. The commissioner was under no obligation to end the government's case.

In this case, Tucker and associates were released on bond after the court determined just cause to forward the case to Judge Parker's court in Fort Smith, Arkansas, with a recommendation that the charged be brought to trial for assault with intent to murder, larceny, and introducing liquor into the territory.[13]

It should be noted, concerning federal jurisdictions that, in 1883, the Northern District was given jurisdiction over what was called the Leased District and included the Comanche Indian Reserve. The dividing line was the 98th meridian just to the west of the old Chisholm Trail. Then in 1888, an act was passed which allowed any marshal of any district to enter Indian Territory and serve process. This would bring much heartache to many deputy marshals a few years after the Paris court was established in March 1889.[14]

In Tucker's case, a complaint had been made by members of the Watson Gang, a warrant issued and served, but the process fell apart at the commissioner's examination due to failure of witnesses to appear on three separate attempts. The case was forwarded due to lack of evidence. There was no free pass for Tucker and his fellow lawmen, simply a delay.

The federal prosecutor of Parker's court, under whose jurisdiction the alleged crime occurred, obviously continued to believe the matter needed resolution and so issued a second warrant. This was not an unusual occurrence. Of course, the accused had a different view of the matter. Outlaws had made the complaints and traveling to Fort Smith would take them away from hearth and home for months without knowing if or when they would return.[15]

According to Tucker the court took a recess during the course of the examination, or trial, for awhile. Judge Bryant and Judge Hare, friends of long standing, "and old topers as well, went out to have a drink together. While they were gone Jameson stole the evidence," said Tucker.

When the judges came back from recess court was resumed. That is when the loss was noticed. Judge Rickets stormed and raved and ordered everyone searched, but no trace of the evidence was discovered. Thereupon, Judge Rickets turned the accused loose. Tucker said, "It was a pretty close shave and I'm grateful to

Jameson to this day. I never knew what became of the evidence. But to have convicted us would have been to help those thieving rascals from over in the Territory."[16]

Tucker's story could not be proven. The court records did not support or deny George Tucker's story of the evidence being stolen or tampered with. The judge did note that on three separate dates in March 1886, the witnesses did not appear, even though ordered by the court. It is possible that someone may have stolen the written complaints or other exhibits from the prosecution.

Tucker might have thought he and his cohorts had pulled a fast one and wouldn't hear anymore about the charges. After all, the complaints came from a known outlaw gang. Though exonerated at Sherman, Texas, or so they thought, it was soon learned that the wheels of justice were turning against them.

Trowbridge and the Watson Gang were definitely a fly in the ointment. The federal grand jury of the United States Court of Fort Smith, with jurisdiction over Indian Territory, charged the group with assault to murder in two cases and theft of $7,000 worth of goods.[17]

United States Deputy Marshal Charley Garrison was given the warrants to serve and he traveled to Spanish Fort and various locations in Montague County and made the arrest of all sixteen men, including the sheriff, deputies, Marshal Tucker, the posse, and the wagon drivers. Deputy Garrison told them everyone would have to go with him to Fort Smith and had arranged for wagons to be used in making the trip.

Preparations were made and the arrestees were carried in the wagons along with bedding and supplies. When night came, they made camp, unhitched the teams so they could drink and graze, and prepared supper. They sat around talking each evening until time to spread their blankets. Deputy Garrison had two possemen with him but according to Tucker, no one had any intention of trying to escape as everyone wanted to stand trial at Fort Smith and have the case resolved. No one was handcuffed and every man carried his guns strapped on his waist. They left Spanish Fort traveling east to Sherman, then turned to the northeast up through present day Durant and up to McAlester, Eufaula, and on northeast to Fort Smith, Arkansas, a distance of around three-hundred miles. It took the party approximately thirty days to reach their destination.[18]

Chapter Seven

Judge Parker's Court

The Territory of Arkansas was admitted to the Union as the 25th state on June 15, 1836. Its name is of *Siouan* derivation from the language of the Osage denoting their related kin, the Quapaw Indians.[1] The 32nd Congress decided a court was needed in western Arkansas and on March 3, 1851, Congress passed a law establishing the district to be domiciled in Van Buren, Arkansas. Though they were separate courts, the Eastern and Western Districts of Arkansas had only one judge. Twenty-years later to the day in 1871, Congress passed a law that shifted the court from Van Buren to Fort Smith, and approved the appointment of a judge solely for the Western District.[2]

Judge William Story was appointed and he called the court to order the first time on Monday, May 6, 1871, in the Rogers Building. In less than two years the building burned. This occurred on November 14, 1872. On November 18, Judge Story moved his court to the old "Soldiers Quarters." The court's future was shaky due to graft and corruption from within the Western District causing a congressional investigation to commence in the spring of 1874.

Bills were introduced to abolish the court in Fort Smith, but the Senate failed to act, however, Story resigned under fire. A new judge, Henry J. Caldwell, was temporally seated while waiting for the appointment of Story's replacement. Judge Story sent seven men to the gallows during his judgeship of the Western District. Judge Caldwell sentenced one man to die at the November 1874 term of court.[3]

On the surface, one may think that Judge Isaac Parker was calloused and uncaring, with a lust for hanging wrong doers. He held the reputation as *The Hanging Judge*. However, when looking at his record, it reveals that a large majority of his convictions resulted in prison sentences. This was a lawless time on the western frontier with the Indian Territory infested with killers, rapists, robbers, whiskey peddlers, thieves, and every kind of unsavory character.

Isaac Charles Parker was born October 15, 1838, and died November 17, 1896. He was the presiding U.S. District Judge for the U.S. District Court, Western District of Arkansas. He served in this capacity for twenty-one years; during the most dangerous time for law enforcement during the western expansion. He is still remembered today as the *Hanging Judge* of the American Old West.

Parker had submitted a request for appointment as the judge of the Federal District Court for the Western District of Arkansas, in Fort Smith and was approved. He arrived at Fort Smith by steamboat on May 4, 1875,

Judge Isaac Parker, 1896. Judge Parker served over the Western District of Arkansas for twenty-one years. *Photo courtesy National Park Service, Fort Smith, Ark.*

and just six days later, on May 10, heard his first case.

In the first term of his court, eighteen men came before him charged with murder and fifteen were convicted. On September 3, 1875, six men were executed at once on the Fort Smith gallows. During his years on the bench, Judge Parker tried 13,490 cases, 344 of which were capital crimes. Guilty pleas or convictions were handed down in 9,454 cases. A total of 156 men and four women were sentenced to death by hanging, but only seventy-nine were actually hanged. The rest died in jail, appealed and were commutated to prison terms, or were pardoned.[4]

Judge Parker's chief hangman was George Maledon. Before becoming the hangman, Maledon was a deputy sheriff; then a turnkey at the federal jail. Later, he was appointed special deputy and his job was supervising the execution of those sentenced to hang. For twenty-two years, Maledon carried out the orders of the court, sending sixty convicted criminals to their death. He shot and killed two men and wounded three others during escape attempts. The 1899 publication of *Hell on the Border* documented Maledon's ties to the executions of the Federal Court, and first bestowed the title of "Prince of Hangmen." Newspapers pegged him "Prince of Hangmen" while others listed him as "King of Hangmen."

When Maledon retired his replacement was another George, surnamed Lawson. His first drop from the scaffold box was Crawford Goldsby, known as Cherokee Bill.[5]

GEORGE LAWSON.

George Lawson replaced George Maledon as Judge Parker's hangman. His first execution was Cherokee Bill. *Drawing from author's collection.*

To the west of Fort Smith was Indian Territory. There were legal systems and governments of these five tribes which covered their own citizens while the Federal Court protected the rights of American citizens. Several famous lawmen served as deputy marshals during the Parker court.

According to Congress, the Federal Court for the Western District of Arkansas was to meet in four separate terms each year; February, May, August, and November. In reality, the court had such a large case load that the four terms ran together. In an effort to ensure that the court tried as many cases as possible each term, Judge Parker held court six days a week, and often up to ten hours each day.

In 1883, Congress changed the jurisdiction of the court, and removed portions of the Indian Territory jurisdiction to Federal Courts in Texas and Kansas. The decreased size of the jurisdiction provided some relief; however, the continued influx of settlers into the Indian Territory, and the resulting problems, contributed to an increased crime rate.[6]

The first executions under the tenure of Judge Isaac Parker took place on September 3, 1875. They were Edmund Campbell, Daniel Evans, William Whittington, Samuel Fooy, Smoker Mankiller, and

James Moore.[7]

Edmund Campbell killed Lawson Ross and his wife in revenge for an insult.

Evans and Whittington killed their traveling companions for the cash and goods they carried. Fooy, a hired gunman, killed a school teacher for $250. Mankiller murdered his neighbor over a land dispute.

Moore, said to be a notorious cold-blooded killer with seven notches in his pistol grip, killed Deputy U. S. Marshal William Spivey.

The first six executed in Judge Parker's court were Edmund Campbell, Daniel Evans, William Whittington, Samuel Fooy, Smoker Mankiller, and James Moore.
Photo courtesy National Park Service, Fort Smith, Ark.

George Maledon said the following in regard to the six men during an 1887 interview with a newspaper reporter:

Six was the largest number ever taken out at one time, and they were, with one exception, fine-looking young men — William Moore, Dan Evans, Sam Fooy, William Whittington, and Ed Campbell, a negro boy. Moore was the first man I ever saw go off mad. He glanced over the immense crowd surrounding the gallows defiantly, and when asked if he had anything to say, remarked that there were worse men than he is standing around looking on. A striking contrast to Moore, however, was Sam Fooy, whose mother, wife, and children were near at hand, and who was well acquainted with many who had come to see him hanged. During the ceremonies on the gallows he stood facing the crowd with a pleasant smile on his face, nodding his head frequently as his eye caught that of some friend. When asked if he desired to say anything, he glanced around and said in a pleasant tone of voice, 'I am as anxious to have this thing over with as these who have assembled to see it, and therefore will not delay matters — farewell to all.'[8]

"There would have been seven to hang this time, said Maledon, "but Ed Butler, a negro, attempted to escape after receiving sentence and was killed by a guard. There have been five

George Maledon served as a jailer and became known as "The Prince of Hangmen," in Judge Parker's court. *Photo courtesy National Park Service, Fort Smith, Ark.*

ansashung at one time on two different occasions since this exe-

This is the only known photograph of Judge Parker holding court. It was taken in the courtroom he used for the last six years of his term. In 1890 the federal court moved from the old barracks building to a new courthouse on Sixth Street. There are no known photographs of the courtroom that was located in the former military barracks and used from 1872-1890.

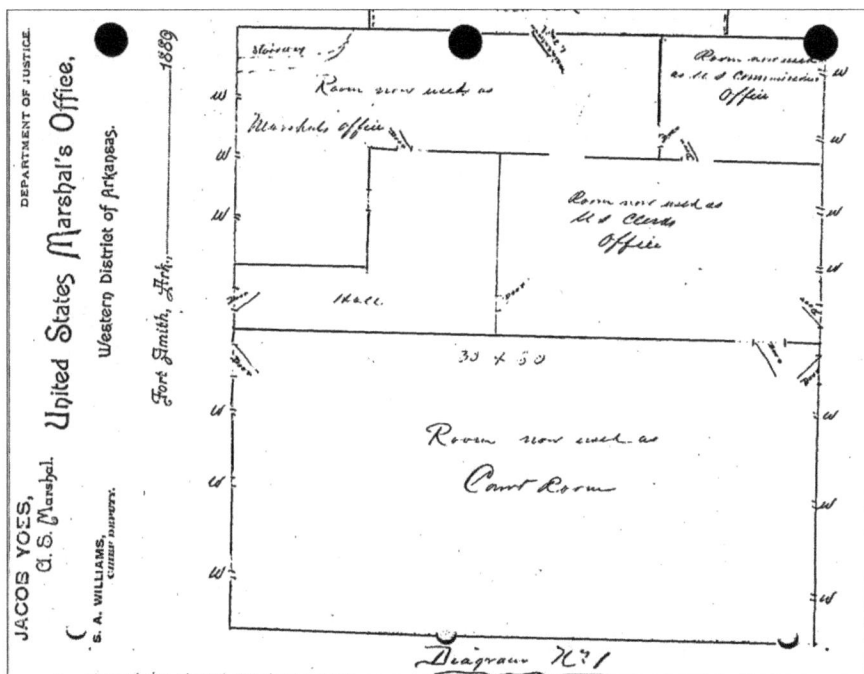

No photographs are known to exist of Judge Parker's courtroom prior to 1890. This 1889 drawing shows the layout of the courtroom and adjacent offices. *Drawing courtesy National Park Service, Fort Smith, Arkansas.*

cution."[9]

The Courts Act of 1889, coming a month after Congress authorized the Supreme Court review, established a federal court system in the Indian Territory, further decreasing the Fort Smith court's jurisdiction.[10]

In the year 1886, the Federal Courthouse in Fort Smith, Arkansas, had its courtroom on the bottom floor. The room was thirty by fifty feet. Off to the right was the U. S. marshal's office, the clerk's office, and the U. S. commissioner's office. Judge Isaac Parker's office was located upstairs. Many court cases under Judge Parker would take place over the next few years in Fort Smith, Arkansas.[11]

* * * * *

George Tucker had stated that he, along with Sheriff McLain of Montague County, Texas, his brother, Bill, cousin, Jack Tucker, all of the possemen and teamsters, were exonerated for the charges of attempted murder and theft of property in the trial at Sherman, Texas. That was an accurate assessment, however, a true bill of indictment was brought against Tucker's party on May 3, 1886, by the Western District of Arkansas grand jury for attempted murder against William Watson and James Trowbridge, as well as theft of property from William Watkins, better known as the Watson Gang. It seems even outlaws could have lawmen charged with crimes.

Those possemen and teamsters charged were Dock Nicks, William Black, James Avis, Frank Avis, Robert Nicks, Phillip Dunnford, John Orr, Isaac Inman, William "Bill" Tucker, Jack Tucker, and William Bagwell. Also charged: Daniel Hurst, John Abner, Jeff Jimerson, Indian policeman F. H. Murray, J. B. March, and "One" Bush. The indictment was approved on May 20, 1886, and the defendants ordered to appear on August 2, 1886.

A copy of the true bill had "110 years of Independence" written at the bottom of the document. Tucker claimed and records confirmed that Deputy U. S. Marshal Charley Garrison, went to Spanish Fort and made the arrest of everyone charged. Little is known of Deputy Garrison's law enforcement and his years of employment are vague.[12]

After that thirty-day trip from Montague County and appearing in court, the defendants gave bond. Those men who went their bonds were Colonel William Cravens, who would be retained as their attorney; Ben Burney, Governor of the Chickasaw Nation, and Captain Sam Sixkiller, U. S. Indian policeman and said to be a wealthy Indian. All were recognized as reputable men in Indian Territory.

After making bond, the defendants returned to Spanish Fort, in the same wagons used to transport them to Fort Smith, until the trial should necessitate their presence in Federal Court. The trial date was set for six months from the date of making bond in Fort Smith.[13]

The group of defendants were all back in time for trial, and established a camp on the outskirts of the town where they slept and cooked their meals. After all, they were required to pay their own expenses. It was in the month of November 1886.

Deputy Marshal Garrison told them to take off their gun belts and leave all weapons in camp. He did not think it would set too good for any of them to enter the courtroom healed with guns. Tucker said, "We were very glad to comply with his request, as he was a nice fellow and had been awfully good to us ever since he arrested us. We knew that he was our friend and that he was, in arresting us, merely performing his official duty." Every morning the defendants stripped off their guns before leaving for the court-room. They threw them in a pile and left a member of their party to guard them while they were gone. When they came back after adjournment of the court, they buckled them on again.[14]

The defendants were likely afraid of Judge Parker, who pre-sided over the court. In Tucker's opinion, the judge was unmer-ciful with criminals and sentenced them to the scaffold without batting an eye. But, Tucker claimed he never feared the outcome of the trial, stating he and his co-defendants were not guilty of anything that merited criminal convictions. Tucker, even in his el-derly years, remembered Judge Parker vividly. He ran into him publicly a few times and faced him twice in his court, this time as a defendant and on another occasion as a witness.[15]

Tucker's description of Judge Parker was that he was a large man standing six-feet-tall and weighing about two hundred pounds and the eyes were his most impressive feature, being large, expressive, and becoming friendly or cold as steel in an instant. In sentencing criminals, they flashed down at them like glints of fire.

Tucker's firsthand account depicted Judge Parker as having a deep, basso, or powerful voice that spoke with dignity. "His voice rolled like distant thunder," said Tucker. "With his powerful voice, he could be heard from anywhere in the courtroom. There was never any question concerning whether he really meant what he said."[16]

Judge Parker lived about a half-mile from the courthouse. He walked to the courthouse every morning, speaking to everyone he met. According to Tucker, Judge Parker was a friendly man, espe-cially to law abiding citizens.

Tucker recalled that a trial was going on while he and his party were waiting for their case to be called. A relative of J. J. McAl-ester, for who the city of McAlester, Oklahoma, was named, was being tried for murder. The defendant was part Indian and the ev-idence against him was extremely far-fetched. Judge Parker saw it and acted accordingly. Instead of writing out his instructions and reading them to the jury, he gave it to them extemporaneously. One could see that Parker did not believe the man guilty, from

Tucker's point of view.

The jury retired to consider the evidence. In a very short time, they returned and announced a verdict of not guilty. There was a roar of applause in the court room. Men threw their hats in the air and yelled like madmen. Among the spectators was Ben Burney, governor of the Chickasaw Nation. This conduct greatly angered Judge Parker. Justice to him was not chivalry; it resulted from a verdict upon the basis of testimony. There was, therefore, according to Judge Parker, no need for demonstration when a verdict was reached, and to impress the demonstrators with the character of the court, Parker ordered every one of them arrested on the spot and fined $50 each for contempt of court. In addition, he give them stern reprimands for acting out in his courtroom. "I've never heard more forceful language from any man," said Tucker.[17]

Colonel William M. Cravens was their defense attorney and was prepared to go up against the prosecutor, Colonel W. H. Clayton, a relative of former governor of Arkansas, General Powell Clayton. He had the reputation of an able lawyer.

This would be a trial by jury and defendant, Jack Tucker, cousin of George, was sitting next to Colonel Craves as they were selecting the jury. Tucker wrote that four of the prospective jurors were Negro women and Cravens asked Jack what he thought about them as jurymen. Jack told him that he wasn't sure, but pointed out that Negroes might be inclined to make it a little hard on Texans. Tucker claimed that defense attorney Craven told Jack that all four of the blacks were women and there was nothing to worry about as he had slept with two of them the night before and planned to sleep with the other two the next night. "After hearing that, we were not afraid," claimed Tucker, "even if most of us had been raised in the South."[18]

First of all, Colonel Cravens was a prominent member of the bar and outstanding citizen. His full name was William Murphy Cravens, son of Jeremiah Cravens and Kitura Murphy. He was born June 26, 1833, in Fredericktown, Missouri. He attended college north of Fort Smith at Fayetteville, Arkansas, and graduated from Cumberland University's law school in 1859.

During the Civil War, he served in the Twenty-first Arkansas Infantry. In 1868, he moved to Fort Smith, Arkansas, where he established a law practice. He died January 2, 1919. He is buried in

This drawing of various people in Judge Parker's court of 1889 shows Judge Parker, prisoner, his mother, attorneys, marshal, and jurymen. The drawing shows white men and a black juryman in the upper center. This adds credibility to the fact that black men did serve in Parker's court. *Drawing courtesy National Park Service, Fort Smith, Arkansas.*

Forest Park Cemetery, Fort Smith. Colonel Cravens son, William Ben Cravens became an attorney also and served in the United States Congress from 1907 to 1913, and again from 1933 until his death on 1939. It is possible that Tucker was trying to impress future readers of his life and those court proceedings.[19]

Also, records prove that black men did serve on Judge Parker's juries but no evidence has been found to conclude that any women, black or white, served. The judge was very strict for court rules and would not tolerate an attorney tampering with or trying to influence jurors. Those people were watched like hawks, often with a deputy U. S. marshal assigned to avoid such things. There are many examples wherein Parker threw the book at people tapering with jurors.[20]

After jury selections were made, the court was called to order. The prosecution's opening remarks made it clear that he planned to convince the jury that the defendants committed assault with intent to kill William Watson and James Trowbridge --- that they committed larceny by confiscating goods from William Watkins' store valued at $7,000 and the introducing of liquor unlawfully into Indian Territory.[21]

Defense attorney Colonel Cravens approached the bench and presented a petition, duly subscribed and sworn to on this the 22nd day of July, 1886; signed Thomas Boone. He confirmed that the charges within the indictment had previously been examined by commissioner Ricketts of Sherman, Texas, and defendants McLain and the majority of his co-defendants who were charged with the assault with intent to murder were discharged by said commissioner in March of 1886. Cravens pointed out to the judge that there were fifteen material witnesses for the defense who were not present and they could not safely proceed to trial without those fifteen men and their testimony. They were: George Roark, Jack Hogue, R. N. Hancock, Eb Hail, Philip Hinson, John Fowler, Henry De Courtney, William Bruch, Alonzo McNeso, A. T. Horton, A. L. Shoemaker, J. D. Wilson, D. M. Smith, J. W. Henderson, and Wade Horton.[22]

All witnesses for the defense who knew Watson and his gang testified that they were bad men for truth and veracity, unworthy of belief under oath, and all were present at the time of the alleged assault, and that Watson and gang fired the first shots and put those charged on the defensive. Trowbridge was seen to open fire after the gun fighting began with a double-barreled shotgun aimed and fired at the defendants.

William Burch was called to the stand and explained his part by stating that he was in charge of the telephone line at Burlington [Spanish Fort] and he transmitted messages to law enforcement from U.S. Indian Agent Owens and from Frank H. Murray, U.S. Indian Police, on the day before the alleged assault. The message received instructed and directed the sheriff to go to Burlington and that the said Murray would there turn over to him the Watson Gang for whom the Governor of Texas had issued his requisitions.

Alougon McNew of Burlington, was called to testify and he stated that it was true that William Watson reloaded his pistol and Winchester when he saw the defendants approaching. He turned and asked his gang if they had cartridges enough to make the fight and said, "I aim to charge for 'em God D---m 'em. I'll meet 'em on the ground." McNew then stated that Watson got on his horse and started riding toward the defendants knowing and recognizing Murray and knew he was a member of the U.S. Indian Police.

As for other witnesses, Cravens said to Judge Parker, "Sheriff McLain does not possess sufficient means and is actually unable to pay the fees of the witnesses and claimed his co-defendants were also unable to pay. Therefore, I pray that they may be subpoenaed at the expense of the United States, in this United States of America, Western District of Arkansas."[23]

Sheriff L. L. McLain took the stand and after being duly sworn before the court said, "My statements contained in the foregoing petition are true as I believe." He had signed the petition on the July 22, 1886.

The prosecutor called W. R. "Bill" Watkins to the stand and he swore that he had been adopted into the Chickasaw tribe. He claimed he made his living farming and running a store where he provided dry goods, ready to wear clothing, boots and shoes and various things for his neighbors. He claimed that on February 21, 1886, the men whose names were on the complaint came and took everything he had in the store at gunpoint. He said that Murray told him he had an order to take the goods because they came from Burlington. He claimed he had a bill of sale from merchant Leforce and his cost was about $200. He told Murray they were his goods and did not belong to Leforce. That was on the 28th that they returned and took his goods. He claimed he told them he would have them prosecuted.

Watkins continued his testimony as follows;

When they came back, there were thirteen or fourteen of them in wagons but one was a covered wagon. Mr. Murray was riding a horse with a rifle across his saddle. They took my goods and loaded them into the covered wagon. His clerk had invoiced the goods at $2,000 but Watkins claimed that did not include other goods he had on hand. He claimed the goods were worth at least $4,000. They took his goods to Burlington [Spanish Fort] in Montague County, Texas, and later moved the goods to the town of Montague. When asked about the shooting, Watkins only mentioned some of the defendants and failed to admit that he or other gang members were shooting. He claimed that Watson was wounded in the arm but could not see Trowbridge. He completed his testimony by stating that he was a citizen of the Chickasaw Nation and Murray was a policeman and was not treating him right.

Watkins was a white man and came to Indian Territory from Grayson County, Texas, in 1866, and had been living just north of the Red River for twenty years. He married a Chickasaw woman and was adopted into the tribe based on the treaty of 1866. He admitted to doing business in Spanish Fort with Mr. Leforce who was in the dry goods business.[24]

The trial lasted eight days according to Tucker and several men from Courtney Flat came to testify against the Watson Gang. Bill Watkins, the man from whom they seized the goods, was bitter against the lawmen. Tucker believed his testimony was given in such a way to have a negative outcome for the defendants, but went too far in his statements and in the end weakened the prosecution's case.[25]

In final arguments, prosecuting attorney, Colonel Clayton, didn't try to convict everyone on the raid, but he demanded the conviction of Sheriff McLain and Marshal Tucker. He stated in his argument that they introduced ten gallons of whiskey into Indian Territory during the raid. Tucker claimed they did not have any whiskey on that trip. But that did not prevent the prosecutor from trying to discredit their character in his argument.

According to Colonel Clayton, Tucker was way down on the list of being *just plain mean*, and Tucker said he had never realized before just how mean he was supposed to be. Introducing liquor was, of course, a crime that carried a two-year mandatory penitentiary term. Judge Parker dismissed the whiskey introduction charges as there was no evidence to support the claim.

Here is where Tucker most likely embellished the truth about Judge Parker. According to Tucker, Judge Parker asked the prosecutor for the amount of whiskey introduced in the indictments charge against the defendants and was told only ten gallons. Tucker quoted Judge Parker's reply, "Why, that's no more than the army of them could easily consume."

Judge Parker would not have excused the transport of intoxicating spirits into the Nations by anyone, including lawmen. It was illegal by treaty, federal law, and Chickasaw law to possess or sell. Many Texans never did understand that both possession and sale were against the law in the territory.

Judge Parker instructed the jury and they went behind closed doors to deliberate the fate of the lawmen and freighters' actions in dealing with a notorious outlaw gang. The jury took half a day to reach a verdict. When they came back, Judge Parker asked if they had reached a verdict. The foreman of the jury said they had. "We find the defendants not guilty on all charges."

Most of the defendants believed they should never have been tried as they were enforcing the law as they saw it. They were acting against a gang of tough law violators. They were acquitted in November 1886.[26]

* * * * *

The principal object of interest that Fort Smith had to show visitors was the notorious Cherokee Bill. Tucker indicated he visited him at the jail but it could not have been in 1886 as Craw-

Crawford Goldsby "Cherokee Bill" and his mother Ellen Lynch. *Photo courtesy National Park Service, Fort Smith, Arkansas.*

ford Goldsby, alias Cherokee Bill was not born until February 8, 1876, at Fort Concho, Texas. The son of George Goldsby, a buffalo soldier of Mexican, white and Sioux descent, and a woman named Ellen Beck, half-black, one-fourth Cherokee and one-fourth white.

When George Goldsby abandoned his pregnant wife and son two years later, Ellen returned to Fort Gibson and sent Crawford to Indian schools in Kansas and Pennsylvania. When he returned, he worked odd jobs until his first run-in with the law in the summer of 1893 at age seventeen.

Crawford Goldsby became an outlaw, known mainly by the alias Cherokee Bill. Responsible for the murders of eight men, he and his gang terrorized the Indian Territory for more than two years during 1893 and 1894. Cherokee Bill became a member of the Cook Gang led by Bill Cook. Their crimes started off small with whiskey charges and stealing horses, but soon led to train robberies, stage holdups, and bank robbery.

On November 9, 1894, Cherokee Bill killed Ernest Melton during a store and post office heist. It was this crime that Cherokee Bill would hang for in Fort Smith, but the road to the gallows had several more twists and turns for lawmen. By some hook or crook, deputy marshals arrested him and he was sentenced to hang for one of his many murders. A half-breed, this outlaw left a trail of crime behind him wherever he went. He was hanged on March 17, 1896, at Fort Smith. He could not by any means, compensate for all of his killings, for he had far too few lives to give.[27]

Tucker claimed they, the defendants, went out to see him. He was in the jail which stood close to the courtroom. Tucker may have been mistaken about visiting Cherokee Bill during his trial in 1886, unless he was referring to another Cherokee Bill. Tucker depicted his confined outlaw as mean, cruel, and desperate, despite the fact that he had not, in legend, acquired so great a reputation as many of his kind who could not match him in crime.

He said Cherokee Bill was always making peculiar noises, and spent his hours in the jail mocking turkey gobblers. His hat was said to be white with a wide red ribbon for band and he kept his hat on all of the time.[28]

*   *   *   *   *

Deputy U. S. Marshal Heck Thomas was one of the lawmen responsible for covering the Western District of Arkansas for Hanging Judge Parker. During the 1880s and '90s many residents of Courtney Flat became acquainted with Marshall Heck Thomas.

Justice had gone wanting on William Watson for a murder he committed on the first day of October 1882. Watson killed a man named John Phelps. For some unknown reason a warrant was not issued until February 17, 1887. Deputy Heck Thomas was given the warrant to serve on Watson and was also given warrants to serve on George and Jasper Doolin, cousins of the notorious outlaw and leader of the Wild Bunch, Bill Doolin.

When Deputy Heck Thomas, posse members Charles Woody and Sam Wingo, arrived at Courtney Flat, just north of Spanish Fort and the Red River, they first went to William L. Beard's residence. "They came by my house and wanted me to go with them

Deputy US Marshal Henry Andrew Thomas. He was better known as Heck Thomas, born January 12, 1850, and died August 14, 1912.

to look for Bill Watson," claimed Beard.

He took them to William Watson's house and they found him at home. Heck Thomas told Watson to come out of the house. The man was arrested without incident. The lawmen took Watson into custody and he remained under guard there in Courtney Flat that night. The next morning, they went looking for the Doolin brothers.

Posse member Wingo took charge of Watson as Heck Thomas and Charles Woody went around behind the house. Once around the house they spotted a man riding horseback toward them from a timbered ridge with open prairie between them. He seemed to be unarmed and both Thomas and Woody recognized him as being one of the men they were seeking, George Doolin.

Marshal Thomas ordered him to stop and Doolin checked his horse a little. "I have a writ for your arrest so stand easy," Thomas said as he pulled his pistol. He repeated himself again telling Doolin he was under arrest. Doolin suddenly turned his horse and started to flee. As he tried to escape, he reached into his saddle pocket. It was obvious that he was going for a pistol.

Thomas and Woody both already had their pistols out and opened fire on the fleeing fugitive. After they fired numerous shots George Doolin fell from his horse to the ground and landed on the other side of a fence from Thomas and Woody. When they got to him they saw a six-shooter lying on the ground near his body.[29]

Wingo had taken Watson around to the other side of the house where a well was being dug. He heard the shots but could not see what had happened. Woody and Beard rode up to Wingo at the well and Woody told him to go get a wagon, that they had just killed George Doolin. While going for the wagon Wingo spotted Jasper Doolin and arrested him on the writ they had for his arrest. He gave up without a struggle. When Wingo took the wagon to the body, "I saw a pistol lying near the body," he said. The lawmen had a writ for both Jasper and George Doolin. The charge against them was for larceny.[30]

Thomas and posse member, Charles Woody, were charged with murder and William L. Beard gave testimony during the trial in Fort Smith on August 24, 1887. In Beard's testimony, he verified the events that took place in the arrest of Watson and helping the lawmen to locate the Doolin brothers. The warrant on Watson for murder and on Jasper Doolin for larceny was served on June 16, 1887, and Heck Thomas and posse men departed with the prisoners for Fort Smith, Arkansas, on June 23.[31]

The court file shows that gang member, William R. Watkins, placed 200 head of cattle and twenty-five ponies up as sureties on Watson's bond. No records have been located to determine the outcome of the murder charge.[32]

The killing of George Doolin would bring a murder charge against Deputy Marshal Heck Thomas and Charles Woody. A descendant of Charles Woody reported him killed by outlaws in February of 1904, at the now defunct town of Belton, north of Tishomingo. However, no records have been found to support the claim.

Chapter Eight

The Rustler & the Horse Thief

Tucker and his deputy were trying to kill Lamb and add another grave to the Spanish Fort Boot Hill.

When federal writer Selfridge conducted her interview of George Redman Tucker, from his manuscript or in person, she also omitted the chapter titled *The Lamb Episode*. Regardless, the story revealed the human side of Tucker.

After his acquittal in Judge Parker's court, Tucker returned from Fort Smith and resumed his position as constable in Spanish Fort. He also continued to hold his commission as a deputy sheriff of Montague County. Tucker wrote that they had the usual run of petty business—drunks, disorderly conduct, fights, just to name a few minor crimes. He was getting new warrants for arrest of criminals on a regular bases as there was much unlawfulness during those times in a county that adjoined Indian country. If they happened to run into those fugitives, they were supposed to arrest them. One of the warrants, in particular, called for the arrest of a man named L. L. Lamb, wanted for cow-stealing near the town of Sherman, Texas.[1]

Marshal Tucker and a unnamed deputy sheriff saw Lamb as he rode into Spanish Fort one day. Lamb stopped at a mercantile store, apparently for supplies and while they did not see from which direction he entered town, they figured he had crossed the Red River from his hideout in Indian Territory.

Tucker discussed with the deputy that they should arrest Lamb, being he had a warrant and the deputy agreed to assist. As they approached Lamb, he was buying some handkerchiefs from the dry goods store. Lamb was being cautious and never got off his horse. The merchant brought the handkerchiefs out of the store and was handing them up to him as Tucker walked up and ordered Lamb to hand over his pistol. Lamb slowly removed his pistol from the holster but instead of dropping it, he palmed the weapon and raised it as he took aim at Tucker.

Lamb pulled back the hammer, but before he could squeeze off a shot at the lawmen, they both drew their pistols and started firing at Lamb. They kept firing until they emptied their guns. Lamb never got off a shot. He was hit hard and the bullets were fired at close range. One round hit him in the face and another round tore away his cheekbone. "I don't know whether we hit him any other place or not," said Tucker.

He figured Lamb to be mortally wounded and waited for him to fall from his horse but he didn't fall. He turned his horse and made a run for it. They hadn't had time to reload but, a man came running out of the saloon and handed Tucker his pistol and he emptied it at Lamb as he made his escape on horseback. Even though Tucker fired six additional rounds at Lamb, he doubted hitting him again as his horse was going too fast.[2]

All Tucker and the deputy saw was dust and realized that, even after being shot numerous times, Lamb got away with nothing but pure courage on his part. "Few men could have taken all those hits and still be able to ride away," said Tucker. He had respect for Lamb's courage but considered him just another outlaw hiding out in Indian country. He figured there was no way Lamb could survive and would die in the brush.[3]

Tucker assumed Lamb died of those gunshot wounds as he was not heard of for a long time. Then, about four or five years later Tucker took a train from Gainesville to Ardmore and to his surprise, he recognized Lamb as a passenger on the train. He made sure his sidearm was close at hand as he was about to met Lamb again. He was surprised that he was alive and seemed well. As Tucker approached him, Lamb smiled, recognizing Tucker immediately. He didn't go for a gun, but began to talk. "You saved me from going to torment," said Lamb. "That one scrape made a man out of me. I saw that I was headed straight for Hell."

"What are you doing now, Lamb?" Tucker asked.

"I have been preaching the Gospel of Jesus Christ," he replied. It seemed that Mr. Lamb had been washed in the blood of the Lamb. On a serious note, L. L. Lamb went on to become a rather famous evangelist which pleased George Tucker. He thanked Tucker over and over again for what had been done to him, and although hot lead had almost ended his life, that hot lead had given him cause to bare his soul and change his life. Tucker and his deputy were trying to kill him and had no thoughts about adding a number to the ministerial profession but, instead, was trying very hard to add another grave to the rapidly growing Spanish Fort Boot Hill.[4]

At this point in Tucker's life, the notches on his gun remained at two, with three or more shot and wounded.

Soon after returning to Spanish Fort, Tucker had to track down another criminal named Gid Beavers, who came to Spanish Fort and stole a horse and saddle belonging to Mr. U. S. Joines. Tucker followed Beavers to the Suggs' ranch, on Beaver Creek, where he found the horse and saddle.

The ranch was owned by Colonel E. C. "Cal" Suggs and his brother, I. D. "Ike" Suggs. After talking with Colonel Suggs, Tucker mounted up and rode to Gid Beavers' mother's little place on Mud Creek, just north of Courtney Flat. He was there, so Tucker arrested him. Beavers gave no trouble, submitting like a child according to Tucker. He was transported immediately to Fort Smith, where Tucker turned him over to the federal officials in Judge Parker's court.

According to Tucker, Beavers was convicted of the theft and sent to the federal penitentiary at Leavenworth, Kansas, however, no record exist to substantiate the claim. It is likely that he was sent to one of the federal prisons in the north, such as Detroit. After serving his sentence, he returned to the Mud Creek country but did not live long after that. "I felt very sorry for him and his mother. He was a half-fool, and so I thought, his crime ought to have been excused somewhat because of that fact." Tucker wrote.[5]

Gid Beavers was listed in the U.S. federal census of 1860 as infant Giddie R. Beavers, the son of John C. and Mahala Sellers Beavers. The family was residing in Tuscaloosa, Alabama. Both John and Mahala died in 1882, and were buried at Spanish Fort. However, Tucker claimed he visited Gid and his mother around 1886.[6]

The Suggs' ranch mentioned by Marshal Tucker was owned by Colonel E. C. "Cal" Suggs. He killed George W. Canterbury near the Suggs' post office in Indian Territory on October 8, 1889. R. P. Short was a witness and this led to bitter feelings between he and Suggs. E. C.'s brother, Ike Suggs, ran into the Short brothers and R. P.'s brother Jeff Short was killed.[7] Tucker wrote extensively of this case in a later chapter.

Chapter Nine

A Lynching Party

Tucker considered the Woodford lynching to be the most important and spectacular case in his career as a peace officer, however, he may not have been there.

In the western movies and fiction books, the sheriff always stood up to the lynch mob, usually a lone, brave man with a scattergun. He always protected his prisoner, even if it meant killing half of the law-abiding citizens in town. He usually backed them down using fear tactics, reasoning, or by threatening to shoot the first man to try and take his prisoner.

Well, it didn't always happen that way in the real world on the American frontier. Few lawmen of the times would likely have been as honest as George Tucker when he wrote about the Woodworth Lynching. Or, was he really being honest? He may not have been completely truthful when he wrote about the lynching in his memoirs.

Court records, in addition to newspaper articles uncovered some previously unknown information concerning the hanging of these men. The so called "Woodworth Lynching," according to Tucker, actually occurred near the Woodford store. There was no such place as Woodworth. The Woodford's store was located in what is now northern Carter County, Oklahoma, or about nine miles west of present Springer and just south of Healdton. It was named for Woodford Smith, an intermarried Chickasaw who had a general store along the south flank of the Arbuckle Mountains. By the time Tucker wrote this passage in 1934, he had been exposed to the popular chain of Woolworth's Five and Dime stores, and simply wrote Woodworth rather than Woodford. The story has appeared in numerous publications since Tucker gave his alleged interview to federal worker Selfridge.

Tucker considered the Woodford lynching to be the most important and spectacular case in his career as a peace officer. The event occurred on or about June 1, 1885, in the Chickasaw Nation.

Arrington Gray was a poor farmer, living on Mud Creek. Along in May, when he needed them most in his farm work, his two horses were stolen. There was considerable agitation about it across the river. Gray was well liked and the settlers felt sorry for him. Besides, the people were beginning to take a strong position against the thieves who had long plied their trade over in the Territory.

George Tucker claimed he was tipped off that Mr. Gray's stolen horses were hidden about eight miles from Spanish Fort on the Texas side of Red River. Tucker reportedly went out to investigate and found them tied in the blackjack timber. Tucker did not find anyone guarding the horses so he decided to have a man go back with him as a lookout from an vantage point in the thicket.

After waiting a while, the lookout saw a man come and water the horses and give them grain. He came and saw to the animals again the next morning. Early on the morning of the third day, Tucker rode back to the hidden horses and waited with the lookout. After a short time, the man came again on his morning routine to water and feed. Tucker stepped out from the thicket and got the drop on him as he loaded a round into his rife and pointed it at the thief.

"Don't move. You are under arrest for stealing these horses." The man raised his hands and Marshal Tucker asked his name.

"My name is Morgan. Billy Morgan," said the guilty party.

"If I ever saw a real thief, you are one Billy Morgan," Tucker said to him. According to Tucker, Morgan was the best example of the thief's countenance that he had ever seen. Tucker took him and the horses into Spanish Fort and placed Morgan in jail and took the horses to the livery stable.

Morgan was surly and refused to talk but Tucker figured he did not act alone. He had been living with a couple of suspicious characters up on Mud Creek named Williams and Moon. Tucker claimed he went up there and arrested both of them on suspicion of horse theft. "They were of the same stripe as Morgan," wrote Tucker. He had no doubt that they were as guilty as Morgan was, but there was little evidence that might be used to convict in court unless one of them could be made to talk.

Tucker claimed that after he had arrested them, he took them from the jail in Spanish Fort and started toward Ardmore to turn them over to the federal officers. He did not explain just who the

federal officer might be. He claimed having five possemen with
him; Jack Tucker, his cousin, Bill Tucker, his brother, John Miller,
Charley Hogue and Cal Turner. Tucker went on to explain that the
prisoners were handcuffed. But they never made it to Ardmore
with the prisoners.

On the third day of the ride from Spanish Fort, they allegedly arrived at the small country store called Woodford. They were
about twenty-five miles shy of their destination when six men on
horseback approached. All had stern expressions on their faces.
When they pulled up to Tucker and his posse, they told him they
were going to take the prisoners.

"I saw that they meant business, wrote Tucker. "Besides, they
were the best men in that whole country, who were trying to stamp
out the thieves and to make life and property safe from depreda-
tion."

Tucker claimed he and his posse put up no resistance as both
factions were evenly matched with six armed men. Tucker believed
it would have been one hell of a fight if they resisted. "Moreover,
I would not have killed one of those decent fellows for all of the
thieves in the Territory," said Tucker.

Being trail weary after two or three nights had left the posse
in less than good humor anyway. They decided to put up no fight
to protect the prisoners knowing that by law they should have
stood up for the prisoners against those who stood in the way of
the legal justice system. Of course, in those days things were far
different from the present, and especially in the attitude toward
thievery.

Tucker identified the six men who did the hanging as Lewis Brewer, Hiram Butler, John Means, Robert Royal, Arrington
Gray, and Lewis McKenzie. Tucker went on to explain in detail
the lynching:

> The lynch mob of six men had the knots already tied in
> two ropes. But they were short one rope for the hanging
> party. One of them asked me for my rope and I loaned it to
> them. They then took the thieves over to a tree, put them
> up on horses, tied ropes around their necks and to limbs of
> the tree, and then drove the horses out from under them. I
> watched them as they were hanged. I remember that Wil-
> liam's rope was too long. He could reach the ground with

his feet by standing on tip-toe, which he proceeded to do when the rope cut off his wind. One of the lynchers cooned up the tree, yanked Williams up off the ground, and tied the rope. That settled him, and the party was over. I lost three prisoners and a good rope and got back to Spanish Fort three or four days earlier than I would have otherwise been able to do. I did get the handcuffs off them before they were hanged. Otherwise, I would have lost three pairs of good handcuffs.

The three men were left hanging from the tree limbs until the next day before they were cut down. Tucker claimed there were a number of men still living in southern Oklahoma in the 1930s who saw those bodies before they were cut down. The news spread quite rapidly about the country and people came on horseback and in wagons to see the result of public indignation. Everybody seemed glad that the thieves had been dealt with in that manner.

There were no cries of distorted justice. Tucker claimed several men were indicted for the lynching, but none were convicted. "In fact, no one was ever brought to trial for it," wrote Tucker.

This statement could not be further from the truth. In reality, the recorded events from court records revealed a completely different story.[1]

Tucker said the episode was forgotten in-so-far as the law officers were concerned but people gave many different versions when talking about the lynching party. Many tales were told and there were differing and erroneous newspaper articles about the affair. Tucker claimed none of them were true and one story laid claim to Tucker lynching the prisoners rather than having to take them to the federal authorities.

It appears that no one has previously investigated the facts of this event. Tucker said the incident occurred west of Ardmore and looking at a map of the region puts the Woodford store in Indian Territory, due north of Spanish Fort, located in northern Montague County, Texas. If he had planned on going to Ardmore, he was far to the west of Ardmore and would have had to cut ninety-degrees to the right, or east, to finish the trip. Unless the terrain prohibited it, he could have traveled northeast from Spanish Fort and rode directly to Ardmore, saving many miles. Tucker did not give a date of the incident and indicated the guilty were not prosecuted.

An unnamed reporter wrote about the lynching in a Hamilton, Ohio, newspaper and said, "At Fort Smith, Jack Hoge [*sic*], High [*sic*] Butler, John Means, Bud [*sic*] McKenzie, and Lewis Brewer are charged with hanging two men named Williams and Morgan, and a boy named Moon, June 15, 1885, near Healdton, Indian Territory. The two men were in custody on a charge of horse stealing and the boy happened along when the lynching was in progress and was hung to keep him from being a witness. All are men of prominent. They gave bond in the sum of $35,000."[2]

The news article provided five of the six names who allegedly hanged the two men and a boy and no record supports the statement of Moon being only a witness. The article was written only a few days after the trial took place in Judge Parker's court in Fort Smith.

The second article from the *Fort Smith Elevator* may have made reference to the same lynching with different names. The article did not mention Moon but did emphasize that all three victims were suspected of horse stealing.[3]

George Tucker was approximately eighty-years-old when he wrote about the Woodworth Lynching and he claims he told it the way it really happened. Was Tucker baring his soul and admitting he turned prisoners over to a lynch mob without putting up any resistance? Was he protecting someone? If it happened as the Ohio news article reported, Tucker and his possemen would surely have been charged for murder of the Moon boy.

Tucker did say he didn't challenge the men who did the lynching because they were the "best men in the country" and other sources mention the men as being "prominent citizens." Well, fact is, they weren't. They were mostly North Texas cattlemen leasing land in Indian Territory and then filling the open range with steers and pushing off those who challenged their right to do so.

In the summer of 1888, the Chickasaw Nation had enough and passed a law forbidding those leasing farmsteads to keep more than ten cows unless they paid a tax of $10 per head. The law also said the tribal stock superintendent could seize sufficient numbers to be sold at public auction to pay the bill if the rancher or farmer refused to pay the tax. The white cattlemen operating below the Arbuckle Mountains met in Ardmore and declared they weren't going to pay and then published their defiance in area newspapers.

When the tribe sent the superintendent and a small force out, they were met by close to 100 armed men who took back cattle the tribe had seized. The ringleaders were arrested by federal deputies and at their examination, were set free because Judge Parker had previously ruled tribes could not tax non-citizens.

The cattlemen were however, put under a huge peace bond and then a few months later most were escorted out of the Territory after the tribe canceled all their leases. In the end, these fine citizens had to either marry an Indian girl or keep their cows out of the Territory. The point is, Tucker's viewpoint was skewed, like most of the time period, when he talked of fine men trying to build up the country because he, like most whites of the time period, viewed themselves as superior to Indians and equated progress with the enrichment of the propertied.[4]

Tucker and his posse let these so called "outstanding citizens" take the law into their own hands by hanging two men and a boy of whom they did not know were innocent or guilty and had not been victimized by them..

As to the actual arrest of Morgan, Moon and Williams, Tucker was probably telling the truth when he said he arrested Morgan after knowing he did steal horses from Arrington Gray and knew that Morgan had house guests named Williams and Moon up on Mud Creek.

Tucker had authority in Montague County, being he was a town marshal and a deputy sheriff and the stolen horses were held in his jurisdiction. It was proper for him to make the arrest of Morgan but not Williams or Moon being they were living in Indian Territory. However, transferring the prisoners to the Indian police was appropriate. It is likely that George Tucker did not participate in the transfer but had instructed his posse to take the prisoners to Indian policeman Beard in Ardmore. Tucker over extended himself on this case, for whatever reason. His actions may have been politically motivated, but for what reasons is unknown.

As far as the "prominent citizens" statement, the following account is noted. The honorable Jonas Wolf, Governor, Chickasaw Nation, filed a written complaint to R. L. Owen, United States Indian Agent, Union Agency, Muscogee, Indian Territory, dated June 5, 1885. In his letter, Wolf requested the removal of sixty intruders from within Indian Territory. Governor Wolf sent another list dated July 23, 1885, requesting an additional five intruders be removed. Owens attached Wolf's letter to his own and followed a complaint to Hon. L. Q. C. Lamar, Secretary of Interior, Washington City, D. C. See appendix for the list of non-citizens provided by Governor Wolf. He requested they be removed from the Indian Nation as intruders and stressed the failure of the government to remove them after numerous requests.

While there were newspaper reports publicizing the lynching of those three men, no action had been taken to investigate or try to identify and prosecute those six men were who took the law into their own hands and committed a triple murder. But secrets are difficult to remain secret.

The victim of the horse theft, Arrington Gray, just happened to visit a local saloon in Gainesville, Texas, and after consuming enough whiskey to get himself drunk and loosen his tongue, wanted to talk. He told two men, Dick East and Walker George, all about the hanging of the three men and bragged of how he himself helped hang all three.

The players in the Woodford Lynching were Tucker's posse (so he claimed) of five men named Jack Tucker, Bill Tucker, John Miller, Cal Turner, and Charley Hague [Hogue]. The horses were stolen from Arrington Gray in the Chickasaw Nation. The horses were alleged stolen by William "Billy" Morgan, William or One Williams, and Thomas Moon. The lynch mob, according to Tucker was Lewis Brewer, Hiram Butler, John Means, Robert Royal, Arrington Gray, and Lewis McKenzie.

The court record file folder header from Judge Parker's court lists Lewis Brewer, Hiram Butler, John Means, John Miller, Cal Turner, Jack Hogue, Robert Royal, Arrington Gray, and Lewis McKenzie. William and Jack Tucker were also listed as pertaining to the case. Ironically, George Tucker's name did not appear within in the court record.[5]

The court was called into session with the opening remarks by the prosecutor as follows: "This is a case of the hanging of three white men in the Chickasaw Nation last June."

Tom Malosces, Dock Cash, Walker George, M. J. Ellis, Sherman Jones, Ocie Moran, and his wife, Mrs. Moran were witnesses and stood before the United States of America's Western District of Arkansas court with Judge Issac Parker presiding and repeated the oath, "I do solemnly swear and believe from reliable information in my possession, that Jack Hogue, Jack Tucker, William Tucker, Arrington Gray, Bob Rail, Ocie Brewer, Hyman Butler, all white men and not Indians, did in the Indian Country, within the Western District of Arkansas, on or about the first day of June, 1886, commit murder to wit: did hang until dead Billy Morgan, William Moon, and Ocie Williams all white men and not Indian."[6]

On Feburary 21, 1887, defendant John Means was disarranged or discharged from the case for unknown reasons.

Testimony in court before James Brizzolara, U. S. Commissioner, charged with murder: Lewis Brewer, Lewis McKenzie, Hyman Butler, John Means, John Miller, Cal Turner, and Jack Hogue. Note that Bill and Jack Tucker along with Arrington Gray were no longer being charged.[7]

To the stand was Addie Moran who testified that Williams, Morgan, and Moon, were brought to her home in Chickasaw Nation and all three had their hands tied and their feet were tied under their horses. Bob Rail [Robert Royal], Arrington Gray, Jack Hogue, and Cal Turner were the men in charge of them. [Jack Hogue and Cal Turner were two of the men charged with the murders] They all came on horseback. They stopped for water and left with their prisoners.

They returned to her house in less than an hour and got supper. They were the same men; Bob Rail, Jack Hogue, Arrington Gray and Cal Turner. Moon, Morgan, and Williams were not with them. They stayed there about half an hour after they got their supper. A hired hand, John Lortner, was at the house.

Under cross-examination Addie Moran testified that some of them said something about someone having taken the prisoners away from them.[8]

Her husband, J. C. Moran, was then duly sworn and testified that he knew all the defendants and stated;

In May or June a year ago Hogue, Arrington Gray, Cal Turner, and Bob Rails passed my house with three men that I took to be prisoners from their arms being tied behind them and their feet under their horses. They stopped at my house and got water and said they were going to Mr. Beard's [Indian policeman] and turn the prisoners over to him. They stayed at my house a short while and went on. They said the prisoners had been stealing some horses. They left and were gone twenty-five or thirty minutes and they came running back and stopped at my house and told me that someone had taken the prisoners from them. I asked them if it was a mob or who? They said masked men took them. They stayed for supper. After supper, they left. The next morning we found the three men hanging from the branches of a tree. Later, a crowd gathered and the bodies were taken down and buried. Doctor Ragsdale searched them. They said they got the prisoners on Mud Creek.

Under cross-examination, Moran testified that he knew Bob Rail personally and Rail told him the first thing they knew the masked men were around them with guns on them and they demanded the prisoners and they gave the prisoners up and cursed the masked men and told them to take the other end of the road. "I asked them if they knew any of the party and they said they did not." The court then adjourned with testimony in the cause to be continued on February 19, 1887.

On the continued date, William L. Deleern gave testimony and said "I went with Mr. Moran the next morning we went four miles south from there and did not find them and then turned back and came on towards home and found them. We found them hanging to a limb."

Mrs. M. J. Ellis, who was Williams' wife at the time was called to the stand and instructed to tell the court what she knew of the incident. Mrs. Ellis said, "The defendants came to my house and took Williams away by force and in reply to questions by her as to when Williams would be back they told her she would never see him again. Sherman Jones was working for Williams when they took him away."

If Mrs. Ellis was truthful in her testimony, Marshal Tucker did not arrest Williams. Williams' home was in Indian Territory and Tucker nor his posse had any authority across the Red River.

According to testimony from Mr. and Mrs. Numan, "The defendants stopped at our house with the three men just at dusk and went to the timber and was gone almost an hour and returned without the three men. They told us to go to the timber and look after the horses of the men. We went to the place indicated and found the three men hanging to trees dead. We also, at the house, heard a person scream and beg in the woods where they had taken the three men."[9]

Those possemen were raked over the coals, so to speak, in Judge Parker's court but no conviction was made on those men. Those charged for the lynching of William Morgan, One Williams, and Thomas Moon, on June 15, 1885, were Robert W. Royal, Lewis Brewer, Lewis McKenzie, Hiram Butler, John Miller, Cal Turner, Arrington Gray, Jack Hogue, and John Means.

Records indicate the murder charge was dropped against Means. Arrington Gray was the alleged victim but some of the court papers had him charged as well. Gray got himself snookered at a saloon in Gainesville, Texas, and boasted about the hanging to Dick East and Walker George. Mr. East's testimony had to be shaky at best due to him having had a case or two of cattle rustling in his background plus an assault with intent to murder.

Ironically, no records were found to indicate any conviction of the masked men who took the law into their own hands. Two of the victims were possibly innocent of any crime but it is possible that Williams did, in fact, steal a horse from Arrington Gray and three men paid the price with their lives. It is also possible that there never was any masked men who took the prisoners away from the posse and hanged them. It is very possible that the posse-men were the guilty party. To add insult to injury, records indicate Marshal Geroge Tucker's only involvement was to have his posse take the three men to the Indian policeman at Ardmore. He was not seen by any of the witnesses.

Chapter Ten
Gangs, Killings & Court Trials

The toughs over in the Indian territory had the habit of running in packs, doing their mischief, and dividing the spoils when engaged in robbery or theft.

The Allison Gang, the Julia Moore case, killing of "Peg Leg," the bully Milton Gardenharrow, the Trout-Fleetwood case, and the trial of Jeff Hooper were not mentioned by Jennie Selfridge for the Oklahoma Indian Pioneer Project. The reason could be because all of these incidents took place while George Tucker was a town marshal in Spanish Fort and prior to his becoming a deputy U. S. marshal in 1889.

Selfridge probably used George Tucker's memoirs to complete her interview for the Pioneer Project but was selective in the process and omitted a number of chapters. The reasons for this could be many, however; it is likely because Tucker was a lawman in Texas during some events, rather than in Indian Territory.

The Allison and Barlow Gangs

According to George Tucker, the toughs over in the Indian Territory had the habit of running in packs, doing their mischief, and dividing the spoils when engaged in robbery or theft. The Allison Gang was well known to everyone in that country. Jim Allison was the accepted leader of the gang. He was a bad man, and would kill anyone who got in his way or sought to prevent him from doing anything he wanted to do.

Despite all this, he was a friend to Marshal Tucker and they had talked on several occasions. "He seemed like a square-shooter, but he was just plain tough — a hard-bitten man who stopped at nothing," wrote George.

He never had to arrest him but would have had the proper occasion ever arisen. Jim Allison died near Woodford around 1932. According to Tucker, after Jim outgrew his youthful period of bravado, he settled down to an honest, peaceful life as a farmer, and became quite wealthy in a moderate sense. With his change, he came to view life differently and was not a bad man to know.[1]

During the years when Jim Allison was on the rage, he was formidable, to say the least. One morning, John Williams rode in to Spanish Fort from across the Red River and said that three men had been killed up in the territory on Mud Creek, near Orr.

The three who had been killed were Bob Reams, Bud Jackson, and John Barlow.[2] Williams was the fourth member of what was known as the Barlow Gang. They had been killed, according to Williams, by three members of the Allison Gang. All had been drinking, and they got into a squabble over the division of some spoils. The Allison outfit had simply shot the others full of lead and he, Williams, had escaped only by running out from under the fire. He had hurried over the river to tell Tucker his story.[3]

Tucker recalled;

Williams was one of the worst scared men I have ever seen. He could scarcely tell me the story, and how it happened. He was simply jittery, stammering around like the coward that he was, and shaking like a leaf all of the time. I knew immediately that it was a case of thieves having fallen out and having taken to their six-guns to settle the squabble. I was, therefore, not very much interested in the whole affair. I knew the victims to be some of the worst toughs on the other side. Nevertheless, I felt it my duty at least to go over and look around.

Tucker took three possemen with him, of whom he considered good dependable men. When they got across the Red River, they spotted about fifty mounted men on the scene. They were riding here and there, excited, and all wanting to do something, but didn't know quite what it was that they wanted to do. All had guns of one kind or another, and as with a typical crowd, they were not gunmen and luckily, didn't start shooting at anything that moved.

Tucker and his three-member posse then approached three men who were lying on the ground. Two of them were dead, but when Tucker checked on Reams, he was still breathing. However, he died before they could put him in the wagon. According to Tucker, Reams was a really bad man and he figured it was the best thing that could have happened to the outlaw.[4]

Then, Tucker and his posse started out to find the killers. They figured one of the Allison Gang members had been hit pretty hard with a bullet, for there was considerable blood along the trail they left. They followed this blood trail for three or four miles and then lost it. Evidently, the wounded man had stopped the flow of blood or bled out. They beat around through the brush and couldn't pick up the trail and gave up the chase. They turned south and rode back to Spanish Fort.

Tucker was not angry or disappointed. The way he figure it, the three possemen couldn't be trusted to hold up in a gunfight with the Allison Gang. They were more adapt at farming than fighting according to Tucker. If he had picked up the trail again and closed on the killers, they would have put up a bitter fight.

"The Allisons would fight, and don't forget that," explained Tucker. "In the second place, the very character of the men who had been killed didn't fill me with any great desire to catch the killers. It was good riddance, the killings. If the men killed had been good honest men, I would have liked to have met the gang. There would have been reason for fighting under such conditions. But as it was, there was little good to be accomplished in further fighting."[5]

The Moore Murders

The following cases mentioned by Tucker were not included in the Oklahoma Pioneer papers interview conducted by field worker Selfridge. These stories are from Tucker's autobiography and newspaper accounts. He was following a date sequence up until this point with some of the incidents occurring while he was a lawman in Montague County and some after he became a deputy U. S. marshal. The Julia Moore case was one where a news article dates it to 1896, about seven years after Tucker put on the deputy marshal badge.

Tucker claimed that an unnamed fellow, proven to be Dick Graham, came to him bright and early one morning in Spanish Fort, He told Tucker that he had seen a dead baby lying on (not in) a grave over in Courtney Flat.

It was lying, he said, only a few feet from the fence along the road. Tucker saddled up and made a hot trail as he rode to the location provided by Graham. After searching around, Tucker discovered the body of a very small baby, probably only a few days old. The body had evidently been buried in a shallow grave, but not deep enough to prevent the hogs from rooting it up.

"It was an awful looking mess, with one arm eaten off completely, and other parts of the body mangled," reported Tucker.[6]

Tucker went on to claim that he searched the place and found an old case knife that was covered with blood. "It had apparently been cast away without any attempt to conceal it and closer investigation of the body showed that the throat had been cut with a fairly sharp blade."

Tucker stated that he moved the body out of reach of the hogs and took the knife as evidence and then went to the nearest house.

According to Tucker, the solution of the crime was not difficult. There was a little nineteen-year-old girl in the neighborhood by the name of Julia Moore who had given birth to an illegitimate child, which had disappeared. Tucker believed he had enough evidence to prove that she had killed her baby so he located her and took her into custody. He arranged transport of the young lady and took her to Purcell, Oklahoma, before U. S. Commissioner Gates. The commissioner refused to grant her bond, so Tucker took her on to jail in Paris, Texas. Later, she was tried, convicted, and given ten-years in the Detroit Federal Penitentiary.

Tucker felt sorry for the young girl, admitting that the crime was a low and vicious one. "She had been raised an orphan," wrote Tucker. "She had been kicked around among rough people and had never had a real chance to make anything out of herself. She took the only way out of a bad situation — and it was against the law, though not particularly against the moral code that she knew. I never knew what became of her."

A news article provided details of the crime and stated the victim was discovered about May 8,, 1896.[7]

This murder was big news in Indian Territory and down in Texas as just about every newspaper in the region printed the same story of Julia Moore killing her baby and the body being eaten by hogs. Tucker only dedicated one page coverage of the Julia Moore case and It seems, however, that Tucker may have omitted an important piece of the puzzle and may have taken credit for solving a murder in error.

The body was discovered on the May 8, 1896, and a little over a month later, on June 14, the newspaper in Ardmore, Indian Territory, reported the murder of Dick Graham. Three men, Dick Moore, his son, Allen Moore, and Henry Rose, were arrested by Deputy U. S. Marshal Selden T. Lindsey. They were taken to Ardmore for an examining trial before Commissioner Gibbons.

The motive for the killing of Graham was the result of bitterness by the Moores for his connection with the Julia Moore case involving the murder of her infant daughter. It seems Julia Moore was the daughter of Dick Moore. Julia Moore was not a poor little orphan as Tucker claimed.

The news article confirmed Tucker's story of taking her to Purcell, bond being denied, and taken to jail in Paris, where she remained as of mid-June 1896. It was Dick Graham who found the dead baby with the almost decapitated body and it was he who found the knife with which the horrible crime had been committed. Therefore, he was the one who rode over to Spanish Fort and reported his findings to Deputy Marshal Tucker.

Tucker's motive for claiming he, himself, found the knife could be that it stood a better chance of acceptance as evidence if he submitted it. For, had Graham been credited with finding the knife, it would have been harder to show the instrument had a connection to the alleged murder near Courtney Flat, in the Mud Creek country, and charged with the Graham murder.

The residents in the Courtney Flat community saw serious trouble beginning between Dick Graham and the Moore faction. His meddling into their private business angered them to the point that Dick Moore, his son, Allen, and Henry Rose, came up with a plan to ambush Dick Graham. Rose was the go-between man and was told by Dick Moore to go find Dick Graham and request his presence at the Moore house, with a false message that the Moore faction wished to calm the matter down and let all become friends again.

Graham figured, wrongly, believing they were sincere and was unaware of their plan. He agreed and started out with Rose toward the Moore house. As they neared the house, the Moores were waiting in the brush to ambush him. As Graham and Rose reached the spot they opened fire on him. Rose walked behind Graham and held back to make sure he would not be in the line of fire when his pals opened the dance. When the Moore faction

Alfred Richard "Dick" Graham was buried in the Crow Cemetery, Indian Territory. *Photo from author's collection.*

opened fire, the battle raged for only a few moments. Graham was able to draw his pistol and return fire. One of Graham's rounds took Allen Moore in the thigh as he fell to the ground, mortally wounded.[8]

Alfred Richard "Dick" Graham's body was taken up to Orr, about fourteen miles from Courtney Flats, and buried in the Crow Cemetery. His headstone reads, born Jan. 10, 1870, died June 8, 1896.[9]

The Killing of Peg Leg

In the case of killing of Peg Leg, Tucker goes back to 1885, while serving as city marshal of Spanish Fort and deputy sheriff of Montague County. In that year, in the hot, Texas weather of August, Marshal Tucker received a warrant for a man whom he claimed was listed only as "Peg Leg."[10]

When Tucker wrote about the event, he could not recall what the charge was against him. He rounded up two possemen to go with him and started up the old Chisholm Trail after him. For unexplained reasons they were mounted on mules. There were no settlements along the trail, so they stopped here and there at cow camps. They received reports that "Peg Leg" had been there and had gone on up the trail ahead of them.

When they reached Bull Foot Ranch, a government station on the Cimarron River, they were told the man they were after was only a few hours ahead and further reported that the man was headed in the direction of Hunnewell, Kansas. They hurried on up the trail and came to Hunnewell, a small town with one hotel, two mercantile stores, two dance halls, and eight saloons. There was no law in the town as the local ranchers took care of the law breakers in the area in their own fashion. Tucker claimed they were joined there by some other officers.[11]

They searched the town for "Peg Leg" and by sheer luck, discovered him in an old abandoned house just after dusk. He must have sensed he was in for trouble so he made a run for it. They drew their guns and cut down on him before he could reach his horse. He fell to the ground. They had killed him instantly.

Later, Tucker pondered over the killing of the man. He wondered if they could have captured him. But, on the other hand, Tucker rationalized that it was August and too hot for a lot of physical exertion. Besides, they had chased him for a long time and the posse was worn out. Tucker expressed it with, "It seems that any mercy that a peace officer might have for a fugitive tends to disappear if the latter puts the officer to a great deal of trouble in making the arrest."

That ended the life of a man known to Tucker only as "Peg Leg." Tucker figured he might have been a pretty good fellow, but believed the chances were that he was another of the desperate criminals who flocked into the Territory for safety. Tucker dedicated only one page on this criminal and did not say if "Peg Leg" had one or two legs.[12]

The body count for Tucker now stood at three. It may or may not have been his bullets that killed Peg Leg, but, at least Tucker was one of the shooters. If we count the three men who were lynched in the Woodworth incident, the total would by six.

The Bully Milton Gardenhire

Tucker's next escapade was to write about "The Bully." For several years, a man whom Tucker claimed to be Milton Gardenharrow [sic] was actually Milton Gardenhire. No records exist for surname Gardenharrow. Milton Gardenhire lived nearby, over in Cooke County, Texas, not very far from Spanish Fort. He was age twenty-two in 1880 and living with his parents and eight siblings.[13]

The bully had been pestering folks around Spanish Fort. He was a cowardly young man who shot people's hogs, cattle, and pets. According to Tucker, the bully was not capable of what he called *more honest crimes*. Any officer of the law held that type in extreme contempt and viewed them as just cowardly. But the bully had acquired a considerable reputation as a bad man, and he apparently enjoyed it very much.[14]

Tucker recalled that one day he and his brother, Bill, were having drinks at the local saloon in Spanish Fort. As they sat at a table they looked the crowd over to see if they had papers on anyone. Tucker claimed he recognized one of the men in the saloon from a picture that had been sent to him and stated that he always carried the pictures with him. He pulled them from his pocket and made a comparison. The man in question closely resembled one of the pictures he carried, that being Gardenhire. Tucker also could not remember what he was wanted for by the authorities, but knew if it was important enough for them to send out pictures they were guaranteed to be bad guys.[15]

In reality, he probably carried a description, but very unlikely photographs. A news article of December 24, 1886, sheds light on the situation. G. L. Scott, sheriff of Grimes County, Texas, reported that he had arrested a T. M. Gardenhire [Thomas Milton], about twenty-eight-years-old, a little over five-feet, six-inches high, weighs about 125 pounds, auburn hair, red whiskers, blue eyes, florid complexion and had been shot through his right arm.

He had in his possession, a mare of the following description: dark brown or black, branded 86 with bar under on left thigh, four-years-old, saddle with pommel broke off and covered with buckskin; saddle was rigged at Gainesville, Texas, by B. F. Melton & Company. He was carrying a Colt .44 frontier six-shooter with ivory handles. Any sheriff wanting such a man will telegraph at once.[16]

Gardenhire saw the Tucker brothers watching him and then saw them looking at a picture. That scared him and he headed toward the door in a hurry. He closed the door behind him as he left the saloon. Marshal Tucker started toward the door and when he opened it slightly he observed the suspect walking across the street. Tucker started running toward him and called out for him to stop.

Apparently, his brother, Bill, was still sitting at his table drinking whiskey. Tucker pulled his pistol and fired into the ground near Gardenhire's feet. He didn't seem to be armed so Tucker wasn't too concerned. But, suddenly Gardenhire pulled a pistol and as he turned toward Tucker he pulled back the hammer and opened fire. Tucker's life probably flashed before his eyes, thinking he was a goner.

Tucker's brother, Bill, had polished off his glass of whiskey and came outside by this time and he later said he thought he saw the bullets coming right straight through George. Gardenhire fired all six rounds from his cylinder toward Marshal Tucker and at close range. But, for some reason, the rounds missed and George didn't go down.

Then, with his pistol empty, Gardenhire turned and ran to his horse, mounted and got away. Bill went over to George to see how bad he was hit but to both men's amazement, none of the rounds hit George. It was like being shot at with blanks. George couldn't believe he had not been hit and blessed his lucky stars. Forty-rod whiskey could have played a significant part is such poor marksmanship.[17]

George and Bill did not give chase but a few nights later, Gardenhire came back to Spanish Fort. Tucker and his posse were on guard and ready for him this time. It was posse member Cook who came upon him on the street and without a word, knowing he was an owl-hoot, raised his shotgun to his shoulder and gave him a blast from both barrels.

The blast took Gardenhire in the body and he was hard hit. He didn't put up a fight but he was not down. Cook ejected his spent shells and started to reload as Gardenhire mounted his horse, and rode off again. He may have been shot in the right arm from Cook's shotgun when apprehended by the sheriff over in Grimes County.

Gardenhire was probably released from Grimes County without being charged. According to Tucker, Gardenhire recovered from Cook's shotgun blasts but after a few months he was found still living and was apprehended over across the Red River in Saint Jo, not far from Spanish Fort. Thomas Milton Gardenhire died at age eighty-seven. in Angelina County, Texas. His headstone reads 1857-1945.[18]

The Trout-Fleetwood Incident

Another of Tucker's cases was that of the Trout-Fleetwood incident. John Trout and Houston Fleetwood were both Indians and lived on adjoining farms. They fell out over a fence line and Trout shot Fleetwood. The latter didn't die right away.

Death records indicate Houston Fleetwood died on May 18,

1888. Mrs. Fleetwood sent word, asking for Tucker to come up and arrest John Trout, as he had killed her husband. So, Tucker made preparations to go.

He got Johnnie March to go as a posseman. "Johnnie March was a big, fine fellow of about thirty-years of age; strong as an ox, but he had little experience in handling toughs," wrote Tucker.

He told Johnnie that he would introduce him to John Trout and that, when Trout shook hands with him, he was to hold on to Trout's hand while Tucker clamped on the cuffs. Tucker claimed he came up with the idea after reading about that trick being used against some of the biggest racketeers in Chicago, by members of rival gangs, and that it has come to be known as "glad handing." The definition of glad handing; being very friendly to people you have not met before, as a way of trying to get an advantage.[19]

An informant told Tucker that John Trout was hiding in a big pasture that belonged to a certain doctor that Tucker knew. So, Tucker and March rode up to the location and searched until they found Trout.

Tucker did his part of the "glad handing" by introducing Trout to March. Then, to Tucker's surprise, Johnnie March put out his hand and did his part like a seasoned veteran. Tucker slapped the cuffs on Trout and he broke down "and cried like a baby," said Tucker.

When Tucker asked him what was the problem, Trout screamed, "I'll be murdered." Tucker assured him that he would protect him, come what might. "And, I would have done it, for Trout was not a mean man."[20]

Tucker took Trout to Gainesville, Texas, and put him in jail. He went almost raving mad when put in his cell. He got released on a writ of *habeas corpus*, but Sheriff McClain was there with a United States warrant. When the judge ordered him released, he was turned loose, but McLain was waiting outside and immediately arrested him. Fleetwood had died while Trout was in the Gainesville jail. Tucker then took Trout to Sherman by train.[21]

While traveling on the train to Sherman, Trout's wife was also on the train and she tried to talk to him but he was trying to appear crazy according to Tucker. So, Tucker worked up a plan to get him to talk to his wife.[22]

Tucker said to Mrs. Trout, "I have some of John's money, Mrs.

Trout. What shall I do with it? He appears to be insane now and I'd like to get the money out of my hands."

"How much do you have?" Mrs. Trout asked.

"About sixty-dollars, I think," replied Tucker. Trout had given Tucker eighty-dollars and when he heard Tucker say he had only sixty, he blurted out, "Don't you have more than that?"

Tucker smiled and said, "Why, John, you seem to have a better memory now." Trout looked wilted and only grunted for a reply. Tucker said, "I have eighty-dollars, John, and now you'd better talk to your wife about what you're going to do, and make some plans that are necessary."

Thereupon, he began to talk to her and they continued communicating until they reached Sherman. At Sherman, he was bound over to Fort Smith, Arkansas. When his trial came up, Tucker and several others were called as witnesses.

Houston Fleetwood had a reputation of being a very quarrelsome person and that fact was brought out in the trial. Trout only received punishment of eight years in the penitentiary, but Tucker believed it was excessive, based on the facts of the case. "Not long after Trout came out of the penitentiary, he was killed over near Ryan."[23]

The following account varies somewhat from Tucker's. Deputy U. S. Marshal W. F. Morton was commissioned in the Western District, Fort Smith, Arkansas, and was under U. S. Marshal Jacob Yoes. In October of 1888, he transported John M. Trout to Fort Smith to stand trial. Robert King's account of the case was that Trout was a Texan and married a Choctaw woman. The killing took place in the Choctaw Nation and Trout was kept in custody for a good while at Sherman, Texas. The woman Trout married owned land adjoining Fleetwood, who had about 10,000 acres under fence and Trout's ranch contained about 5,000 acres. The argument they had was caused by joint possession of the land. Trout's fence was cut several times and he accused Fleetwood. During a quarrel Fleetwood was killed and Trout fled to Texas where his brother was also being held on larceny charges.[24]

Chapter Eleven

Incident at Red River Station

Red River Station was a good place to find fugitives hiding from the law, especially when they were having a dance.

Tucker continued writing of cases that were never published and the Jeff Hooper case was no exception. Tucker received a warrant for the arrest of a cowboy named Jeff Hooper, who allegedly killed another cowboy over in Indian Territory. Deputies kept on the lookout for him, and his elusiveness indicated he might have pulled up stakes in favor of some other section of the country. Tucker did not know the details or facts of the killing. But Tucker knew it was his job to arrest him on the warrant or kill him, if he could find him.[1]

Tucker and Cook were up at Red River Station one night. They were having a dance and Tucker knew this was a good place and right time to find those who were fugitives of the law. Tucker believed they took more chances in having fun than in their work. There was a large crowd at the dance, a much larger crowd than Tucker had ever seen at a dance in that section of the country. It was one of those, "everybody and his brother were there." They finally spotted Jeff Hooper in the crowd and he appeared to be having the time of his life. Around Hooper was a dozen cowboys and Tucker didn't know how many were friends of Hooper. It was a dangerous undertaking to attempt to seize him if he were surrounded by his friends, according to Tucker.

Tucker decided it would be best to wait until Hooper was out on the floor dancing and informed Cook that they could just walk up to him and put the handcuffs on him before his friends had time to learn of the arrest. They waited patiently. When Hooper asked someone to dance, Tucker and Cook were ready.

"After the first milling was over we walked out to the set he was in, put the cuffs on him, and quietly left the building," said Tucker. Few people noticed the arrest and Hooper offered no resistance. They hurried to their horses, mounted, and, "rode like

91

hell away from Red River Station," reported Tucker.[2]

Back at the dance, according to Tucker, news filtered through the crowd that they had arrested Hooper and some of his friends began to get excited. Meredith DeCrow [*sic*] was a rough and ready cowboy tough. He tried to organize a group of friends to overtake the Tucker party. It seems DeCrow had too much to drink and pulled his pistol out and began shooting up the dance. He ended the show spectacularly by shooting himself in the leg. The deputy marshal at the station came in and took DeCrow into custody.

According to Tucker, that ended the rescue attempt. He wrote that DeCrow was taken to Fort Smith when it was learned that he was wanted for killing a man over at Courtney Flat. Tucker was not aware of DeCrow's crime while at the dance arresting Hooper. At Fort Smith, DeCrow was convicted of the killing and sent to the penitentiary for a number of years.

"He was a pretty good fellow but when he was drinking, he was inclined to be overly courageous, to the point of being dangerous and when he wasn't drinking, he was a good, hard-working cowboy," according to Tucker.[3]

Tucker's story differs from two other accounts. One was a story from Robert King's *Oklahoma Marshals and Deputy Marshals*. He stated that on January 14, 1885, Deputy U. S. Marshal James Guy captured a white man named Meredith Crow who killed Cub Courtney on July 12, 1879, in the Chickasaw Nation.

It seems both men had been on bad terms over unknown issues. On that day, Cub Courtney was passing by a house and saw Meredith Crow standing out front. Crow quickly stepped inside the house, pulled his pistol and fired two rounds at Courtney as he closed the door behind him. Courtney pulled out his Winchester and leveled the rifle as he rode his horse toward the front door, shooting as he rode.

Suddenly, defiant Meredith Crow bolted outside through the front door with a double-barrel shotgun in his hands. Courtney turned to flee as Crow fired both barrels at his retreating foe. He was at close range and both blasts hit Courtney in the back. He fell from his horse. The shotgun blast resulted in almost instant death. When Deputy Marshal Guy tried to serve the warrant of arrest to Crow, he resisted arrest which resulted in him being shot in the leg.

The third account: "Meredith [Meridith] Crow was a white man of about thirty-five-years of age. He killed Cub Courtney on June 8, 1875, in the Chickasaw Nation. He then fled to Texas. Courtney was barely out of his teens but was old enough to be lusting for the Widow Thurman who was also being courted (successfully) by a Thurman Pitts.

Courtney was jealous and one day while he was visiting a neighbor of the widow, she, not wanting to see Courtney, slipped out the back. Courtney rode from the neighbor's to the Thurman house, parked his horse and fired a shot into the window, thinking Pitts was there. Then Courtney began cursing loudly and proclaiming his ability to take on all comers. Bad mistake. Pitts was not present but Crow was and he stepped out and put a bullet through Courtney's brain.

After Crow's arrest, an attempt was made at trial to portray him leaving the house to talk some sense into the brash boy, but the jury didn't buy this fable and convicted him of murder. Later his sentence was commuted to life and he was sent to Detroit, Michigan, to begin serving his sentence."[4]

Sergeant James H. Guy, of the United States Indian Police, was killed while trying to arrest the Lee Gang for whiskey peddling, cattle rustling, and horse stealing in late April, 1885. Guy was also a commissioned U. S. deputy marshal of the Fort Smith court. The fight took place on Caddo Creek, about ten miles south of the Arbuckle Mountains.

Basically what happened was Guy, along with Andy Roff and a posse went to serve a warrant. The Lee place was a stone and log block house with a lot of open ground around it. As Guy approached, the men inside opened up and killed him and three men of the posse. The rest of the posse was unable to find shelter close enough to assist so they abandoned the fight.[5]

The Roffs were pretty well off so they offered a big reward for the Lee outfit. Some months later, Heck Thomas and a detective out of Texas, together with Jim Taylor and Jim Shattles, located Jim and Pink, Lee brothers, while they were trying to cut across Bill Washington's pasture in Love Bend, near Preacher Strother Brown's place.

This was also pretty open country, hilly, but at that time mostly brush free. Heck Thomas and crew had the high ground and the advantage and they didn't waste it. They shot the Lee brothers to pieces. It was shortly after that shootout that Heck Thomas began his career as a deputy marshal out of Parker's court. His capture of Della Humby, the last member of the Lee Gang some two years later, is a story which has often been repeated.

Preacher Brown was a black man and he and Jim Webb, Bill Washington's foreman, got into it over a fire Brown started accidentally which burned a good bit of Washington's pasture. In the debate, Webb shot and killed Brown and was on the run. The famed black deputy, Bass Reeves, caught up with Webb some time later at the Bywater Store near Woodford, at the southwest end of the Arbuckles. The gunfight they had was probably one of the most exciting tales of the old west.[6]

Deputy Marshal George Tucker claimed he had Cook take Hooper on to Fort Smith. After the usual preliminaries, they held his trial. The stockmen stuck by him and he was acquitted. It was generally said that the cowmen got him out of it, but Tucker could not figure out why they "stuck so tight to him."[7]

The *Montague Democrat* carried a story as follows;

> Jeff Hooper, charged with the murder of Jim Christian, one mile south of Spanish Fort in June 1894, was tried Thursday. It will be remembered that Hooper is the man that Sheriff Raines brought back from Tennessee last March and who had just served a sentence of five years for killing a man in Tennessee. The jury returned a verdict of not guilty. It is unclear if these are not the same men as in Tucker's story.

Additional information from various newspapers only clouds the case with the following: On April 10, 1887, Jim Christian, part Chickasaw Indian and white man Bud Luttrell, were murdered at Rooster Creek, Pickens County, Chickasaw Nation. Suspects in the murder were Alex Juzan and Steve Bussell. Juzan was subsequently killed three days later while resisting arrest by Indian Policeman Dave Hardwick. Bussell was later arrested by U.S. Deputy Marshal Charles Leflore. Luttrell, being a white man and not Indian, resulted in Bussell being indicted in the U.S. district court at Fort Smith, and tried by Judge Parker in June, 1887.[8]

During the trial in Judge Parker's court, testimony given was of a very conflicting nature. The date of the killings was confirmed as April 10, 1887, near Harney, in Chickasaw Nation. James Christian and Bud Luttrell had taken custody of a prisoner named William Hamilton who was delivered to them from south of the Red River, likely by Marshal Tucker.

They were driving along the road in a buggy with the prisoner in tow. Hamilton was the only witness to the killings and at the time of the incident, claimed that Alex Juzan and Steve Bussell were hidden behind the bank on Rooster Creek and as the buggy entered the stream to cross, Juzan shot and killed Christian while Luttrell was shot twice and killed by Steve Bussell.

This was the story Hamilton told to Indian policeman Hardwick and another man named Jim Bounds who arrived only a few minutes after the killings. Hardwick followed their tracks and formed a posse to take up the chase. Three days into the pursuit Hardwick and his posse were hiding in the brush watching Juzan's sister's ranch. They didn't have to wait long as they spied Juzan and Bussell riding up. The posse was fired upon and they returned fire. Juzan was killed but Bussell escaped with a slight head wound.[9]

A reporter claimed he had it on good authority that Aleck Juzan told his wife, on the morning before he was killed by the officers, that he did, in fact, kill Christian, but that he did it in self-defense. He told her that he and Bussell met Christian, Hamilton, and Luttrell on the trail and that Hamilton assailed him with abuse accusing him of theft.

Then, according to Juzan, Hamilton reached for his Winchester and he had to kill him in self-defense and then Luttrell reached for his Winchester and it was to protect himself that he killed Luttrell. The reporter added that the story was given as a statement of a dead man, and as the other side of the great tragedy which is now racking the Chickasaw Nation.[10]

Christian's widow offered a reward of $500 for the arrest of Bussell and on about June 1, 1887, he was captured by Captain Charlie Leflore of the United States Indian Police and taken before Commissioner Tuft at Muskogee who bound him over for the alleged murder of Bud Luttrell and sent him to jail. At this examination William Hamilton, the only eyewitness to the killing, was not present.

In the meantime, the friends of Bussell were not idle and on a Sunday, Miss Lucy Thompson, aunt of the prisoner, arrived in Fort Smith. Through her attorney she made application to the court for the release of her nephew, Steve Bussell, on bond on the ground that he had no hand in the killing of Christian and Luttrell. She claimed he was merely a witness to the tragedy which she was ready to prove. It so happened that Captain Leflore arrived in Fort Smith on the same day as Miss Thompson and had witness Hamilton in custody.

During Hamilton's testimony in Judge Parker's court, he stated that he had been arrested in Grayson County, Texas, by Hardwick and Christian on April 9, and before crossing the Red River into the Nation the party bought three quarts of whiskey and all were drunk when the killing occurred.

He admitted to being in the buggy with Christian and Luttrell who had joined them in the Territory and as they were driving along they met Juzan and Bussell. Juzan greeted them with a hello but Christian told Juzan to go to hell and called him a cow thief. Hamilton claimed that Juzan and Bussell dismounted from their horses and Christian had his Winchester between his legs and raised the rifle in an attempt to shoot Juzan, but the latter was too quick for him as he raised his rifle and shot Christian in the head.

Christian's rifle dropped and Luttrell grabbed it and started to get out of the buggy when Juzan shot him in the shoulder, causing him to drop the weapon. Luttrell then ran around in front of the team when Juzan shot him again, breaking his neck. Hamilton said only three shots were fired, all by Juzan.

When questioned as to why he had changed his story as he first stated that Juzan and Bussell were in ambush and killed the men without warning, he claimed that when he started to tell the truth to Hardwick and Bounds, they pulled guns on him and told him if he didn't tell a different story they would kill him.

Christian's brother testified that Hamilton told him privately that the killings that took place, the shooting was done from behind the creek bank, not up close and visible, and that he and Hamilton examined the ground and saw where the men had kneeled down behind the bank and then followed the tracks in the bed of the creek to where their horses were concealed. Hamilton claimed that when Juzan dismounted, he let his horse go and during the shooting the other horse of Bussell's broke loose and followed the other horse. Christian's brother countered that claim by stating there were no horse tracks anywhere near where the killings took place.

Bussell was released on bond in the sum of $10,000 and Mrs. Thompson furnished the bond.

Bussell always maintained his innocence of the crime and alleged that it was Juzan who did all the shooting. Regardless, he was convicted on September 28, 1888, and sentenced to be hanged on April 19, 1889. His sentence was later commuted to "life" and he was back in Indian Territory by 1902, a free man.[11]

This was only one case of many feuds in the Territory. This one started when the Overton faction had Dick Sacra and Alex Juzan arrested for cattle theft. Juzan and Bussell retaliated by killing Christian and Luttrell, who were of the Overton party. Later, Jim Mayer of the Overton crowd was killed by Dud Luttrell and John Christian severely wounded. Luttrell fled to Texas and a black man named Campbell went to jail for wounding John Christian. Milton Overton killed Sacra, and then died from the effects of confinement in jail. It is unlikely that the feud ended anytime soon after the death of Sacra.[12]

While some of the above stories occurred when Tucker was a local lawman on or before 1889, and some on or after 1889, when he became a deputy United States marshal, he concluded his career as a local peace officer and moved forward to an interesting career as a federal law officer, a hired gunman in the Wyoming Cattlemen's War, and other police work.

Chapter Twelve

First Years as Deputy U. S. Marshal

George Tucker was one Healdton, Oklahoma citizen who was an honored guest at the Ardmore Pioneer day program. He became a deputy marshal in 1889.

When 1889 rolled around, George Tucker was still the town marshal of Spanish Fort. He wrote, "the Indian Country was full of criminals and others who would become criminals." It is clear that he was still in the dual role of town marshal and deputy sheriff of Montague County. George never mentioned what his salary was as a deputy sheriff. He did say that when he was first hired as the lawman for Spanish Fort he was paid five dollars per day and probably remained at that rate for a few years.

As the town started to shrink in population due to being missed by the railroad, he likely saw the handwriting on the wall. He apparently wished to remain in law enforcement and it is likely he could have survived on the salary as a deputy sheriff in case he lost his job as constable of Spanish Fort. But, George was reading a newspaper one day and saw an advertisement from U. S. Marshal R. B. Reagan of the newly established Federal Building, Eastern District of Texas.

The headquarters was located at Paris, Texas, not far from Spanish Fort. The notice called for brave young men who could ride, shoot straight, and walking on the right side of the law. George applied for a job as U. S. deputy marshal and rode over to Paris for an interview. It is debatable exactly who interviewed George and one would think Marshal Reagan would be the one. However, evidence indicated George did not meet Marshal Reagan until sometime after he was hired.

George Tucker's long experience as a lawman easily qualified him for the job but he was told a deputy drew no salary. He was to be paid a small fee for serving warrants and would be paid mileage for travel with the marshal deducting a large percentage of the funds. But George agreed and was given a badge.[1]

The comprehensive breakup of the Fort Smith court's jurisdiction became law on the first day of March, 1889, when President Benjamin Harrison signed legislation defining Indian Territory as that area bounded by Kansas on the north, Arkansas on the east, Texas on the south, and Oklahoma Territory on the west. That same act also established the District Court of Indian Territory and gave it authority over the whole as described. The new court was headquartered at Muskogee, in the Creek Nation, and had original jurisdiction over all offenses except those punishable by death or imprisonment. The court was also given authority of civil suits with damages of $100 or more between American citizens, or American citizens and Indians. The Muskogee court was officially opened on April 4, 1889, but did not get down to the business of trying cases until June 3.

A third provision of the March legislation transferred jurisdiction of felonies punishable by imprisonment or hard labor committed within the Chickasaw Nation and the southern half of the Choctaw Nation to the Eastern District Court of Texas. Elsewhere, the act gave the United States circuit courts for the Western District of Arkansas and the Eastern District of Texas continued exclusive jurisdiction in Indian Territory over all crimes and misdemeanors punishable by death. The same act established an administrative court at Paris, Texas. This court also had jurisdiction over federal matters in the Texas counties of Lamar, Fannin, Red River, and Delta.

The bill then authorized two court terms per year, one beginning on the third Monday in April and the other on the second Monday in October. Under other language in the bill, the Wichita, Kansas, federal court continued to have felony jurisdiction over the northwestern quadrant of Indian Territory, excluding No Man's Land (the present Oklahoma Panhandle,) which was assigned to the Paris court.[2]

Before the enactment of the bill, the Eastern District of Texas included the eastern half of Texas and stretched from the Red River to the Gulf Coast. The administrative court was then located at Galveston, and the bench was filled with the person of Chauncey B. Sabin, appointed by President Chester A. Arthur in 1884. However, Sabin never filled the bench of the Paris court for in the weeks before the first term he was terminally ill.

This happenstance prompted presiding Circuit Judge Don A. Pardee to appoint Judge Alex Boarman[3] of Shreveport, Louisiana, to fulfill Sabin's duties. Arrangements were then made for the staffing of the Paris court beginning with the appointment of H. H. Kirkpatrick as commissioner. The reasoning behind his selection was he had for years been a deputy marshal in the region and it was felt his presence would add to the stability and effectiveness of the court. Owing to time constraints in Senate ratification of other appointments, initially he was also given the role of court clerk.[4]

The exact date when Tucker became a deputy is open to debate. The first article naming him as such is found in May 1889, when he arrested W. L. Purcell of Montague County, formerly of Abilene. Tucker arrested him and took him to Paris on a warrant charging him with the theft of horses in the Indian Territory.[5]

On July 19, 1933, George Tucker was honored at the Ardmore Pioneer Day program. The *Daily Ardmoreite* newspaper reported, "George Tucker is one Healdton citizen who will be an honored guest at the Ardmore Pioneer Day program. He became a deputy marshal in 1889."

George wrote about his early years as a newly commissioned deputy marshal and was still living in Spanish Fort in 1889, acting as police chief or constable while also serving as a deputy sheriff of Montague County. When he wrote his memoirs he claimed to be thirty-five years of age in 1889. His editor, Major Alley changed it to thirty-four years of age. George did not particularly love the job of law enforcement, but admitted there was a certain exhilaration that one gets out of "the job of hunting men. Man hunting is different from any other kind of hunting as the hunted is more resourceful," according to Tucker.

George noticed in the newspapers that United States Marshal Richard Reagan at Paris wanted some deputies. After careful consideration Tucker decided to apply for one of those positions. His reasoning was not dissatisfaction with the way he had been treated by the people of Spanish Fort. But, he thought of the federal deputy position as being a better job than that of keeping the peace in a small town. He saw it, from frequent contact with deputy marshals as being sent out on cases while the routine or petty work of a constable would not have to be done. Besides, there was a chance to make a great deal more money as a federal deputy, since the deputy received a fee for an arrest and good liberal mileage allowance for taking prisoners to Paris or Fort Smith, or wherever they were supposed to be taken. Of course the U. S. marshal would take a sizable cut from his fees and mileage.[6]

The United States Eastern District of Texas Court had been established in Paris, Texas, which lies in Lamar County. The northern district court sat at Dallas, but its jurisdiction was in north central Texas, to the north and west of Dallas. The jurisdiction of the Eastern District Court was extended to the Indian Territory, which made that court one of the most important in all of the West.

The Indian Territory was full of criminals and others who would become criminals upon the least provocation. Of most importance was the hard fast rule that a deputy was to make arrests within his assigned district and was prohibited from going, as example, from the Eastern District over to the Northern District to arrest someone. This would cause great problems and hardships for the deputies of the Eastern District in the not too distant future.[7]

When Tucker applied for the job of deputy marshal he was soon notified of his appointment and claimed that it came as a surprise. He had acquired a good reputation as a constable and deputy sheriff of Montague County. He realized that the marshal wanted men whom he could rely upon to bring in those for whom warrants had been issued. Being a deputy marshal was non-political but the deputies had to serve under a marshal who was politically appointed and subject to come and go with presidential elections every four years. In the years ahead, Tucker would serve under two democratic and two republican appointed marshals. When Tucker was first appointed R. B. Reagan was marshal.[8]

Reagan had a colorful prior record as sheriff of Cherokee County, Texas, and was noted for either capturing or accepting the surrender of John Wesley Hardin, in 1872. Hardin had been wounded by a young man named Sublett while playing ten pin bowling and drinking. Sublett shot Hardin with a shotgun and Hardin fled. He was seriously wounded and arranged to have himself arrested so he could receive medical treatment and the Reagans nursed him back to health.[9]

Being Tucker and his family lived at Spanish Fort, he was allowed to work his cases from there for quite a while. Each time he left Paris with a warrant and returned with his prisoner, he would be given another warrant and back again to Indian Territory to make another arrest. This resulted in infrequent trips home so he decided it was best for him and family to give up residence and friendships in the little town of Spanish Fort and move to Paris.[10]

Tucker readily admitted that he and the other deputy marshals did not always get their men even though he felt as though a good peace officer was suppose to get them. They received erroneous reports which he called "punk tips" and many criminals gave them the slip when they almost had them in their hands. "It's the way with police work," wrote Tucker.

Richard B. Reagan was the U. S. marshal of the Eastern District of Texas when Tucker was appointed deputy marshal in Paris, Texas. Reagan was an experienced lawman, having been a sheriff. *Photo from author's collection.*

Right after being appointed George Tucker received his very first deputy marshal assignment. Even though he worked under Marshal Reagan for only a short time, he considered Reagan a fine marshal to work for under any and all conditions. Tucker was coming into his own as a member of the warrior clan. This best describes these young lawmen who for whatever reasons, decided to work in the capacity of a federal lawman to go after criminals and do their best to bring them to justice. Tucker didn't know it at the time, but he faced some hard times ahead. Some say we cannot control fate; that what will happen will happen. Regardless, Tucker surely had a protective angel looking out for him, at least up to this point. In all the arrests made so far, and there had been many, Tucker had not received even a scratch.

George Tucker's first assignment as a newly assigned deputy U. S. marshal was an arrest warrant given by U. S. Marshal Reagan. The man Tucker was to arrest was Mack Hicks. It so happened

Federal Court Building and Post Office in Paris, Texas. It is a three-story brick building. Handwritten on the front, "Papa to Rosa Louise" *Photo from Joe E. Haynes Collection.*

that Hicks was living just across the river from Spanish Fort and Tucker was working out of that location at the time. Tucker knew him quite well and "I liked him in a general way. It would be almost an evidence of imbecility," said Tucker. Hicks was wanted for horse stealing which was a rather serious charge in those days.[11]

Tucker contacted one of his posse, a first cousin, Jack Tucker, and asked him to go along with him as backup and they mounted their horses, making sure rifles and handguns were fully loaded, and rode north across the Red River. Then they rode up Mud Creek a short distance until they came to Hicks' house.

Hicks was outside, crouched down, hidden in a fence corner. He had evidently heard or seen them coming for he had grabbed an old muzzle loading musket and hid behind the fence. Hicks threatened them not to come any closer or he would make a fight of it.

Tucker's thinking was Hicks couldn't do much damage with that old musket so he and Jack simply closed in on him and took his gun away from him. Jack grabbed it out of his hands and threw the old relic as far as he could send it out through the blackjacks.

Once Hicks was in custody, Jack went back home to Spanish Fort as Tucker had Hicks saddle a horse, then took him back to Paris. Mack Hicks had an uncle in Paris who owned and operated a hardware store and he asked Deputy Tucker to keep Mack out of jail and promised he would make the necessary bond in the morning.

Tucker wasn't sure what to do being he knew Mack well and wanted to treat him right. But Tucker did the right thing by telling the uncle, in the presence of Mack Hicks, that he had no authority to make such a decision. He further stated that it would be up to Marshal Reagan to do whatever he wanted to do in the case. Had Tucker been out on the road with Hicks, "I would not have hesitated to make a decision in such a matter." However, Tucker did not say what that decision would have been.[12]

Reagan happened to get wind of the arrest and walked up in the presence of Hicks and his uncle. Tucker introduced himself to Marshal Reagan and told him what Mack and his uncle wanted. Tucker believed that Reagan instantly realized his predicament so he ordered Tucker to throw Hicks into jail. According to Tucker, the marshal was not afraid to take responsibility. "And he always tried to help his deputies whenever it was possible for him to do so," said Tucker.[13]

After Tucker put Hicks in jail, Reagan took him up to the Lamar Hotel where, after drinks, they had their first talk together. "I had never met him before that day," confessed Tucker. He considered him a pleasant fellow to talk to and was such a man as to inspire confidence in others. "He was a fine marshal to work for under any condition," said Tucker.

One would assume that when a person was hired as a deputy U. S. marshal that he would have been interviewed by the boss, that being the residing U. S. marshal. In this case, Tucker states that he had no contact with Reagan until after making his first arrest as a newly assigned deputy. This means he was hired by someone other than Reagan.[15]

The first known photograph of George Tucker was taken in 1891 and the names and photograph came from Susan Swain Peters, John Swain's second wife. She listed number twelve as unknown. He is Deputy George Redman Tucker.

Susan married Swain on April 15, 1891, after he had been a

deputy U. S. marshal for about four years. She was born Charlotte Susan Ryan on January 6, 1873, to Thomas Granville Ryan and Martha Davis in Huntsville, Tennessee. Before Susan reached her teens the Ryan family's ideal life was turned upside down by the death of her mother. At about the same time her father was elected circuit court clerk.

The position required constant travel and, as he lacked means to have someone care for Susan, she accompanied him on all his trips. During these years Susan picked up many tom-boyish habits, including a fierce independence toward making her own decisions and the scandalous practice of riding a horse astraddle like a man.

In the mid-1880s, Mr. Ryan, his son and two of the girls moved to western Kansas. They remained there until shortly after the 1889 land run and then moved to Indian Territory to settle at the tiny

Eastern District of Texas, 1891 - This photograph was taken in 1891, probably at Paris, Texas and deputy marshal John Swain's second wife, Susan Swain Peters numbered and named them: 1. Bill Henderson, 2. John Swain, 3. J. J. Dickerson, 4. Heck Thomas, 5. Bill Little, 6. Will Weaver, 7. Matt Cook, 8. H. H. "Hilly" Lindsey, 9. Bill Stewart, 10. John Walner, 11, Jim Chancellor, 12. Unknown [George Tucker,] 13. Louis Eichoff, 14. Bill Huchinson, 15. Chris Madsen, 16. Ran Dickerson (little guy in the middle.) *Photo courtesy of Mike Tower.*

community of Alex, southwest of Purcell. There, Judge Ryan and his son were occupied managing farms for some of the wealthier Chickasaw while seventeen-year-old Susan entertained herself by accepting a position as a school teacher.

Susan became an American preservationist and matron at the Anadarko Agency, who worked to promote Kiowa artists. While working as a matron for the Indian Agency, she discovered the talent of the young artists who would become known as the Kiowa Five and introduced them to Oscar Jacobson, director of the University of Oklahoma's art department. She was honored by the National Hall of Fame for Famous American Indians and both adopted by the tribe and given a Kiowa name in 1954. They named her Kom-tah-gya. She was inducted into the Oklahoma Women's Hall of Fame in its inaugural year, 1982.[16]

Chapter Thirteen
The Land Rush

The first men who had rode out ahead of the others was not playing the game fair but they got the best pick of lands. They had already planted their flags.

Tucker was sent on a case which just happened to take place at the right place and at the right time. On April 22, 1889, at high noon, the first land rush in America was unleashed. Settlers raced to claim land in the Unassigned Lands, most of modern day Canadian, Cleveland, Kingfisher, Logan, Oklahoma, and Payne counties.

George Tucker was one who observed this first land rush as he stood on the banks of the North Canadian River while on a hunt

Oklahoma land rush April 22, 1889. Photo is a reenactment of the land rush shown in the 1931 film, *Cimarron*, directed by Wesley Ruggles, starring Richard Dix and Irene Dunne.

for an outlaw. If true, Tucker pinned on his deputy U. S. marshal badge before April 22, 1889. He would have had no authority as a town marshal or deputy sheriff to be that far north looking for a fugitive.[1]

There were seven land runs in Oklahoma: The land run of 1889 took place at noon on April 22, 1889, and involved the settlement of the Unassigned Lands, with an estimated 50,000 people lined up for their piece of the available two million acres.

The Unassigned Lands were considered some of the best unoccupied public land in the United States. The *Indian Appropriations Bill of 1889* was passed and signed into law with an amendment by Illinois Representative William McKendree Springer, that authorized President Benjamin Harrison to open the two million acres for settlement. Due to the *Homestead Act of 1862*, signed by President Abraham Lincoln, legal settlers could claim lots up to 160 acres in size. Provided a settler lived on the land and improved it, the settler could then receive the title to the land.

A number of the individuals who participated in the run entered early and hid out until the legal time of entry to lay quick claim to some of the most choice homesteads. These people came to be identified as "Sooners." This led to hundreds of legal contests that arose and were decided first at local land offices and eventually by the U.S. Department of the Interior. Arguments included what constituted the "legal time of entry."[2]

September 22, 1891 — Land run to settle Iowa, Sac and Fox, Potawatomi, and Shawnee lands.

September 23, 1891 — Land run to settle Tecumseh, the pre-designated location of the county seat of County B, later renamed as Pottawatomie County.

September 28, 1891 — Land run to settle Chandler, the pre-designated location of the county seat of County A, later renamed as Lincoln County.

April 19, 1892 — Land run to settle the Cheyenne and Arapaho lands.

September 16, 1893 — Cherokee Strip Land Run. The Run of the Cherokee Strip opened nearly 7,000,000 acres to settlement. The land was purchased from the Cherokees for $7,000,000.

May 23, 1895 — the last land run to settle the Kickapoo lands.[3]

Not long after Tucker handled the Hicks' case, he was sent up north of Oklahoma City to arrest a man by the name of Charley Bowie. He rode up along the North Canadian River looking for Bowie and it was when the run was made of the newly-opened lands. Tucker dismounted and was standing out on the bank of the river. He had a brand new Winchester and was looking it over when riders caught his attention.

"Men were riding like the wind, carrying little flags," said Tucker. He saw the main line of people farther back who were riding all sorts of animals and every vehicular contraptions imaginable.[4]

Some of those who came along later, thinking that Tucker was guarding a claim from jumpers, offered him money for it. "I remember especially one fat, old Dutchman who came past riding horseback. He was quite out of the race then. He stopped a moment and asked me how much I wanted for my claim. I suppose that I could have sold something that I did not have, but I didn't care for that kind of profit. Being a deputy United States marshal, I was prohibited from staking out a claim. The poor old Dutchman rushed on after his brief stop with me. I hope that he found something on across the country some place," said Tucker.

Tucker got to use his Winchester that day. As the line of people moved across the country, the wild animals rushed ahead of the line. Tucker shot at wolves as they sped past him and saw lots of antelope, deer, and wild turkeys pass by.[5]

"Since that time, I have heard so much about the openings and the runs, and have known so many people who participated in them. Needless to say, I'm glad that I got to see a small corner of it, for it was a sight to be remembered. It was so frantic, so hectic, so seemingly crazy and hurried! And I've often wondered how many fellows slipped in ahead of the line to get the better lands. Or rather, I hope that oil was discovered only under the lands that were honestly staked."[6]

Chapter Fourteen

The Killing of Charley Bowie

He had no use for officers of any kind as they were merely convenient marks at which to shoot.

Tucker recalled when Bill Carr handed him the warrant for the arrest of Charley Bowie, the charges were rape and horse-stealing. Bowie was noted as one of the toughest young men in the country and when killed, he was barely grown. However, "he left a record of crimes behind him that many a veteran criminal would have been proud to own." said Tucker.[1]

"I give you these warrants for Bowie," said Carr. "If you kill him, I'll buy you a new suit of clothes." Bowie was a dangerous character and while deputies were searching for him, Tucker did not believe they were too anxious to meet up with him.

One morning, Deputy Tucker, along with two possemen, D. N. Terry and C. L. Hart, went up between Fleetwood and Red River Station. Hart had died only a few years before Tucker wrote this story in his memoirs. He wrote that both of the men were fine possemen. They were riding along the river from Red River Station to Fleetwood, which the latter town was situated in Indian Territory. "I remember that we had a bottle of bitters with us. We had been nipping at it all morning. It was pretty cold," said Tucker.[2]

"Give me another drink," said Hart. "I feel as though I could do some shooting this morning."

They were on the lookout for Bowie, and had planned to reconnoiter the country up around the Bowie home. They approached the house with considerable care. Finally they saw Bowie standing in the yard. They also noticed that his mother was washing clothes with steam rising from the pot of boiling water setting over a fire. Old Man Bowie was also outside, standing by the fire watching his wife boil the clothes but was swearing at the officers as Tucker and his two possemen rode on up to the house.

When young Bowie spotted them, he ran into the house. They knew there would be trouble from the young hellion. "He was only seventeen-years-old. "When young fellows are mean, they're worse than old ones because they take much desperate chances," said Tucker.

Tucker decided the best way to prevent Bowie's escape, at least from the back of the house, was to send Terry around behind the house to prevent a back way escape. Hart and Tucker stayed out front. Charley's father, Old Man Bowie, was still out in the yard watching his wife do her washing. According to Tucker, he was one of the toughest men he had ever known, and he claimed he had seen no end of criminals in his over fifty years as a police officer.. "He had no use for officers of any kind as they were merely convenient marks at which to shoot," said Tucker. Bowie proclaimed, "By God, you'll not take my boy!"[3]

Bowie yelled at his boy, saying, "Don't come out of the house, son!"

Tucker yelled back, "Bowie, I'm going to take your boy. If I don't take him alive, I'll take him dead!"

But Old Man Bowie was not to be calmed and kept up his storming while Mrs. Bowie said nothing. Then Tucker said he was going to burn the house down if the boy didn't come out and surrender. That only ignited additional anger from the old man. It made the situation much worse.

Old Man Bowie yelled to his son saying, "Kill every damned one of them if they start toward you, Charley!" That was enough to ignite courage from the kid and he started shooting at the posse from inside the house.

Tucker and his men sought cover quickly and began a steady return fire at the house. It was determined later that Tucker and his posse shot seventeen holes through the light frame house before finally hitting Charley Bowie. They were shooting Winchesters and after they wounded him, he came out of the house. They then withheld fire. He was hit hard.

Bowie said, "Don't shoot me anymore, you have killed me." They came up to him. He was in a pitiful state, but still standing. He shook hands with the three lawmen and said, " I don't blame any of you at all."

Tucker took his saddle blanket from his horse and spread it on the ground, then laid him on it. His father began to simmer down a little after he witnessed what had happened.[4]

"Do you see what you did," Tucker told him. He was pretty wrought up against the old man.

"You killed your boy, or made it necessary for us to do it," Tucker told him. Hart was excited and said he was going to shoot the old man because it was his fault they had to kill the boy. Hart was new at man hunting and this was one of the first killings in which he had participated. Tucker told him to back off even though the old man deserved no better than his son.

After Old Man Bowie finally calmed down, Tucker told him that he was indeed sorry about the whole matter, but he had to do his duty as a sworn deputy marshal.

Bowie indicated he understood but Tucker knew that it was folks like Old Man Bowie that made the young men so lawless.

Tucker wrote, "The sorriest feature of the whole episode was when the mother came over to where the boy lay dying. I can truly say that I never felt so sorry for anyone as I did for her. I don't know what sort of a woman she was, but it was too much for her to see her boy dying right before her eyes. She got down with him, crying bitterly. I could damned near have killed the old man then, simply because of the pain he had caused his wife. It was a sad case, the saddest one that I ever saw in all my career as a police officer."[5]

The Territorial Topic, dated October 19, 1889, stated that W. H. Terry was working with Deputy Marshal George Tucker and C. L. Hart in October of 1889, when they went to serve a warrant of arrest on Charley Bowie alias "Charlie Davis" who was wanted for stealing horses at Lexington, Chickasaw Nation. The nineteen-year-old Bowie had taken refuge at his father's home in Fleetwood, Chickasaw Nation. The deputy marshals, with a posse, surrounded the Bowie home demanding Bowie to surrender. Bowie refused, telling the deputy marshals he would kill them if they did not leave. Tucker moved back to bring reinforcements forward. Bowie, seeing an opportunity to escape, left the cabin firing as he ran. Deputy Marshal Terry shot the fleeing outlaw with his Winchester rifle striking the horse thief in the right nipple, killing him instantly. The deputy marshals went to court in Paris, Texas, to report the shooting. Of course Tucker, never mentioned a posse except to say they were Hart and Terry and Tucker did err when he pegged Terry with initials D. H. rather than W. H. which was his correct name. Perhaps it was the "Bitters" they were drinking.

Regardless, Tucker's story appears to hold water as to who actually killed him. If the story was correct, the three deputies fired seventeen rounds through the walls of the house. Only one of those bullets struck Charlie Bowie but it was a killing shot as Bowie was found inside mortally wounded.

According to Tucker's story, "Following the Bowie killing, there was considerable criticism of me. It was rumored that I had needlessly killed the boy. Of course, only the tough element really believed it. Nevertheless, I wanted the criticism stopped. So I asked to be indicted for the killing. I had a good friend on the grand jury, Frank Hammers, and I went directly to him."

Tucker told his friend Frank that he wanted to be indicted for the killing of Bowie and Frank thought openly that it was a rather strange request and asked Tucker why he wanted to be indicted for a justified killing. "Because I want to stop all these rumors," said Tucker.[6]

Tucker claimed that he knew there was no danger of being convicted on the charge. The indictment was voted as per his wishes, and he said he was brought to trial. "Bud" Birmingham was the prosecutor.

"He was one of the best friends that I've ever had. He didn't try very hard to make a case against me. Judge Bryant was the presiding judge in the case, and he was another good friend of mine. A lot of tough characters came down to testify against me. But Judge Bryant refused to hear their testimony. Then he gave a directed verdict of not guilty to the jury. That ended the case and also the rumors against me. There never was anything to the charges. We killed the boy because he wouldn't surrender and we gave him every chance to give himself up to us," proclaimed Tucker.

The Bowie killing caused a great deal of concern at the Eastern District Court in Paris. After the deputies returned from the Bowie farm, Tucker sent a telegram to Dickerson, the United States marshal who replaced Reagan, telling him that Bowie resisted arrest and put up a fight so they had to kill him in trying to arrest him.

The message was sent from Belcher, Texas, which was in the Northern District which was outside the jurisdiction of the Eastern District where they were assigned. Dickerson became worried because he thought Tucker had killed a man in United States Marshal Knight's Northern District, headquartered in Dallas. There was considerable rivalry and bad feeling between the marshals and deputies of the two districts. This would eventually lead to an investigation and the firing of a number of Eastern District lawmen.[7]

"We're all in for it now," Dickerson told some of his deputies in Paris. "Tucker has killed a man in Knight's district."

"Don't get worried without the facts," J. D. Mynett [also went by Mynatt] replied to Dickerson. Tucker had known Jeff Mynatt for years

George A. Knight, U. S. marshal, Northern District of Texas. He was confirmed by the Senate on January 27, 1890. He resigned April 4, 1892.

and got to know him much better in the next few years as a fellow deputy marshal. They were thrown together many times in working criminal cases. According to Tucker, Mynatt was one of the best deputies that ever wore a badge.

"George never killed a man outside his district in trying to make an arrest, you may bet on that," Mynatt assured Dickerson. "He might have killed someone over there as a personal affair, but not as an officer."

Anyway, Dickerson sent orders for Tucker to report to him at Paris. Tucker complied immediately. Mynatt met Tucker at the train station, saying that the old man had his feathers all ruffled up about the affair. When Tucker told Mynatt that the killing had taken place up on the Fleetwood farm in the Territory, he seemed greatly relieved.

"You ought to have known," Tucker said to Jeff, "that I had more sense than to go outside my district to kill a man."

"That's what I've been telling them all along," was Jeff's answer.

Tucker hurried to U. S. Marshal Dickerson's office to tell him about the true facts of the affair. "Everything was all right when he learned the true facts of the case," said Tucker. "He was a good-hearted fellow, the best I ever worked under as a peace officer."

He was appreciated by his deputies as he always tried to protect them from criticism and interference and he stood against seeing innocent men suffer from crimes of which they were unjustly accused, according to Tucker. He went on to say;

"I remember once that he took me along with him when he was sent to hang three men who had been convicted of murder. He went out to do the job and didn't even take a gun. Of course, I had my guns with me. After the three were disposed of, he asked me if I would have shot any of them if they had started to run. 'Sure,' replied Tucker."

Tucker was of the opinion that Marshal Dickerson didn't take his guns because he was hoping that the condemned men would try to get away and that Tucker would not shoot them. "He had me figured wrong; for I would have considered it my duty to kill them if the had tried to escape."[8]

At another time, to show what kind of a fellow he was, Dickerson told Tucker that he would refuse to execute the two Ball boys and Bob Bardwell if they were found guilty of the murder with which they were charged. It was common practice for most districts to carry out their own executions and in this case, it seems the U. S. marshal was the hangman. Of course, hangings were not so common in the federal districts because the convictions were subject to approval by the Supreme Court and those somewhat egotistical judges of that era believed they had to discipline frontier judges.

However, Judge David Bryant, of the Eastern District of Texas, was a brilliant student of law and had very few of his convictions over-turned. Author Howard K. Berry's book, *He Made It Safe To Murder*, stated that an attorney named Moman Pruiett earned the title "King of Acquittal," by getting more murderers off than any other lawyer in history.

As for the Ball brothers and Bardwell "You needn't do it," Tucker told him. "We'll hang them for you if the court orders them hanged."

The three men were convicted, but they maneuvered until they received a new trial. Finally, they all beat the rope. Two of them were sent to the penitentiary for life. However, as was the case with so many of the crooks that the deputies put their lives on the line, they were later pardoned. The only positive note in the affair was that Marshal Dickerson didn't have to refuse to hang them.[9]

As to the jurisdiction of the Eastern District Court of Texas for crimes with death penalties, the *Denton County News* reported on July 19, 1894, that nine men were to be executed on September 8th. Sheb Williams was the marshal. On September 29, 1894, the *Galveston Daily News,* gives the names of the men, their crimes, and other details of the event.

Williams' obit as given by his daughter gives the total he hung as an even dozen. From its inception, the court never posted less than eight murder cases per docket. It is unclear as to the number of men Dickerson hanged, if any.

Tucker dedicated a chapter in him memoirs about the Bowie affair and indicated that the case caused him considerable trouble, even though he had requested an indictment against himself in an effort to discredit the rumors that he and the other lawmen had killed a boy when they might have taken him without such dire measures.

The criticism finally died down. Three years after they had killed his boy, Tucker had a conversation with Old Man Bowie, Charlie's father. They were on a train and Tucker saw the old man a few seats ahead of him. Tucker decided it would be best to not say anything to him, for Tucker figured the old man still held the killing against him. After a while, Old Man Bowie happened to spot Tucker and motioned for him to come up and sit with him. Tucker went up and sat down.

"You killed my boy," he said, by way of opening the conversation.

He had already testified in the trial that he was responsible for the boy's death. It seemed curious to Tucker that he would make such a statement to him so long afterward.

"I didn't know, though, exactly how he felt towards me," said Tucker. "He had been tried for resisting an officer as a result of our attempt to arrest the boy. I had not wanted to see him prosecuted at the time and had said so, but was powerless to prevent it. And he had admitted that he was responsible for the boy's death."

"Yes, I killed your boy," said Tucker. "And I shall always be sorry for it."

"Oh! Don't think that I hold it against you," he replied. "You know, my boy's death put me to thinking about things. And I decided to lay aside my evil ways. I was a worker for the devil in those days. I can see it now! I'm exhorting. I'm trying to catch up on my work for the lord."

 He wished Tucker good luck before their talk ended. Tucker noted that he certainly was a different man from the one that he had heard cussing on a morning three years earlier.

Tucker finalized his feeling about the visit with Mr. Bowie by stating;

> He was the second man I had got into the pulpit, and though I don't pretend to have been so good a Christian myself, I was certainly glad to see such complete changes come over persons who had been so uncivil before. And I do not approve of such a method of converting crooks into Christians. It seems such a pity that people can't do the right thing without having to be shaken out of their boots by some dreadful event. And I always felt that Old Man Bowie would have to spend long hours in his work for the Lord in order to overcome the evil work that he had already done in the world. For, so long as I live, I shall always hold him personally responsible for the death of this boy.[10]

Chapter Fifteen

The Whiskey Runners

It isn't against the law to have it here; and if we get across the river, we don't give a damn for all of the deputies in this whole section of the country.

It was previously believed that George R. Tucker and Jeff Mynett were good friends. When Tucker wrote about his life as a lawman he revealed proof that he and Mynett were, in fact, very good friends.

As deputy marshals, Jeff and George were spending the Christmas holidays at Spanish Fort. Tucker still had family there but it likely that Mynett did not and was there only as a friend. It was probably Christmas of 1891, Tucker claimed they celebrated in Spanish Fort to talk over old friends and to get away from work for a while.

One day they were in the saloon talking and having a few drinks of whiskey. While they were sitting at a table, three white men, peddlers according to Tucker, came in and walked straight up to the bar. They told the saloon keeper to fix three sacks of whiskey up for them.

The saloonkeeper, like the lawmen, knew what was up but had no scruples against selling whiskey to anyone who could walk straight and fork up the money. He knew they were going to run it up into Indian country. Tucker knew the saloonkeeper was a good man who didn't want to see anyone get into serious trouble.[1]

Accordingly, he warned the three men that there were two deputy marshals sitting there in the room and warned them that they had better leave by the back door. If they had taken the advice of the saloonkeeper, the deputies would never have had a run-in with them. But they were stubborn, and insisted that they would carry the stuff out the front door, right out over the lawmen.

"What? You don't think that we give a damn for two puny marshals, do you?" one of them shot back at the saloonkeeper.

"Well, you'd better not flaunt your gun in their faces, or they

118

might resent it," returned the saloonkeeper.

"You fix up the liquor and we'll take it out of here. It isn't against the law to have it here; and if we get across the river, we don't give a damn for all of the deputies in this whole section of the country," the spokesman of the trio replied.

The trio saw themselves as really tough hombres and maybe they were. Due to their failure to heed the saloonkeeper's advice, he went ahead and filled the three sacks with bottles of whiskey.

They paid him and proceeded to walk right by the deputies. Tucker saw it as, "I really believe that they thought they didn't give a damn for any number of deputies. Jeff and I certainly didn't want to get into any scrap while we were on our vacation, but we couldn't let such a challenge go unanswered. I asked Jeff what he thought we ought to do. He was willing that we give them a little run for their money."[2]

"But, we have no horses," said Mynett. Henry Denny, one of Tucker's prior possemen was there and he had a horse. He agreed to loan Tucker the horse but Mynett couldn't find one at the moment. Denny had his horse and an extra so they mounted up and took out after the three peddlers, leaving Jeff Mynett nursing his glass of whiskey.

They trailed the trio across the Red River into Indian Territory. Once the whiskey peddlers were across the river they started shooting their guns and yelling like wild Indians. Tucker and Denny were not far behind them. Tucker wasn't sure if the trio knew they were being followed but assumed they did not. They were following close enough that they could see them and hear them shooting and yelling.[3]

Tucker knew the country well and especially Indian Country to the north side of the river, as he had scouted and worked it for about fifteen years. He claimed to have covered almost every foot of it while looking for criminals. Based on his experience, Tucker believed he knew about where the runners were going.

He knew a shortcut through the timber, so he and Denny dug their spurs into the horses and hurried to where they thought the two trails would meet up on the flat. They got there before the peddlers came along. They stayed in the timber and dismounted and stepped back into the brush. Soon, they were within hearing distance and suddenly the trio was right on Tucker and Denny.

They stepped out of the brush in front of them and Tucker said, "Ok men, give up."

Their leader, Loshie Bradburn, apparently had no intention of obeying the order, for he started to pull his six-gun down on Denny. Tucker was prepared as he already had his Winchester up and cocked.

"I didn't take very careful aim, for there wasn't time. But I let him have it," said Tucker.

Bradburn was hit hard and fell from his horse like a ton of bricks. His brother, Joe Bradburn, turned tail and ran like the devil out through the woods. They took the third peddler, Bill Merritt, without any trouble.

Tucker wrote, "If either of the others had been as tough as Loshie, it might not have been healthy for us. But they didn't have the iron in their constitutions that Loshie had."

A grim situation turned into a somewhat funny affair. According to Tucker, when Loshie went down, they figured he was finished. As he fell, Denny also fired his six-gun at him, hitting him in the side. The bullet only grazed the skin but broke a bottle of whiskey in Loshie's coat pocket. When that whisky soaked into his skin, he thought it was blood.

Loshie yelled out, "Don't shoot anymore, I'm done for!"

That surprised Tucker, for he supposed he would be stronger than that after the way he boasted back at the saloon. Tucker took Loshie's gun and threw it away. When Tucker looked him over he discovered that his bullet from the Winchester had torn away the top half of one of his ears.

"The situation became somewhat funny then, said Tucker. "I had only bobbed his ear, just marked him, as some of the old fellows used to mark the cattle that they turned loose in the woods."[4]

They took Loshie and Merritt back to Spanish Fort. Mr. Allen dressed the mutilated ear. "I can still remember Doc cutting off a piece of the ear that was hanging down like a pendant," said Tucker.

They took Bradburn and Merritt to Paris and put them in jail where they remained for a long time prior to their trial as no one would go their bail. Tucker refused to add resistance to their arrest, being he thought they had enough trouble to satisfy the liquor running offense.

Colonel John Hodges, a lawyer in Paris, asked Tucker if he was going to testify against Loshie?

"No," Tucker told him. "He will have enough on his hands with the liquor charge. I have nothing against him as a fellow. In fact, I rather like him when he's sober."

"Then I'll let Judge Bryant know how you feel about it," Hodges said.

He was as good as his word according to Tucker. When Loshie was brought to trial, Judge Bryant threw out the resistance charge. Tucker figured it was much better that way. Tucker saw Loshie as a good-hearted fellow except when he was fired up with whiskey. Then, he was mean and ready to fight with plenty of courage.

Tucker liked him, and respected him, as one fighter admires another. Tucker thought Loshie was killed a short time later in Tishomingo, but when Tucker wrote of the incident, he had forgotten the facts about that case.

Tucker may have been mistaken about the demise of Loshie Bradburn. On August 3, 1894, A Fort Smith, Arkansas newspaper, *The Elevator,* printed a story about Deputy Marshal Abner McLellan. The report stated that McLellan was killed on July 20, 1894, west of Caddo, in Choctaw Nation during an attempt to arrest Gerald Bryant on a larceny charge. Bryant was followed by a posse to the home of a man named Bradburn, six miles from the scene of the murder where the cabin was surrounded and at daylight he was killed as he tried to escape. It is not know if this was Loshie.

This Bradburn was referred to as first name of Loshie by Tucker. However, he is probably Lish Bradburn, convicted of murder and sent to Leavenworth around 1900. He appealed his conviction and the details are as follows:

In *Bradburn vs. United States, 1901;*

Decided: October 4, 1901, Indian Territory Court, Murder, claims self-defense, Flight from the state. This is a case upon a charge of murder. The facts of the killing were that the defendant and the deceased, one John Evans, had a misunderstanding with regard to a small indebtedness claimed to be owing by the deceased to the defendant. On the day of the killing (and the killing is admitted by the defendant) the two rode off together for the purpose of going to the home of a man by the name of Stair, whom the deceased claimed really owed the debt. Their object in going to Stair's was probably to settle their differences. On the way, when no one was present save themselves, the defendant killed the deceased. He immediately informed the neighbors of the occurrence, claiming that deceased had provoked a general quarrel with him about the debt, and had obtained a rock, with which he was trying to strike defendant, when he [the defendant,] in order to avoid the blow, struck him with his fist upon the neck, and unintentionally killed him. Shortly thereafter defendant fled the country. Upon the person of deceased, about the face and neck, there were found some two or three bruised places, where he evidently had been stricken. About one year after the killing the defendant was arrested, and indicted and tried for murder, the trial resulting in a conviction for manslaughter, and the defendant was sentenced to imprisonment for ten years. During the trial exceptions were saved to the admissibility of certain evidence, the charge of the court, and to what was claimed to be improper language of the attorney representing the government in his closing argument to the jury. The case is regularly appealed to this court. The conviction was overturned.

The attorney at the court proceeding had Bradburn pegged in the same light as Tucker based on his comments as follows: On a trial for murder, defendant, on cross-examination, testified that he had been arrested, charged with stealing cattle, and acquitted, and had had a fight with deputy marshals. In his closing argument, counsel for the government said. "That rooster [pointing to defendant] has been stealing cattle and fighting deputy marshals until he has become a desperate dare-devil, and he did not care what he did."

The court documents list him as Lish Bradburn, indicted for murder, convicted of manslaughter, and conviction reversed. Of the inmates listed at Leavenworth Penitentiary Inmates, 1895-1931 was Bradburn, Lish, inmate #2188 and again, #4073. The death of Lish or Loshie Bradburn seems to be lost in time. However, it is likely Lish was the same Bradburn Tucker dealt with.[5]

Chapter Sixteen

Bully John Thrasher

A young boy was walking up the road during the gun battle. A bullet hit him squarely in the forehead, blowing his brains out.

George Tucker titled the next chapter of his life as "John Thrasher" and he tells a sad story, but one that is typical of the times of an unsettled and wild area of the west.

George had close ties with his brother Bill who owned and operated a mercantile store in Atlee, Chickasaw Nation. Bill was often a posseman for George and put his life on the line on more than one occasion. He took a bullet in the arm during one chase. While George Tucker failed to say much about his family, he did mention his son, Bert, when writing about John Thrasher.[1]

When Bill Tucker's wife died in 1946, a news article gave a report on this pioneer family who came from Franklin County, Arkansas, to Hill County, Texas. By 1880 they were living at Spanish Fort, in Montague County. Bill opened

William H. Jefferson Tucker Family

William H. Tucker family. The names of his wife and children were not written on the back of the photography. William "Bill" was George Tucker's brother and posseman. *Photo from author's collection.*

123

a mercantile business in Petersburg, Indian Territory, but it was some time before Mrs. Tucker could be reconciled to crossing the river and making her home in "uncivilized Indian Territory."[2]

Eventually she did cross the river and they lived at Petersburg until 1902 when they moved to Sugden and went into the mercantile business again. They moved to Waurika in 1907 but eventually made their home in Childress, Texas, where Bill died.

In George Tucker's story he stated his brother, Bill, owned and operated a store in Atlee, Indian Territory, but it was likely Sugden. That is based on a newspaper advertisement in 1904, which read; "Rock bottom prices, our motto: Large scales and small profits at W. J.[*sic*] Tucker & Co. at Sugden."[3]

George Tucker's son, Bert, was born in 1880 and he would have been grown for George to allow him to take part in a showdown with the use of weapons. Therefore, sometime during 1904, the following took place. George Tucker's brother ran a store up in the Territory and he and his boy, Burt, were visiting him.

George related that Bill was having some trouble or was being threatened with trouble from a fellow named John Thrasher. According to Tucker, he was a big bulldozing man, who liked to bully everyone he could. He had a buddy who ran with him named Bill Edwards and was as big a bully as Thrasher.

Tucker's brother was a rather peaceable sort and didn't want trouble with anyone, but, according to George, he was a Tucker, had been a posseman for George, and he believed all Tuckers could fight if they had a need to do so, and with some Tuckers it didn't take very much provocation.[4]

Thrasher made his threats around through the community that he was coming up to the store some day and just take it over. Tucker's brother told him about it when he and Burt came up to visit. Tucker said, " We might have something to say about that if he tries it while we are here, and we don't know when we are going to leave."

George and son Burt took positions on the porch of the store and waited. George had his Winchester and Burt a six-gun. They didn't have long to wait before Thrasher and another man drove up in a wagon. They had Winchesters in their laps and when they saw two men on the porch with weapons, they opened the show and started firing at George and Burt.

The Tuckers returned fire and drove them off. They made a hasty exit from the scene and Tucker didn't think they hit either of them seriously. It would have been easily forgotten and laughed about but unfortunately it turned tragic. A young boy, named King Prater was walking up the road during the gun battle. He had been hunting and was carrying a red fox-squirrel in one hand and a little target rifle in the other hand. A bullet hit him squarely in the forehead, blowing his brains out.

"It was, to put it simply, a damned shame," said Tucker. "He was coming home with his prize kill."

Thrasher and Edwards never came back to bother George and his brother after that, according to George. The fact of the matter was that John Thrasher was killed by John D. Williams in July, 1904. The homicide was ruled "a justified killing."[5]

The killing of the boy led to some hard feelings against them and indictments were made against George and his son, Burt. Deputy Marshal Frank Fore, an old friend of Tucker's, came and arrested them and took them to Chickasha.

W. B. Johnson, of Ardmore, was sent by the court to make an investigation of the affair. He determined and reported that the Tuckers were not responsible for Prater's death and that the killing was a result from pure accident. So the judge threw out the indictment and discharged them.[6]

William Benjamin Johnson was appointed United States Commissioner at Ardmore, Indian Territory, in 1890. He remained in Ardmore the rest of his life and died on April 22, 1939. He resigned from this position and formed the law firm of Johnson & Cruce.

Later another Cruce joined the firm. He was Lee Cruce, who became the second Governor of Oklahoma. On January 14, 1898, President McKinley appointed Johnson attorney for the United States Courts for the Southern District of Indian Territory. He was reappointed in December 1901, by President Theodore Roosevelt, for another four years and he continued as federal attorney until 1906.

Therefore, based on Tucker's statement that W. B. Johnson came and investigated the incident, would indicate a time frame of between 1898 and 1906. Additional information from Fore indicates this incident occurred in 1898.[7]

Frank Fore was a deputy marshal from 1892 to 1898. A news

article of 1893 stated "Deputy U. S. Marshal Frank Fore arrested John Savage on charge of violating the law governing the sale of intoxicants in the Choctaw Nation, and he will be required to defend himself in court. We believe one of the charges is for selling Choctaw beer some time ago."

His service record lists him as Fore, D. F. Then, on November 6, 1898, Frank Fore brought Dowdy Tucker (George Tucker's nephew) from the Rock Island country on a bench warrant charging him with murder. He was placed in the jail at Ardmore. Being Fore's service ended in the latter part of 1898, and Johnson was made federal attorney in January, 1898, we must conclude that this incident had to occur during 1898. Fore died in 1905.

It is unfortunate that Indian Territory was still a violent place in 1898. It had been so for many years prior and would continue for years to come. There were many ways this accident that resulted in the death of an innocent young boy could have been avoided.

Two men faced two others who had made threats and opened the dance in front of Bill Tucker's store. Winchester rifles were powerful weapons and had long-range stopping power. Hollow-point rounds, or controlled expansion rounds, are preferred by today's law enforcement. This is because the bullet flattens out on impact and has more stopping power but does not continue on its path and risk injury or death to an innocent bystander.

In this case, it was likely a stray bullet that hit the boy and a hollow-point versus a standard round would have made no difference. Was there a better way of dealing with Thrasher? Possibly! George Tucker was a deputy U. S. marshal and Thrasher probably knew this. George's son, Burt, was around eighteen-years-old and probably should not have been allowed to take part in the affair, unless Tucker appointed him a posseman to assist. Today's forensics could have determined which bullet hit the boy, but not in 1898.[8]

* * * * *

During Tucker's first year as a deputy marshal, he and other deputies were called upon to head to Richmond, down in Fort Bend County, to deal with the serious trouble of the Jaybird and Peckerwood War. Some called it a riot, while others called it a war. The Jaybirds were part of a Democratic association while the

Woodpeckers were Republican.

The control of the black vote was the main issue. Family divisions helped bring on a terrible fight in front of the courthouse on August 16, 1889. Deputy Marshal Tucker was there and when he wrote about the mettle he named it the Jaybird and Peckerwood riot. This story, like many others from George Tucker has never been published.[9]

The Woodpeckers (many of whom had been Republican during Reconstruction) included a number of whites and virtually the entire African American population of the county. The Woodpeckers had controlled the county government by winning elections since the Reconstruction Era.

The Jaybird faction, which included a majority of the white population in the county, wanted to oust blacks and their white allies from the county administration. Murders were committed against persons in each faction in 1888 and 1889.

On August 16, 1889, a gunfight broke out at the county courthouse, in which four people were killed, including the sheriff. The Jaybirds won the fight and seized control of the county government soon afterward, with the collaboration of Governor Lawrence Sullivan Ross, who established martial law in the county. The effects of the post-reconstruction feud echoed in local politics for decades. The Jaybirds effectively disfranchised the African Americans in the county by using a "whites-only" ballot in preliminary party voting from 1889 until 1953, when the United States Supreme Court ruled that this was unconstitutional.[10]

As Tucker remembered there were some black men elected to the county offices, including the county clerkship, and some others whom Tucker had forgotten over time. The Democrats didn't like it and apparently they did not refrain from showing their displeasure. This was, of course, East Texas and there had been trouble there ever since Reconstruction times.

Finally, a riot broke out and Sheriff Garvin and three deputies were killed while trying to restore order. Others, on both sides of the riot, were also killed during the rioting.

U. S. Marshal Dickerson received an emergency call for help so he gathered twenty-five deputy marshals and hurried to Richmond, the county seat of Fort Bend County. The deputies were given warrants for forty people, both Republicans and Democrats.

It took a while to pick them all up but according to Tucker, they nabbed every one of them. They took them over to Galveston and lodged them in the city jail. Tucker was of the opinion that they were all released on bail within a heartbeat.

A month or so later, the deputies were called back to Galveston to guard the court while the forty men returned and were being tried for the rioting. There were twenty-five deputies from Paris, and U. S. Marshal Fricke brought ten deputies over from the Western District of Texas in order to help maintain peace.[11]

They were armed with Winchesters and six-guns as the lawmen patrolled along the streets of Galveston. Tucker stated that they all wore the big white hats that are so common on the plains and the people of Galveston were not used to seeing such antics or such people. They eyed the deputies as though they were monsters. "I suppose that we didn't look very good to them, for we were a pretty hard lot," said Tucker.[12]

Nothing of unusual importance happened at the trial. All of the defendants eventually went free. It's always difficult to find out who did a specific act when a mob is rioting. But Tucker believed that the old judge who tried the case was afraid to convict anybody. Tucker said, "People who live in swampy country are not particularly healthy. Their lives are out of fix. They are swarthy. You don't want to fool with a fellow whose liver is out of fix-he'll kill you before you know it. Those people down there were of that sort."[13]

Chapter Seventeen
Train Robbers & Horse Thieves

I knew that he was a skunk, that he would not shoot anybody when by himself, because he lacked the nerve to do it on his own responsibility.

According to Deputy Tucker, a notorious character went by the name of Judge [*sic*] South. Actually, he was referring to Jud South. When Tucker wrote his autobiography years later, he had likely forgotten that he went by Jud and not Judge.

Tucker wrote, "Judge South was not a judicial officer but was a 'wampus cat' during the times I knew of him." Tucker described the outlaw as being over six-feet tall, and weighed more than two hundred pounds. His formidable appearance was enhanced by a huge black beard. "And he had a reputation as an outlaw that demanded respect," wrote Tucker, "even from the deputy marshals. He wasn't the usual saloon tough fellow. He was more intelligent and more resourceful and he wasn't in the game for petty personal things. If there was ever a man who earned the title of being as cold as steel, I think Judge South was that man," concluded Tucker.[1]

Tucker laid claim to the marshal sending him, along with five possemen to arrest South in Indian Territory. Tucker and his posse had heard that South was staying up on Mud Creek in the Chickasaw Nation.

When Tucker wrote about the incident he had forgotten what charge was listed on his warrant for arrest, only that he did have a warrant as well as one for a character named Bob McFarland. McFarland was said to be staying with Jud South at someone's residence.

They scoured the country along Mud Creek very carefully. They eventually came up on a house where a man by the name of Bill Luke lived. As they approached on horseback they spotted Jud South and Bob McFarland in the yard on the east side of the house. Tucker and his posse approached the house from the west side, hoping to get as close to them as possible before they could "flush and run."

The lawmen were doing just fine as they made their careful approach. They decided to dismount and then started forward again very slowly on foot. Tucker was feeling confident that they would be able to sneak right up on them. Then, a dog started barking.

"Luke had a damned watchdog that hadn't seen or heard us until we were very close to our prey," wrote Tucker. The dog began to bark furiously. The lawmen rushed forward on foot but the pair of outlaws saw them and McFarland broke and ran for the house with Jud South right on his tail.

They were in close range by that time, and McFarland made it inside. Just as South was about to enter the house, Tucker leveled his sawed-off shotgun at him and shouted, "I'll kill you if you make a move."

South froze, having just grabbed hold of the door. He didn't move a muscle. He just stood there like a statue holding on to that door. Tucker's finger went to the trigger three or four times and almost shot South down as he was convinced he was going to have to kill him rather than take him alive. He expected South to break at any second and "I was going to let him have it if he made a move."

One of the posse members walked up to South out of the line of fire and took his six-gun from his holster as he remained frozen to the door. Then he took South over to Tucker who slapped the handcuffs on him.[2]

Deputy Tucker could not give himself a sigh of relief as he realizeda dangerous man remained inside the house. In the meantime, they heard someone jack a cartridge into a Winchester, figuring it was McFarland. "I heard the click that no one who has ever used a Winchester would mistake for anything else," said Tucker. He claimed he had no fear of McFarland, even though he had a loaded rifle inside that house.

"I knew that he was a skunk, that he would not shoot anybody because he lacked the nerve to do it on his own responsibility. If Jud South had been in the house with him, he would have fought like a wildcat."

But, it was most fortunate in apprehending Jud South before he got inside. According to Tucker, "once on his own, McFarland's guts turned to butter. It wasn't long before he threw down his

Winchester, put his hands in the air and walked out of house and told the posse he was giving up."

The homeowner, Bill Luke, was a minor player and made no trouble for the lawmen. He remained in the yard during the entire proceeding. He seemed to be an innocent sort of fellow, "but stupid," said Tucker. Luke was not a criminal, he merely harbored criminals. That wasn't good in Tucker's book but the only saving grace to having criminal fences about the country is that the lawman knew where to go in search of criminals.[3]

As far Jud South, Tucker knew he had a prize package. South was believed to be the outlaw who had robbed a train near Fort Worth. Tucker wanted to see if he could have a witness identify South as the train robber being there was a thousand dollar reward being offered by the railroad officials. This was a reward that a deputy U. S. marshal could accept. Had it been a federal reward a deputy could not make a claim.

The railroad people hatched up a scheme for Tucker to bring Jud South from the Fort Worth jail to a street car and put him on the back end of the car without his handcuffs. Seated in the car was to be "Old Gabe, the African American porter who had been on the train and saw the man who robbed it. If the porter could identify Jud South as the train robber, Tucker was to receive the reward of one thousand dollars that the railroad officials were offering for his apprehension.

Tucker upheld his end of the plan and put South on the street car. Old Gabe identified him as the one who robbed the trail. Then, Tucker took South back to the jail. Later on, a hard pill had to be swallowed by Tucker, as the railroad officials refused to pay the reward, "which meant that they merely took a thousand dollars out of my pocket," wrote Tucker.

Tucker failed to note that railroad officials almost always withheld paying rewards if there were no convictions. No record could be found to indicate that South was ever convicted for any train robbery.

According to Tucker, *alias* Judge or Jud, or Judd South was a tough nut to crack and actually, was never cracked. When Tucker and his posse took him to the jail in Fort Worth, the police had to register him, as was the usual custom with newly arrived prisoners. When they asked him what his name was, he refused to answer. So the officer, who was asking him questions, said that he would register South as Mr. Train Robber. Jud, or Judd, or Judge, replied that he would just as soon be registered under that name as any other that he knew.[4]

There was a murder charge out of Fort Smith pending against a person who answered to the description of Jud South. So, Deputy Tucker took South from the jail in Fort Worth to Paris. From Paris, Tucker and posse members took South to Fort Smith to stand trial while Bob McFarland remained in the Paris jail.

South was reported to have killed an Indian police officer by the name of Naked Hand. Again, Tucker was actually referring to Indian policeman and Deputy U. S. Marshal James Nakedhead, not Naked Hand. They were unable to convict South for lack of evidence to make the murder charge stick.[5]

Tucker's party then brought Jud South back to Paris where he and Bob McFarland were tried on a charge of horse stealing. The evidence, according to Tucker, supported them stealing ten head of horses from around Sapulpa. The indictment from the Eastern District of Texas stated that Jud South and one Bob McFarland, both white men and not Indians nor citizens of the Indian Territory, nor any nation of tribe of the Indian Territory, on the first day of April 1895, did steal certain horses from Jim Owen and John Minton valued at two hundred dollars. The indictment was read on December 23, 1895. The document was signed by commissioner H. H. Kirkpatrick.

An additional document filed in the court by the commissioner stated that Jud South and Bob McFarland did shoot the horses on the same date of the theft, April 1, 1895. The document gave no other details but it was believed that South and McFarland were being chased and when Owen and Minton caught up with the pair, they shot the horses.

Tucker doubted they were guilty of that crime, but the court convicted South just the same. "We never found out what his real name was. He was indicted and tried under the name of Judge South. But no one thought that was more than a convenient handle for him," said Tucker.

When the presiding Judge was sentencing him after his conviction for horse stealing, he called for Jud South to stand. South made no move to comply for quite a while. The courtroom got very quiet. At last, he said, "I reckon that I'm the fellow you want."

Then he stood up and received the sentence but it didn't seem to bother him. "If he felt anything at all, he didn't show it," said Tucker.

The only other time Tucker saw South was at the federal prison in Detroit, Michigan, where he was incarcerated. Tucker said he often wondered whatever happened to the mysterious Judge South. It seems that McFarland was acquitted of his alleged crime or crimes and "was sanctified and the Salvation Army got him out of it," said Tucker.

* * * * *

In his book, *Deadly Affrays,* author Robert Ernst wrote that South had a number of aliases. He went by Jud or Judd South, Judd Southern, and Judd Silvers. There were three train robberies mentioned. One was at Belle View [Bellvue], Texas, on December 1, 1886, Gordon, Texas, on January 29, 1887, and Ben Brook [Benbrook] on June 3, 1887. Suspects were Ben and Jim Hughes and Sam Baker, all of the Hughes Gang out of Indian Territory. They were all eventually arrested and taken to Dallas, Texas, and tried in November.

Baker was acquitted and Jim Hughes released being he had an alibi. Ben Hughes received a conviction with ninety-nine years prison time but on appeal had his conviction overturned. He was a free man. The gang kept a low profile until 1894 when a train was again robbed at Gordon, Texas, in the same spot as six years prior. Texas Rangers and deputy marshals from the Northern District out of Dallas took the trail up into Indian country. They eventually located the suspects around Muskogee. They were Shirley Smith, Ben Hughes, and Jud South.

The lawmen were joined by Indian policeman and Deputy U. S. Marshal James Nakedhead. When Hughes and South were cornered in a house Marshal Nakedhead was killed by the outlaws. Hughes was arrested but South escaped through the bushes. Both Hughes and South were eventually tried for the murder in Fort Smith but both were acquitted for lack of evidence.[6]

Tucker was not involved in this shootout and there was no mention of Tucker being there. Jud South remained at large, wanted in the train robbery at Gordon, Texas. At first glance, it seemed that Tucker might have fabricated the arrest and transport of South to Fort Worth. However, a newspaper article, *Fort Worth Gazette*, Fort Worth, Texas, June 12, 1895, supports Tucker's claim and is worthy of repeating here as follows:

> Yesterday, June 11th, 1895, Deputy Marshals George R. Tucker and A. J. Tucker arrived here, having in custody two men named Jud Smith *alias* Jud Southard *alias* A. J. Anderson and Bob McFarland, who were arrested last Sunday near Mud Creek, twenty miles east of Ryan in the Indian Territory. These two men were captured on the strongly grounded suspicion that they were engaged in the robbery of the Pacific express car at Gordon, Texas, October 19, 1894. They were found by the Tuckers and a posse of four other men at the house of one Bill Luke, and were sitting behind the house in the shade when the officers came upon them. When they officers came up the called to South and McFarland to surrender, but both of them showed a disposition for a fight. McFarland caught up his Winchester and South started for the door of the cabin for his rifle, but finding that he was shut off from reaching it by the officers, he started to draw a big six-shooter which he wore in his belt, but the officers told him if he made a movement to shoot they would cut them to pieces with bullets, and six-guns were leveled in their faces. South and McFarland concluded finally to surrender, and accordingly dropped their weapons and threw up their hands. They were taken at once to Duncan and committed before the United States commissioners. South or Anderson doggedly refused to tell his name, but he was recognized as the man who was with Ben Hughes, who was captured by Sam Farmer at Checotah last fall, when South, or Anderson as he was then known, escaped through the brush.

> Special Officer H. L. Sisk of the Pacific Express company has been on the track of South and McFarland for some time, and they were run out of their hiding places in the mountains of Palo Pinto County. They had been in the neighborhood of the place where they were captured only four or five days.

> The officers say that South is one of the most dangerous men they are acquainted with. He is a giant in size, and is said to be a man of very reckless character. McFarland is an Erath County man. Old Gabe, the porter on the trail that was robbed at Gordon, states that the men captured very closely resemble

the robbers. South and McFarland are wanted at Paris, Texas, on a charge of horse stealing, and will be taken there today, where an effort will be made also to identify them as parties connected with the Gordon express car robbery.

Therefore, Tucker was not fabricating his story about Jud South and Bob McFarland in his memoirs concerning the Gordon train robbery. There was no evidence to prove that anyone was ever convicted for the Texas train robberies and without convictions, no rewards were honored.

Author Robert Ernest has several articles about the trial of Ben Hughes and South/Smith. They were both found not guilty because the Texas deputy marshals did not have arrest warrants for either of them when Nakedhead was killed.

The time line of the Hughes Gang and Nakedhead's death follows: On February 27, 1895-Deputy U.S. marshals S. N. "Sam" Farmer and J. M. Britton, Northern District of Texas, attempted arrest of the Hughes gang and Deputy Marshal James Nakedhead was killed. Ben Hughes was shot in the arm and surrendered after his wife was arrested. Jud South hit the bushes and escaped. The dead body of Nakedhead and prisoner Ben Hughes arrived in Muskogee the same day. The next day, the 28th, Shirley Smith surrendered in Checotah. On March 1, 1895, James Nakedhead was buried in Tahlequah. The next day, March 2nd, deputies Farmer and Britton took Ben Hughes and Shirley Smith to Fort Worth, Texas, arriving at 4:40 p.m. The prisoners were transferred to Dallas and jailed.

On May 18, 1895, Texas Ranger Captain Bill McDonald arrested Ben Hughes' brother, Jim, in Palo Pinto County and took him to jail in Dallas.

Then, on June 11, 1895, deputy U.S. marshals George Tucker and A. J. "Andrew or Jack" Tucker arrived in Fort Worth with Jud South and Bob McFarland. During the last week of November, Ben Hughes and Jud South are in Fort Smith Federal Court charged with murder of Deputy Marshal Nakedhead. The trial was set for December 3 but delayed at the defense request. Then, during the first week of January 1896, Hughes and South stood trial, The verdict was "not guilty" due to the deputies from the Northern District of Texas not having arrest warrants. The larceny case against Hughes was dismissed. A Writ of Removal was issued against Jud

South, allowing Texas authorities to pick him up.

On December 23, 1895, Jud South and Bob McFarland were in Federal Court, Eastern District, Paris, Texas, for horse theft in Chickasaw Nation. The horses were valued at two-hundred dollars and the defendants shot the horses when they could not escape undetected with the horses. According to Deputy Tucker McFarland was released and Jud South was convicted and sent to federal prison in Detroit.[7]

In 1896, the Hughes brothers move to Oklahoma Territory and started a ranch in Caddo County. On June 3, 1897, Jud South was tried and found guilty of horse theft and given five years in the Huntsville prison.

* * * * *

On October 20, 1902, Deputy U. S. Marshal Lute Houston was murdered by the Casey Gang. Deputy Houston was hanged and his body riddled with bullets near the Hughes' ranch. On March 3, 1903, James Hughes, Will Crossland, and S. G. Littrell were arrested for the murder. A preliminary hearing was held beginning April 20 to April 23, 1903. Littrell was released but Hughes and Crossland were charged with the murder. They were finally tried and declared not guilty.

The Hughes brothers raised horses on their ranch and were noted for harboring criminals. Brothers, Ben and Jim, headed the Hughes gang of criminals. They were friends with Bert Casey who was one of the most violent of the outlaws to operate out of Oklahoma Territory. He had his own gang and they were responsible for several savage murders, including the eleven-year-old son of Dr. Zeno Beenblossum, Deputy U.S. Marshal Luther "Lute" Houston, and Caddo County Sheriff Frank Smith and his deputy, George Beck. One of the most senseless killings attributed to Casey was his judging the range and accuracy of his new Winchester rifle by shooting a farmer working in his field some 400 yards away.

Belonging to Casey's gang at different times were Fred Hudson, Ed Lockett, Joe Mobley, George Moran, Bob Sims, and Pete Williams. James and Ben Hughes also participated with the gang; although opinions differed as to whether they were members or employees.

Most of the gang members were called as witnesses in the

Hughes and Crossland trial. However, the Hughes' ranch was Casey's hideout. Casey was finally stopped by two of his former gang members, Fred Hudson and Ed Lockett, who were given deputy U.S. marshall commissions and promised a pardon if they captured or killed Casey. They killed him in 1903. His body was unclaimed and he was buried in the Boot Hill section of Summit View Cemetery in the territorial capitol of Guthrie.[8]

The Hughes Gang kept a low profile until 1911 when, on November 11,   was convicted of grand larceny in Custer County, Oklahoma, and sentenced to four years in prison. After his release, it seems he changed his lawless character or became smart enough to evade arrest. He died on June 5, 1945.[9]

Chapter Eighteen

Law Reform & Transport of Prisoners

*We will wear our guns Judge. It's the custom out here, for deputy U. S.
marshals to go armed.*

Federal field worker Selfridge found it appropriate to publish
Tucker's transport of prisoners and also published Tucker's
account of Judge Bowman's ill conceived reform ideas. Ideas that
probably worked back on the streets of the civilized and somewhat peaceful eastern cities. But, the Judge must have failed to
realize that he was out west in an untamed and somewhat lawless
area of the country; a place where a man was just plain dumb to
go unarmed; especially a lawman.

Tucker knew that the judge was green as a gourd for that part
of the country and gladly participated in a plan the deputies came
up with to change the judge's way or thinking about matters of
personal protection.[1]

Tucker wrote in his memoirs that there are always those who
do not understand the necessary facts in law enforcement. Especially where there are certain important things to know about
criminal law enforcement in Indian Territory before statehood
came. "It was a tough place. The crooks from other states came
in large numbers, and they didn't get any softer by coming out
here," said Tucker.[2]

Tucker made reference to a federal judge whom he pegged
with the surname of Bowman. Actually he was Alexander Boarman, but Tucker was not the only one to call him Bowman. The
newspaper made the same mistake. Boarman was the seventh
federal judge of the Western District of Louisiana and served the
courts from 1881 to his death in 1916. He was born in 1839. He was
sent to Paris, Texas, in April of 1889, as a special judge to assist in
residing over criminal cases, pending appointment of a new federal judge for the Eastern District of Texas.[3]

According to Tucker the judge had some personal ideas about
the proper way for deputies to go about their work. They were not

to provoke trouble. Tucker confirmed that he hailed from Louisiana where policemen wore billy clubs rather than six-guns and he sought to arm the Texas deputies in like fashion. According to Tucker it was about the same as taking willow switches out to bring in the gunmen of the territory.

On November 21, 1889, a newspaper printed the following account: "It is reported that the judge of the U. S. Court at Paris, Texas, has decided that no deputy marshal has a right to carry a gun into the Indian Territory in making an arrest, and, at the last session of the grand jury in his court, he instructed that it find a true bill against every deputy charged with killing in endeavoring to make an arrest."[4]

On one occasion, Judge Boarman and some of the deputies had taken a train and departed Paris on their way to Sherman. Some of the deputies approached the judge to pass the time of day with him.

"How dare you approach me with those guns on," Judge Boarman said heatedly.

"Oh! It's the custom out here, Judge, for deputies to go armed," one of the deputies replied.

"I'll change that," he declared. "I shall relieve you of your duties right now." Judge Boarman did likewise to every armed deputy that he encountered. The deputies had gotten themselves into a fix as the judge was really in earnest about the whole affair. The deputies didn't like it at all. They felt naked without firearms. Something had to be done. So, someone came up with a plan to deal with the dilemma. The deputies on board fixed it up with a gambler from Ardmore, who happened to be on the train, to work a little shenanigan on the judge. Jim Hughes was the gambler's name. Hughes agreed to the plan to come through the train and assault the judge by slapping him.[5]

Hughes did his part of the job well. The judge was sitting there in all his dignity. Hughes walked up to him and jammed the judge's Katy [Cady] hat down over his face. Then, he drew back and hit him, giving him quite a rap.

"His hat crumpled up as though it had been a wet rag," said Tucker. "The judge was really scared."

He sent for Deputy Tucker to come and protect him. Tucker had been seated in the coach just ahead of him. When a deputy came and told Tucker that the judge wanted him to go back to his car and protect him, Tucker jumped up and went back and sat down beside the judge. He had his six-gun in plain view so the judge couldn't miss it.

By way of opening the conversation, Judge Boarman asked, "What kind of people do you have out in this section?"

"Oh, they're damned tough," Tucker replied.

"Are they are in the habit of going around hitting people," asked the Judge?

"Yes, and they may do even worse than that. One has to be prepared to meet almost any emergency in this country. That is the reason people carry guns out here. If you don't, some bully may decide that he wants to whip you," Tucker replied.

"I'm beginning to see, now," Judge Boarman replied, just as earnestly as he had scolded the deputies a short while before. He went on to say, "I was wrong when I told the deputies that they would have to discard their guns."

The judge called all of the deputies whom he had relieved of duty and re-instated them immediately. Tucker said he rode on to Sherman, Texas, with Judge Boarman. He didn't think the judge ever learned that Jim Hughes' attack on him had been a made up job. It really didn't matter one way or the other according to Tucker, being Boarman didn't understand the West anyway. Visualizing deputy marshals performing their duties with policemen's billy clubs would likely bring laughter to a tough gunman's face when a deputy tried to arrest him.[6]

Additional insight into the character of Judge Boarman took place in November 1889, while the judge was continuing in his capacity as a special judge for the Eastern District due to the illness and incapacity of the official presiding judge.

A news article stated that a rancher by the name of Cal Suggs had been arrested and lodged in the Paris jail. When he went before Judge Boarman, bond was set at $20,000 and while the judge was out of town Deputy Marshal Letherman allowed Suggs to be released on bond. The problem was that the bond had to be approved with the judge's signature and this did not occur.

Judge Boarman instructed Deputy Marshal George Tucker to go to the Sugg ranch and arrest Mr. Sugg and "do not return until you have him in custody."

Judge Boarman severely reprimanded Deputy Marshal Letherman, who had Sugg in custody, and said, "If you should ever discharge another prisoner that is to be tried in my court, under such circumstances as Sugg has been discharged, I will send you, Deputy Letherman, to jail for an indefinite period."

Tucker discussed his dealings with the Sugg family in another chapter.[7]

* * * * *

"While the convicted criminals were normally desperate in jail, they became ever more desperate on the way to prison," wrote Tucker. Little has been published about the transport of federally convicted criminals in the Texas and Arkansas areas during the 1800s and early 1900s. In addition, very little has been published about transport to jail upon arrest.

In the western movies we saw transport wagons with bars that made their route through the territory and picked up prisoners at various jails, chained, caged, and taken to Fort Smith to await the dreaded Judge Parker's judgment; many times it was the noose. For those sent to prison, we think of Yuma or Leavenworth but not New York or Detroit, Michigan. But, that is where those convicted in Texas and Arkansas where sent. Tucker provided a good account of those transports.

Tucker claimed that during his years as a deputy U. S. marshal, he made only two of those transport trips "I went then only

Detroit House of Corrections cells and passageway during the 1890s. This is a look at the layout of a cell block and guard station. *From Robert N. Dennis collection of stereoscopic views.*

because I wanted to see the country, as I had never been north before."

Tucker talked about the method used in transporting "batches" of convicted prisoners to the penitentiaries in the north. The first trip for Tucker was as a member of a group of deputies that took sixty prisoners to Detroit, Michigan. The other time, he took part is helping to transport eighty-five convicted criminals to Brooklyn, New York. They came back through Chicago from Detroit on the first trip. On the New York trip they returned by way of Washington, D.C. Tucker said he enjoyed both of the trips, but would not have liked a steady diet of that sort of thing. "I much preferred to work in the field. There was more spice to it," said Tucker.[8]

On the Detroit trip, Tucker recalled there were twenty-seven deputies and the U. S. marshal who made up the escort. The prisoners were handcuffed and shackled in special coaches and the deputies kept a close watch over them. The biggest job was in feeding the prisoners. No meals were served on the trains. The lawmen made plans in advance on where they would stop and feed them. Upon stopping, the prisoners were unshackled and marched under heavy guard into the dining rooms, seated, and handcuffs unlocked so that they could eat. Then, after the meals, the cuffs were put back on and the prisoners were marched back to the rail cars and shackled again to the coach floors.

In those days, blacks and whites, in most cases, did not socialize, visit, or dine together. Tucker said;

> The only time that I ever ate between two Negroes was at St. Louis when we were making the Detroit trip. I was going along unlocking the prisoners. There was a vacant seat where I finished unlocking my section. I flopped down into it before I noticed who my companions were. When I looked around, I was surprised to find that they were two big Negro bucks. However, I was too hungry to stand on ceremony or social prejudice, so I rushed at the food the same as if I were seated among the boys. My recollection of these trips is that the deputies had a hard time getting enough to eat. They were so busy feeding and looking after the prisoners, there wasn't any time to eat their own meals.[8]

On those trips, according to Tucker, many of the prisoners were pretty tough customers. They were more desperate on the way to the penitentiary than they had been before. Some picked their shackles. They would use almost any kind of small wire or metal to do it. Most were not successful. Tucker remembered one old doctor who used the spring out of his watch to pick his shackles. He got the spring fast in the lock and broke it off, so that the shackle keys would not work. They had to cut the shackles off him, but gave him a new pair right away. They delivered every man whom they started with on every trip. They never lost a prisoner.[9]

* * * * *

Deputy U. S. marshals of modern day are probably treated somewhat better than deputies whose duties were to serve warrants in Indian Territory. Often times newspaper reporters would get an incident a little wrong and at other times seriously wrong. Many times, the news article doesn't give the complete story and sometimes distorts what really happened. The misspelling of names was common.

A news reporter in Gainesville, Texas, gave a misleading account of an incident of Deputy Marshal Jeff Mynett, often spelled Mynatt and sometimes Minot, and Deputy George Tucker. The reporter, named Walker, after receiving a serious beating from Deputy Mynett, continued to report misleading and false information. This account from Tucker's prospective has not been previously published. He titled the incident as "Personal Affrays" and said, "The title might lead one to believe that I was always seeking trouble, but that is not the case. Fighting was common on the frontier. Most everybody, sooner or later, found himself engaged in a squabble of one kind or another. I really didn't have much time for personal altercations, for I was engaged in rounding up criminals most of the time. But, I engaged in two set-tos that are worthy of being mentioned."[10]

The first of those was the Mynett fight at Gainesville. Tucker claimed he was not an active participant, "But before I was through with it I had come to believe that I had about ruined the town of Gainesville," Tucker said. In Tucker's opinion the entire matter started over a rather insignificant piece of foolishness conducted by a newspaper reporter named E. B. Walker.

Jeff Mynett had been sent up to Rush Springs in the Territory to arrest a woman charged with bigamy. He found her without difficulty or resistance and started back to Paris with her. When they arrived at Gainesville, they had to change trains. The woman had two small children with her and a bundle of clothes that she was carrying in an ordinary pillow slip. When they started down the platform to the other train, Jeff asked her to let him help her with the luggage and the children. But she was sullen and angry at Jeff for having arrested her.

She "lowed" that she could take care of herself and that she would much rather do it than to accept the aid of some people that she knew. So, Jeff, who seemed to understand how to deal with such cases, let her make her own arrangements, which she did. She took a child on each hip and the pillow case in her teeth and started to walk to the other train. And she made it without the assistance of Jeff or anyone else.

Everything would have been all right if Walker, a reporter on the Gainesville paper, had not seen the affair. The next day's paper carried a note to the effect that Jeff Mynett and family had passed through Gainesville on the day before en route to the federal court at Paris. Rather than leaving it there, reporter Walker made an assumption and went too far by writing that Deputy Jeff Mynett passed through Gainesville with a notorious woman wanted for adultery and went so far to indicate she and her children were his family. At least, that appears to be the way Jeff Mynett took it. Two news articles were published in the *Galveston Daily News*.[11]

The first article was somewhat accurate by stating Marshal Mynett assaulted Walker due to Walker stating Mynett passed through the city with a notorious woman, which Mynett viewed as slanderous. Tucker points out that a Mr. Darwin was editor of the paper and Walker was a reporter.

The second article goes even further and accused Mynett and two of his companions with the assault and made it look as though they ganged up on Walker. According to Tucker this was far from the truth as he pointed out in his memoirs. He emphasized that Jeff had to notice the squib, and he saw the rather course insult that was intended.

Many fellows would have passed the whole thing off as a joke, but according to Tucker, Jeff was not of that stripe. He was a gentleman in his relations with other people, and he demanded the same treatment for himself. Mynett had married a very fine woman from Palestine, Texas, the daughter of Bill Foster. She came of a very good family. They knew that she would in all likelihood notice the lampoon and might think that he was not quite a model husband. The more Jeff thought of the affair, the madder he got. Finally, he went to his boss, Marshal Dickerson and told him about it.[12]

"I'm going to whip somebody if retraction is not made," he told Dickerson. Mynett received encouragement from the marshal as he said, "I wouldn't think a damn thing of you if you did not." Of course, Tucker saw Dickerson's reaction as characteristic of him and figured he was that sort of a man.

Jeff made preparations to go to Gainesville. He did not ask any other deputies to accompany him. He would have gone by himself but Jim Chancellor and Tucker decided to tag along to see that he didn't get too raw of a deal. Tucker said, "After you have gone through many dangerous situations with such a fellow as Jeff Mynett was, you do not feel like seeing him imposed upon by others. Ours was a real feeling of loyalty for each other. And that brief statement will suffice to show why I went along with Jeff to Gainesville. I knew that there would be a rumpus, but I wasn't particularly afraid of those things. I'd already been through my share of them."[13]

When the deputies arrived in Gainesville, Jeff looked up Percy Darwin who ran the paper. Chancellor and Tucker went with him to talk with Darwin at some location away from the newspaper office, probably Darwin's home. In a very polite manner, Jeff asked Darwin to correct the error.

"As a matter of policy," said Darwin, "we never correct anything that we publish in the paper."

"Then," said Jeff, "if I understand you correctly, you refuse to make the retraction?"

"I see no reason to depart from our usual policy," was the answer that Darwin threw back at him.

"Well," said Jeff, as his temper started to rise. "Somebody is going to take a damn good licking here in Gainesville."

Darwin saw that he was getting pretty close to trouble, so he began to explain. He believed that Mynett was a fellow of his word. He decided to get himself out of the situation by giving Jeff the name of the reporter who wrote the articles in question. He told the deputies that a fellow by the name of Walker had written the articles. He was merely trying to escape a beating. Tucker believed that he ought to have taken the responsibility on himself and not given Mynett the reporters name.

Jeff was ready for a showdown and he and Tucker went into a nearby saloon. According to Tucker, Chancellor did not go with them but failed to remember where he went. Jeff knew his anger might get the best of himself and didn't want to go armed into the argument, so he gave his six-gun to Tucker. Then, he laid his coat on a table in the saloon and he and Tucker walked outside on their way to the newspaper office.

As they entered the newspaper office a man was seated at a desk writing. Jeff walked up to him and asked him if his name was Walker. Walker replied that it was. Just as he started to rise, Jeff hit him a terrible blow to the face. He hit him so hard that he knocked him to the floor. He was unconscious. Jeff began kicking him. He kicked him several times, knocking most of his front teeth out.

Just then, a man who was one of the printers, started for Jeff with a big club. Tucker pulled his six-gun on him and said, "I'll bore you if you don't stand back." Tucker was protecting Mynett and wasn't going to let anybody climb on his back, even though Tucker thought that Jeff was a little too harsh with Walker. Walker was a small man; Jeff was big. Jeff might, at least, have refrained from kicking him after knocking him out.

"But that was Jeff's business. Walker had insulted him and Jeff had a right to protect him honor," explained Tucker.

They walked out of the printing office and then back to the saloon, where Jeff got his coat and Tucker returned his gun. Pretty soon, the police came and arrested them.

"We were expecting it," wrote Tucker.= "They threw us in jail. It was the first time I'd ever been on that side of the cage wire, but I didn't worry much about that. I had seen a lot of good fellows thrown in jail, and I'd put some of them there myself."[14]

Later in the afternoon, they took the deputies out of jail and before a justice of the peace. "We pleaded guilty to disturbing the peace and paid our fines to both the city and the county." They thought that would be all. "But the damned rascals threw us back into jail on a charge of rioting," said Tucker.

Marshal Dickerson heard about the fight and he hurried over to Gainesville and did what he could for the pair. He got them a separate cell away from the drunks and human rats that one usually finds in a county jail. And he brought them some new bed clothing being the old bedding appeared to have been used ever since the jail was built according to Tucker.

Finally, on the fifth day after the fight, the district judge returned to Gainesville from his circuit. Frank Daugherty, president of the bank, was waiting for him. "Several rich fellows of the town went upon our bail along with Daugherty," wrote Tucker. Bonds were set at $2,100 each, which included Chancellor who had not even been in on the fight. But that didn't make any difference. He was charged just the same.

The three went back to work until the date of the trial. They hired the best attorney in Gainesville to defend them. His name was W. O. Davis. When the case was called, they asked for a change of venue. There was a great deal of local prejudice against the deputies. No fair trial could be received there. The change of venue was approved and the case was transferred to Denton County, which lies just to the south of Cooke County, in which Gainesville is located.

Jeff was tried first, for he had been the principal actor in the play. He didn't have much of a defense. He escaped the penitentiary, but got a fine of five hundred dollars and costs. Tucker came up next. The case against him seemed to be worse than that against Jeff, for Tucker had pulled a gun, while Jeff had used only his fists and his feet.

Emery Smith was the prosecutor and Tucker claimed they were old friends. They had been associated together in the Montague County court from back in the days when Tucker was city marshal and deputy sheriff while living in Spanish Fort. Regardless, it probably didn't make Tucker feel too good when Smith came to him and said, "George, I've known you a long time, but I'll have to send you to the pen"

"Just do your duty," Tucker told him, "and everything will be all right."

Then, Tucker got a very lucky break. Judge Barrett, the district judge, took sick, and was forced to quit the case. In his place they selected a local Denton attorney and the trial proceeded. After some little jockeying between the attorneys and the judge, they agreed to let Tucker plead guilty to the charges and take a fine of one hundred and fifty dollars and costs.

"I was to glad to get off with that," proclaimed Tucker. Chancellor got one hundred dollars and costs. That little assault by Mynett cost the three deputies a total in fines and costs of $1,200. They didn't have enough money to pay the court but figured it was worth it. Marshal Dickerson was a stockholder at the City National Bank of Paris and went on their notes so they could borrow the money.[15]

There was one other item of interest about the case and that involved the defendants settlement with Davis for his fees as attorney. He told them that each man owed him two hundred dollars. Somehow, they scrapped up the money and went up to his office to pay him. Each man counted out two hundred dollars and laid the money on his desk. He picked up each separate bundle and counted it to be sure that the proper amounts were there. Then he began pulling bills off the piles. He handed each of them one hundred dollars. They were surprised. Tucker summed it up by saying, "It is the only time that I ever saw such a thing happen and I've spent most of my life in the company of lawyers. I thought that I knew lawyers and their ways, but I decided then that I would have to make an exception in my general rules."[16]

Chapter Nineteen

A Clash Between Districts

Washington sent an investigator to fire us deputies.

Deputy Marshal George Tucker was instrumental in helping to lay the foundation for the successful recruitment of Texas gunmen to hire on as Regulators to fight in the Johnson County, Wyoming, Cattleman War of 1892. Had it not been for these previously unpublished events, it is very unlikely that the war would have taken place. At least not with a few of deputy U. S. marshals and the recruiter, Tom Smith. Tom Smith and other deputies had been fired as the result of a federal investigation.

According to Tucker, U. S. Marshal George A. Knight, from the adjoining Northern District of Texas, headquartered in Dallas, made complaints that the deputy marshals of the Eastern District, headquartered in Paris, were arresting persons inside his district which was not within their proper jurisdiction. Marshal Knight had made his threats that he would send some of Marshal Dickerson's deputies to the penitentiary if they didn't stop poaching in his territory."

We always thought that he was jealous of us because we got the good cases from the Territory," wrote Tucker.[1]

To investigate the controversy, the federal government sent down an investigator by the name of McDougal from Washington. He went to Paris and all of the deputy marshals were called before him. He had charged Tucker with arresting three men in Marshal Knight's Northern District.

Tucker was one of the last deputies called to testify by McDougal. All of the others who had appeared before him had been discharged. Tucker was just as guilty as the rest for arresting criminals from the northern part of Knight's district. Tucker wrote, "I got gloriously drunk for the investigation. I fully expected to be discharged, and I didn't care if I did. I knew the charges against me, so I fixed up a lot of damned lies about them."[2]

Investigator McDougal accused Deputy Tucker of arresting Wild Bill Cawhorn [sic] at Nocona, Montague County, on an unspecified date. Montague County was in the Northern District. It was true, but Tucker told investigator McDougal that he had followed that desperado all the way from Bush Creek in the Territory: and that he "had him close enough from time to time to see him out in front." Tucker insisted that he never actually overtook him until reaching Nocona.

"It was just one of the damned lies that I'd concocted for the occasion," wrote Tucker. According to Tucker, McDougal swallowed it, hook, line and sinker, and complimented him on his good work. He apparently didn't know that Tucker's "good work" consisted of a vivid imagination and a not too clear concept of truthfulness. "He told me that the law would bear me out. I was more surprised than elated."[3]

Tucker explained the situation as, "The law most certainly would not have borne me out if he had known the true facts of the arrest. I was intruding on Knight's territory."

Tucker had been looking for a man who was allegedly hiding out around or near the town of Henrietta. Tucker went there but was unsuccessful in locating him. After completing an extensive search Tucker figured he has spent sufficient time there, decided to return to Paris. He boarded the early morning train for Paris which made a stop at Nocona.

Tucker decided to depart the train and have breakfast at one of the local cafés. While having breakfast an old friend of Tucker's, Henry Denny, came over and told Tucker that he had just seen Cawhorn over in Arthur Croxton's saloon sacking up some whiskey to take over into the territory. "He was a noted whiskey runner, but my warrant charged him with assault to murder," wrote Tucker.[4]

To be in accordance with the jurisdiction rules between the two districts, Tucker could have waited and followed him across the river into Indian Country and arrested him there. However, Tucker decided to arrest him in the saloon and take him to Paris. He considered it foolishness to go to the trouble of following him across the river and then making the arrest.

Tucker walked over to Croxton's saloon and approached Cawhorn. Tucker wrote, "He offered no fight at all, either to being arrested or to being taken to Paris. He didn't even have his guns on him. I suppose that he had hidden them over on the other side of the river as he came over. Anyway, I took him to Paris. But McDougal said that the law would bear me out,"[5]

McDougal also charged Deputy Tucker with arresting a man named Walker George in the Northern District. Tucker told McDougal that one of his possemen had brought George to him at Nocona and that Tucker only took charge of him and transported him to Paris.

The inspector told Tucker that he did his duty in that case, for it was his job to relieve possemen of their prisoners at the earliest opportunity. Apparently, Tucker was telling the truth regarding this particular case and he claimed that he was truthful.. George was arrested by one of Tucker's possemen over in the Territory and only a switch in officers took place within the jurisdiction of Knight.[6]

Tucker was also questioned about the arrest of Percy Williams in Montague County, again in the Northern District. The facts were about the same as with George, except that Williams had been arrested in the Northern District and not in Indian Territory. However, the arrest was made by a posseman and not by a deputy marshal, making it legal.

"We were not too good to steal a man off him [Marshal Knight] now and then. After he became so outspoken about us, we did do everything that we could to pester him," said Tucker.

The Paris deputies learned that they could escape the regulations if they used possemen to arrest the criminals. The regulations applied only to the marshal and the deputy marshals. "So, we used one posseman to make the actual arrests, and then we took charge of the prisoners. Those were the facts in the arrest of Williams, but McDougal didn't get the technical point. He merely insisted that it was my duty to relieve the posseman of his prisoner when I had the opportunity," said Tucker.[7]

After all the firings of deputy marshals, Tucker heard that McDougal intended to lay him off with the others. But he never did. One of Tucker's friends told him that McDougal appeared quite surprised when he heard that he was still working. He said that he thought he had told him that he was to quit also.

"It would have been just as well if I had been laid off with the rest of the boys, for I didn't make anything out of my work. They [fired deputies] would meet me at the train when I brought a prisoner in and would demand part of my fee," said Tucker. Deputy marshals were not paid a salary in those days. They were paid a fee, mileage, and reward money, if posted and not a federal warrant. A deputy was paid six cents a mile for travel, two dollars for making arrests, and fifty cents for serving subpoena, etc. The officers were not paid a salary until the fee/travel practice was abolished on July 1, 1896, when the marshals were put on annual salaries.[8]

The unemployed deputies, all in fun, would threaten to take the money from Tucker after his returns with prisoners. He usually gave them money "for the poor devils had to live, and with many of them I'd already gone through hell," said Tucker. "Tom Smith was of these old partners. He was a fine, brave, big fellow. I would usually divide with him. Poor Smith! Some years afterward, he was killed by a Negro on the train just inside the Territory."

Some historians gave Tucker credit for being on that train. He was not. Dave Booker was with him and after Tom Smith was shot, Dave, in a heartbeat, drew his pistol from his holster, returned fire, and killed the black man.[9]

Chapter Twenty

Wyoming Cattle War of 1892 — An Overview

The Johnson County, Wyoming, war was a clash between large and small cattle ranchers in northern Wyoming. An invasion took place in April of 1892. In later years the incident would be remembered grandiosely with various titles such as *The Johnson County War, The War on Powder River, The Wyoming Range War,* and others. Deputy U. S. Marshal George Redman Tucker dedicated a lengthy chapter on the affair but he gave his own perspective about the affair, based on the fact that he was there and lived it. He said, "I have no intention or desire to rehash what has been previously written." Accordingly, for Tucker, the Wyoming Cattle War of 1892, was "one hell of a war."[1]

Wyoming was ideal for raising cattle and by 1880, many cattlemen from Texas and other states, moved in to capitalize on the fruits of good cattle country. This resulted in overstocked range and low beef prices. Then, the harsh winter of 1886-1887 took a heavy toll on the stock and ranchers had to cut back. Many cowboys were laid off. Some of these out of work hands remained in the area and homesteaded small spreads. Most of those small operators maintained small herds. Most of the land for grazing stock was "free range" and not owned by anyone.

The increasing number of small ranchers alarmed the big cattlemen of the region and they used their influence to gain passage of the *Maverick Law of 1884.* This law made it illegal to brand a maverick (cattle, regardless of age, found roaming the open range without a mother and without a brand) except under orders of the foreman of each roundup district. Another provision of the law required high bonds for bidding on mavericks. This made it difficult for small ranchers to start or enlarge their own herds. To the disappointment of big cattlemen, the Maverick Law did not stop the so called illegal branding of mavericks.

For one to fully understand the law and the need for the law is rather simple. A farmer raises crops; a rancher raises cattle whose crops are the calves and when it comes time to sell them they must have a brand burned into the hide. Whoever put his brand on cattle became the owner of those critters. Once the calf becomes older it leaves the mother and can no longer be linked to her. The Maverick Law gave the honest rancher some recourse against those who used a free hand in branding mavericks.[2]

The first book written about the range war was A. S. Mercer's *The Banditti of the Plains*, published in 1894. Mercer gave an angry eyewitness account of the range war, or in his words "cattlemen's invasion." The book was successfully suppressed and few copies reached the public. Since then, it has been republished. Most historians have questioned some of Mercer's conclusions about the range war. However, they have supported his grim assessment of the small homesteading rancher struggle, created because the larger ranchers believed their less affluent neighbors, if not themselves thieves, supported those who were.

The large ranchers fully intended on executing alleged rustlers and terrorizing their supportive network. To this end, Mercer stated that a band of fifty-two cattlemen and hired gunmen invaded Johnson County in April 1892. He reported that these gunmen besieged and killed the bravest man in Johnson County and in turn, found themselves besieged by the homesteaders and later being placed in the protective custody of the United States cavalry with further legal and illegal maneuvering permitting the invaders to go unpunished. Hence, the term "Johnson County Invaders" became a common term when referring to the hired gunmen.

In 1930, Frank M. Canton's autobiography was published and titled *Frontier Trails*. He related his experiences as a lawman in Wyoming and Oklahoma and his book has long been considered a classic work. Dr. Edward Everett Dale, professor of history at the University of Oklahoma, edited Canton's memoirs and the book was published again by University of Oklahoma Press in 1966 and titled *Frontier Trails: The Autobiography of Frank M. Canton*.

Frank Canton, self-admitted friend of both Ella Watson and Nate Champion, moved to Oklahoma after the Wyoming affair and became a respected U. S. marshal. About fifteen years later he somehow arranged a meeting with the Governor of Texas in which he admitted to being Joe Horner, a Texas fugitive, murderer, bank robber, cattle rustler, stage robber, and jail breaker. Horner was sentenced to twenty years in the penitentiary for bank robbery in Uvalde County, Texas and bank robbery in Comanche, Texas.

Taking Canton's years of working in law enforcement into account, the governor pardoned him for his crimes. Although we have no comment from Tucker on Mercer's book, Tucker was incensed over Canton's statements. When he sat down his own remembrances of the event he discredited Canton as a danger to others and himself and considered his book to be "garbage" with little truth about the details. Tucker did have something to say in his assessment about Canton and him shooting himself in the leg.[3]

Six-Guns & Saddle Leather was written by Ramon F. Adams and the University of Oklahoma Press published it in 1954. The book is a bibliography of books and pamphlets on western outlaws and gunmen. A second edition has also been written. Adams gives an account of the Wyoming war.

Yet, another account was provided in 1959, by Charles B. Penrose, the official surgeon accompanying the cattlemen who led the invasion. It was entitled *The Rustler Business*, Douglas, Wyoming: Douglas Budget, 1959, and was originally written in 1914, but published for the first time in 1959. This was followed by Helena Huntington Smith's in-depth account: *The War on Powder River: The History of an Insurrection*, New York: McGraw-Hill, 1966 and remained the standard for years.

In 1967, Wyoming Governor Jack R. Gage, wrote *The Johnson County War Is a Pack of Lies & Ain't a Pack of Lies*, Flintlock Publishing Company. More recently, renowned author and Texas state historian, Bill O'Neal, gave his account with *The Johnson County War*, published by Eakin Press in 2004. O'Neal gave an excellent account of this historic event. As one can see, there are many accounts of that cold month of April 1892, on the high plains of Wyoming's cattle country.

One book that is rarely mentioned was written by R. B. David and titled *Malcolm Campbell, Sheriff, Casper, Wyoming*, Wyomingana Inc., Casper, Wyoming, 1933. Campbell, was the first sheriff of Converse County, Wyoming, in 1888. He was instrumental in the capture of Alfred Packer, the notorious cannibal. Campbell was also sheriff during the Johnson County Cattle War in 1892. He wrote that the conflicts between large cattle companies and smaller settlers led to the death of up to twenty-five people. Tucker stated that Mr. David gave a true account, generally speaking, of the range war.[4]

The events of this cattlemen's war became highly mythologized as a symbolic story of the "Real American West" and became a major source of lore and legend for many years and probably for many generations to come. Over the years' variations of the storyline have come to include some of the west's most famous historical figures and gunslingers; its variations serving as the basis for numerous works of fiction for novels, films, and television stories.

What is most interesting about the Wyoming affair is the fact that a few of these hired guns had been recently fired from federal service as deputy U. S. marshals and were being subsidized monetarily by Deputy Marshal George Tucker. It should be noted that George Tucker was the only Texas gunman who was allegedly still actively employed as a deputy U. S. marshal and apparently never had a break in service upon his return to Texas. Most of the fired deputies were rehired upon return as they were seen in a positive light rather than as hired killers.[5]

A photograph was taken, preserved and titled *Invaders at Cheyenne*. A second photograph was taken of the same group and titled *Invaders of DA Russell*. However, the poses of the group are

Invaders at Cheyenne. This photograph was taken at DA Russell, near Cheyenne and the group of men were hired gunman by the large cattlemen in Wyoming. *Photo courtesy of Jim Gatchell Memorial Museum, Johnson County, Wyoming.*

somewhat different as George Tucker was in the first image but his half-brother, Starling Tucker, was sitting in his spot, number 40, in the second one. Names were added to the *Invaders of DA Russell* copy. The photographs were taken at Fort D. A. Russell near Cheyenne, Wyoming, in May, 1892.

The identities of the men in the photograph are attributed to Mr. A. B. [Arthur Bruce] Daniels. Mr. Daniels was a saloon keeper in Douglas, Wyoming, according to the 1910 federal census records. He was from Wisconsin and left home during 1870, at age fifteen. He went to several states before going to Leadville, Colorado, where he was a freighter for the mines.

In 1882, he freighted up to Laramie and used Rawlins as his station until moving to Rock Creek. From there he freighted to Fort McKinney and Sheridan. Then, in 1886, he moved to the new town of Douglas and built a two-story building with the lower floor for a business and the second floor for secret meetings. He was a Royal Arch Mason and an Odd Fellow. He later owned the First National Bank and was a partner of a large ranch. He was a member of the Wyoming Stock Growers Association [WSGA] and knew all the powerful men in Wyoming by 1892.

It is very likely that he visited with the invaders and after obtaining a copy of the invaders' photograph was able to match the faces to names. Later, Mr. Daniels moved back to Wonewoc,

Invaders at DA Russell. This photograph was also taken at DA Russell but the poses are different from the first image and numbers and names were added. *Photo courtesy of Jim Gatchell Historical Museum, Johnson County, Wyoming.*

Wisconsin. It is believed that he donated the photograph with the names to the Wyoming Pioneer Association on August 31, 1956.

The names were handwritten below the image. The original photograph was taken by Charles D. Kirkland and was titled, *Johnson County Invaders, Prisoners at Fort D. A. Russell*. A third group photograph was taken, same location and someone convinced most of the men to remove their hats. Most of the so called "regulators" were from Texas and were gunmen, some having been prior deputy U. S. marshals.[6]

It is inconclusive how Mr. Daniels knew the naming patterns. However, the only logical evidence is that he was present when the photograph was taken and obtained the names personally from them. We do know that George Tucker was in one photo, and his half-brother, Starling Tucker was likely photographed in another group photo. Many of the faces appear to match the names but there is no proof that the naming patterns are one-hundred percent accurate.

Invaders at DA Russell without hats. This photograph, same location as two previous, was taken with hats removed. However, Dave Booker and one other man did not take their hats off. *Photo from author's collection.*

Chapter Twenty-One

Hired Guns Were Deputy Marshals

Not to laugh, not to lament, not to judge, but to understand.
Baruch Spinoza
17th Century Dutch philosopher

Most of the regulators, or invaders came out of Texas and twenty-three were reported to be from the Paris, Texas, area. However, only twenty-one were accounted for. Many were, or had been, deputy U. S. marshals who had been fired or were on leave of absence. On the other hand, Tucker will lay claim that many of the so called hired guns were nothing but saloon toughs, street brawlers, and trouble makers.[1]

According to author Bill O'Neal, only nineteen Texans were taken prisoner from the TA Ranch to Fort McKinney. O'Neal went on to say reports persisted one or two defenders slipped past the besiegers. "When the list of prisoners was compiled, two Texans were missing: Tom Smith and Bob Martin." The inventory of weapons did not record any weapons belonging to these two men. Martin disappeared but Smith rejoined his comrades in time for the group photo.

The hired gunmen O'Neal lists in his book are Smith, McNally, Jerry Barling, Pickard, Dudley (aka Green), Snarl [Starling S.] Tucker, Alex Hamilton, George Dunning from Idaho, Alex Lowther, Bob Barling, Jeff Mynett, Dave Booker, George Tucker, J. A. Garrett, Wilson, Bill Little, Armstrong, Bob Martin, Benson, Schultz, Buck Garrett, Willey, and Johnson. So it appears there were twenty-two Texans including Smith while nineteen were taken prisoner and listed by the military. Smith and Martin slipped out before the troops arrived.

A Buffalo newspaper stated there were a total of forty-five men charged and named twenty-one Texans as follows: William Armstrong, Alexander Hamilton, William Little, Alexander Lowther, Thos. Smith. Buck Garrett, J. C. Johnson, J. D. Mynett, J. Barlin, S. S. Tucker, B. Willey, J. M. Buford, K. Riekard, B. C. Schults, W. H. Tabor, G. R. Tucker, A. R. Powers, D. E. Brooks [Dave Booker], W.

A. Wilson. M. A. McNally, and Robert Barlin.

Major Walcott was the self-appointed leader of the invaders. He was a former Union Army officer from Kentucky. When the invaders surrendered to the U.S. Army, Major Walcott presented a list of all firearms belonging to each man. They were new weapons provided by the cattlemen. The list showed make, caliber and serial number of each man's arms as well as cartridges, and cartridge belts. Robert Murray located the list in the U. S. Army records in the National Archives and published in *Shooting Times* magazine, July 1967.

George Redman Tucker's pistol was a single action .45 caliber Colt, probably M1878. His rifle was a 1886 Winchester, .40-82. His second Winchester was a 1876, .40-60. His half-brother, S. S., or Starling Tucker's pistol was a single action .44 caliber Colt, M1883 and his rifle was a 1886 Winchester, .45-70. Both were well armed. Almost all of the pistols taken were single-action Colts in either .44 or .45 caliber.

The list continues as follows: Alex Hamilton, pistol, Colt .45, rifle: Winchester 1873; K. Pickard, pistol: Colt .44, rifle: Winchester 1873; J.C. Johnson, pistol: Colt .45, rifle: Winchester, 1886, .45-90; J. A. Garrett, pistol: Colt .45; rifle: Winchester 1873, .44; D. E. Booke [Dave Booker], Colt .45, rifle: Winchester 1873, .38. Other weapons taken were; B. Wiley, pistol: Colt .45, rifle: Winchester 1873, .38; J. D. Mynett, pistol: Colt .45, rifle: Winchester 1886, .45-90; J. Barling, pistol: Colt .45, rifle: Winchester 1886, .45-90; W.A. Wilson, pistol: Colt .44, rifle: Winchester 1873, .44; F.M. Benford, pistol: Colt .45, rifle: Winchester 1873, .38; Bob Barling, pistol: Colt .45, rifle, Winchester 1886, .40-82; B.C. Schultz, pistol: Colt .45, rifle, Winchester 1873 .44; William Little, pistol: Colt .45, rifle: Winchester 1873 .38; M.A. McNally, pistol Colt .45, rifle, Winchester 1873 .38; Will Armstrong, pistol: Colt .45, rifle: Winchester 1873 .38; Buck Garrett, pistol: Colt .45, rifle: Winchester 1873, .44.

Chapter Twenty-Two

The Lost Wyoming Range War File

George Tucker wrote his version of the Wyoming Cattleman War in his unpublished and untitled memoirs. For all these years, the manuscript has been in a file at the University of Oklahoma Library, at Norman. The manuscript was first edited by professor John Alley of the University, apparently to be published as a book, but was only used, in most part, for an interview by Jennie Selfridge around 1936.

Selfridge stopped at page seventy-one of Tucker's manuscript. This was likely due to the political climate of the times, as no one wanted to print any versions of the Wyoming affair that would differ from what had been written by Frank Canton. It is unclear exactly why Tucker's manuscript of his life was never published as a book. His full story has been tucked away and somewhat ignored for almost a century.

Then, just a few years ago, Bill O'Neal, who apparently opened that drawer at the Oklahoma University Library, found Tucker's manuscript. He referenced parts of it in his book about the Wyoming range war. Tucker's account of the Wyoming affair is likely one of the most accurate based on the fact that he was there, was a hired gun, was a Lieutenant under Tom Smith, and was still employed as a deputy U. S. marshal. He was in the middle of it all.

Many of the hired guns or regulators were fired deputy U. S. marshals, but Tucker still carried his badge, or so he claimed. Tom Smith had been fired from his position as a deputy prior to the trip as well as Jeff D. Mynett, Dave Booker, and Bill Little. Buck Garrett would later become a deputy marshal and sheriff of Carter County, Oklahoma. All were rehired upon returning to Texas.[1]

A number of historians have claimed that gunman Booke [*sic*] was the Texas Kid. There never was anyone named Booke documented. There was Dave Booker, prior deputy marshal out of Paris. He was a quiet, soft spoken man but was quick and deadly with a gun in his hand. He was the deputy marshal who killed the murderer of Tom Smith, not George Tucker as some reports indicated. Regardless, he was not the Texas Kid.

George Redman Tucker's half-brother was the Texas Kid. Wyoming reporters mentioned him often in the newspapers but only referred to him as "The Texas Kid." Bill O'Neal, in his book on the affair, listed his name as Snarl Tucker. His was not Snarl, but was Starling S. "Starl" Tucker, He was born in Franklin County, Arkansas, in 1869 and he was age twenty-two in Wyoming. But, he was, for a fact, the Texas Kid.[2]

Known as the Texas Kid, twenty-two-year-old Starling Tucker shared the same father with George Tucker. Starling killed Nick Ray and later he was killed by his cousins at a dance in Indian Territory. *From group photo, courtesy Jim Gatchell Historical Museum, Buffalo, Wyoming.*

George Tucker despised Frank Canton and his written character assassination was probably the primary reason for his autobiography on the range war being omitted from publication. Tucker dedicated fifteen pages of his autobiography to the Wyoming war and titled the chapter "The Wyoming Cattle War: 1892."

The first time that Deputy George Tucker heard of plans to take a group of Texas hired gunmen to Wyoming to arrest cattle rustlers was early in the spring of 1892. Tom Smith and other deputies had been fired and were out of work. Only a skeleton crew remained available to perform duties out of the Paris district.

Tucker was one of the few deputies who was not fired due to the clash between districts. He was providing some financial aid to those men from the fees, travel pay, and occasional rewards that he received. Tom Smith, with whom he had worked with for years, had made arrangements with some Texas cattlemen who had ranches in Wyoming, to recruit a bunch of good, courageous gunmen to help them. They told Smith they would pay the men well and that the job would be short in duration. They left the impression that they were going to arrest cattle rustlers. That was just to their liking. As deputy marshals, Tucker and his fellow deputies had been doing just that kind of work for years. "Nobody liked a cattle or horse thief," said Tucker.[3]

Smith talked to a lot of men in Paris, Texas. Some had a reputation of being good with guns and some were nothing but saloon bullies. Smith needed an army of guns and if some were only tough, that didn't seem to bother him. He told them of the opportunity to be paid well to go with him to Wyoming and clean out a nest of cattle rustlers and outlaws.

All of the prior deputies were hanging around and needed jobs desperately, so they listened to his call and agreed to go with him. Tucker told his friend Smith that he would go when Smith made his pitch telling Tucker all about the deal. But meanwhile, Tucker went on working as a deputy, just the same as if nothing had happened.

Preparations were made to entrain the party and they left Paris while Tucker was away making an arrest. The party would be going through Gainesville, Texas, on the way to Denver, Colorado, and it so happened that Deputy Tucker was in Gainesville when the train of hired gunmen was scheduled to pass through, so he went down to the train to see he friends.

"They all put at me to get on with them. I had, as I said, promised to go. But I also had two prisoners in the Gainesville jail that I had arrested up in the Territory. I was then on the way back to Paris with them," wrote Tucker.[4]

Under the circumstances, Deputy Tucker told them that he couldn't go. Smith was insistent. Tucker told Smith that he had already been out about fifty dollars in expenses while catching the prisoners, and didn't want to lose that money. Smith said he'd gladly give his friend Tucker the fifty dollars as he was needed him as his lieutenant and would get another deputy to take Tucker's prisoners to Paris.

That left Tucker without further argument so he agreed to go. A deputy by the name of Reynolds was on the train. It was agreed that he would take the prisoners to Paris for Tucker. Little is known of Deputy Reynolds and only one newspaper account was found that mentions him. Deputy Reynolds, no first name listed, arrested and brought to justice, Galee Taylor, charged with the murder of U. S. Postmaster A. H. Glaze. Ben Sargis killed Glaze because he would not return a forfeit of ten dollars on a horse he had bought on time from Glaze, a year before. It was claimed that Taylor furnished Sargis the gun to do the killing. That is a good example of such violent behavior in those times over a ten dollar issue. So, Tucker crawled on the train, and thus became a member of the Texan army that was going to free Wyoming from the cattle rustlers.[5]

The group which Smith had gathered to go to Wyoming was a combination of gunfighters, brawlers, and misfits. There were some good men, and, according to Tucker, some who were worse than no men at all. He wrote, "I didn't like the looks of things very well, but I kept still. I didn't care a great deal of what happened. Later, in the evening, I told Tom that I could use my fifty dollars, but he told me that he was merely kidding about it, and that he had to tell me that to get me to go. I didn't like it very much, but then Tom was too good a friend of mine for me to raise a squabble with him over so paltry a sum."[6]

When the train stopped at Henrietta, Texas, a well-armed young man boarded the train. As they were pulling out of Henrietta, for Denver, Tucker saw that the young man was none other than his half-brother, Starling "Starl" Tucker, who was to play a prominent part in Wyoming. Tucker claimed Starl was only seventeen-years-old when he climbed on board that train that day. However, according to records he was twenty-one or twenty-two years of age in 1892.[7]

When they were recruiting men back in Paris, Starl had asked Tucker if he could go, so he was probably living with Tucker or his brother Bill, or possibly Jack Tucker, a cousin. Tucker told him that it was no place for a boy. Starling balked and let Tucker know that he was a man grown, not a boy. Records prove he was an adult, not a boy as Tucker indicated. Tucker claimed that he feared for Starl's safety, being he was so young; afraid he would get into trouble.

Tucker proclaimed that his brother "didn't have a bit of sense. That boy was as mean as they come and always wanting to kill somebody."

It made the seasoned man hunter, George Tucker, wonder why one of his half siblings was so deranged. Tucker said that once in Wyoming, Starling got his wish about killing folks and became know, for only a short time, as "The Texas Kid." And while Starling Tucker, alias Texas kid got his wish, it ruined him in Tucker's assessment.[8]

Tucker reported there were twenty men from Paris on the train when they pulled into Denver. They were met there by the stockmen, the large ranch owners of Wyoming who were fetching them up there to arrest cattle thieves.

The regulators were given new guns. They had brought their six-guns and Winchesters, which were of .44 caliber. "We threw away the latter and were given guns of larger calibers, some of them .45-90, some .52-40, and others .38-55," said Tucker. "It looked like a war, to see them handing out the new guns. They were dandies, to be sure. At Denver, we also loaded on [the train] wagons and horses and saddles."[9]

After leaving Denver, Tucker claimed that he began to have suspicions regarding their real purpose in Wyoming. Soon after the train started out, they pulled down all of the blinds and locked the doors of the coach. "What does this mean," Tucker wondered to himself. He asked himself why deputy United States marshals had to move secretly into a country simply because they are going to arrest a few cattle rustlers? In Tucker's words it was apparent that some of the hired guns from Texas were still active deputy marshals. But, no one said anything. The men were tired after the long trip and as they traveled toward Cheyenne, most of the men slept in their seats.

When the train arrived in Cheyenne, the regulators didn't get out of the locked coach. The train took on more horses, saddles, and equipment. They weren't detained long in Cheyenne. Running on to the north, they soon arrived at Casper. The coach was unlocked and the men unloaded everything; horses, wagons, saddles, and equipment.

Though it was May, it was spitting snow from the north. Tucker's memory may have eluded him, being it was April and not May when the trip was made. He said, "I thought that I'd freeze to death. My Texas blood was too thin for a Wyoming May winter. After we'd gotten all the troupe together, we hit out for the Tisdale ranch, about sixty miles to the north on the Powder River."[10]

Once they reached the Tisdale ranch, they prepared to stay for the night. The Tisdale cowboys told them that there was a big dance over at the K. C. Ranch and that the rustlers were there. So, being they were up there to deal with rustlers, plans were made

This drawing shows the wagon loaded with pine and spruce boughs, set afire, pushed up against the cabin and burned during the siege at the K. C. Ranch. Artist unknown.

to intercept them at the dance. The Texans got up in the middle of the night and filed out across the country toward their objective. They arrived there a little before daylight and surrounded the ranch house. Everything was done as quietly as possible; and the people in the house gave no sign of being alerted.[11]

Tucker and his group of gunmen lay in wait behind any cover they could find. Some had taken positions in an old stable that stood between the ranch house and the river. Just at daylight, a man came out of the back door and walked on down the path toward the waterhole. Some of the invading men stepped out onto the path as he approached them. They pulled their guns on him and took him into custody quietly and without trouble. The man was then taken to the stable.

After questioning him, it was determined he was not one of the so-called rustlers. Pretty soon, another man emerged from the back door, and started walking down the same path. He was taken in the same manner. They proved to be two trappers who had stayed at the ranch house that night and had gotten up early so they could be on their way. They told the invaders that there were only two alleged rustlers in the house.

They decided to settle back and wait. After a while, one of the two remaining men in the house came out by way of the back door. He stood near the house urinating. Starl Tucker was lying next to his brother George and, "begged me to let him kill him," wrote Tucker. George refused to let him do it, believing it would be plain murder to kill the man.

But Tom Smith, who was close by, whispered to George and said, "Do you think the kid could hold steady enough to get him?" Tucker agreed that Starl probably could, knowing his brother was a good shot and had nerves of steel. That led Tom Smith to say, "Let him go ahead, then."[12]

After Smith gave the go ahead, Starl Tucker raised his rifle and pulled down on the man. The bullet hit him and knocked him to the ground. "But the bullet didn't kill him and when he began to wriggle around, we all began to shoot at him," said Tucker.

Despite their efforts, he crawled into a basement entrance. There was no longer a need for secrecy, so everyone began to shoot at the house. Tucker claimed that the man Starl Tucker shot was Nick Ray, and seen as a rustler. "Nathan Champion was the other man inside the house. He would answer our shots," said Tucker.

While they were peppering away at Champion, Jack Flagg, another man believed to be a rustler, came along. He and a boy were riding on the front gears of a wagon. The boy was driving. When they got close enough to see them good, one of the cowhands yelled, "That's Jack Flagg!"

Major Whitcomb cried out, "Kill him!" The regulators all began to shoot, not only at Jack Flagg, but also the boy. They put the whip to their horses and ran out of range of the gunfire. On reaching the top of a low hill, they stopped the team, cut them out of the harness, and rode them away "like wild Indians," said Tucker.

Some of the gunmen gave chase but didn't get close enough to do any harm and the last they saw of Flagg and the boy was watching them race up the road toward .[13]

Tucker reported that Buffalo was the stronghold of the rustlers. Any probability for success of the regulators expedition was destroyed when Flagg got away. "He would give the news to the rustlers and they would be down on us like hungry wolves. We were too small a force to meet them in an open fight. Most everyone in our party seemed to realize that, if we did anything more, we would have to do it in a hurry," said Tucker.

They went back to get Champion. Time was important, and it

was decided that they should burn him out. They loaded an old wagon with pine and spruce boughs, fired it, and pushed it up against the house. The house caught fire almost immediately.

They knew that Champion could not stay inside much longer. Just as the roof was falling in, Major Whitcomb went to Tucker and told him to get on his horse and instructed Tucker to kill him when he came out of the house. As Tucker was getting on the horse, he heard a gunshot and knew that Jeff Mynett had just killed Champion, "for Jeff was waiting for him," said Tucker. "We examined him and found some papers on him, including a short story that he had written during the day. We left him lying for the coyotes and lit out for the road toward Buffalo.'"

The gunmen pulled out and got as far as the T. A. Ranch that evening. The ranch owner's name was named Harris. They were tired and hit the blankets early. They were awakened at daybreak by gunshots. Bullets were dropping around the ranch house and the stables. Tucker believed it was the rustlers who came to take them on. He didn't know how many there were but enough to surround the regulators. "From the number of shots that came our way, there seemed to be a large force of the rascals," said Tucker.[14]

They fought for three days there at the T. A. Ranch. Finally, Major Whitcomb directed the construction of some temporary breastworks made of logs, on the edge of trenches. Some of the defenders took positions behind the logs and they were relatively safe there. Others were in the ranch house. There wasn't much the defenders could do except keep out of the way of bullets coming their way. They couldn't see anything to shoot back at.

Tucker referred to Jack Tisdale as a fine old English gentleman. He and Tisdale were sitting on a log on top of the breastworks one evening. They had been cramped down all day but as evening came, things quieted down. They were sitting there chatting about their fine predicament. Suddenly, a bullet came along and cut the brim of Tisdale's Katy hat. They made a joke about the fact that one couldn't depend upon appearances in Wyoming. They decided it best to crawl back into the burrows.

"At least, they couldn't get bullets into us down there," said Tucker. Billy Irwin, foreman of the Ogallala Ranch, started to run from the entrenchments to the ranch house. A bullet tore off the heel of one of his boots.[15]

It wasn't the firing from the so-called rustlers that was so bad as no one had yet been hit hard. The problem was lack of food and ammunition. The regulators were traveling, light, of course, and couldn't take many provisions along. Very foolishly, they depended upon freighters and chuck wagons to bring provisions up. But how could the drivers get the food and ammunition in to them when we were completely surrounded by a strong force?

The answer was, of course, that they couldn't get through the lines. Three of their provision wagons were taken by the rustlers. But, they did have plenty of water during those three days of being under siege and had enough good beef. However, on the third day, the beef had been depleted and they were reduced to eating raw potato rations. Tucker was of the opinion that regardless of how good a fighter a man may be, he simply cannot do his best on a raw potato diet. He concluded his opinion with, "And it was a feeling of relief when I saw the soldiers coming."

The politicians had finally pulled strings so that the United States soldiers who were quartered at Fort McKinney, only fourteen miles away, could come and rescue the regulators. The sheriff of Johnson County tired to keep the soldiers from interfering. He wanted to be the one to take them. "He had been elected by the rustlers and was distinctly partisan. But the higher officials of the state were on the side of the ranchers, and fortunately, so for us," said Tucker.

The regulators surrendered to the troops with the condition that they not be turned over to the civil authorities of Johnson County. Major Wolcott, one of the leaders, negotiated the terms of the surrender. Tucker elaborated with, "I have often thought that we were rather cocky, considering the circumstances that we were in at the time. For, it would not have been long before we would have been starved out of our stronghold. And if we had started out, we would have been picked off one at a time. To escape, timely, would have been impossible, and most of us had decided to stick it out until we were killed."

Before Major Wolcott went out to meet the troop commander, he told the men that he would wave a handkerchief over his head if they were to march out. They watched in suspense for the signal and when it was given there was a general feeling of relief for all factions of the seige.[16]

The mere escape from the rustlers' bullets didn't mean they were through with the cattle war. The regulators who went to Wyoming thinking they were in the right, were prisoners, and would most likely be tried for a number of crimes.

But, the temporary relief was more than acceptable to them. The soldiers—there was only a handful of them—took them to Fort McKinney. They were kept there for two days. The sheriff was working like fury to get them turned over to him, but all of his telegrams were futile. Tucker claimed that the sheriff had captured two or three of their men but did not provide their names.

The government made sure that the sheriff turned them over to the soldiers. On the third day of custody, the troops escorted the group to Gillette, in Campbell County, which lies just east of Johnson County. Soldiers from Fort Russell met them there and took them back to Cheyenne by train. Once in Cheyenne, they were turned over to the civil authorities for a brief time. They tried *Habeas Corpus* and exhausted every county except Laramie, the county in which Cheyenne is located.[17]

The trial was ultimately held in Cheyenne. The two trappers, eyewitnesses to the regulators being at the K. C. Ranch, were thought to be out of the country, but the civil authorities had picked them up. The cattleman then got busy and sent them out of the state. "We didn't want them at the coming trial," said Tucker.[18]

While in custody, the group was trying to get bail. They got into an argument with the district attorney. According to Tucker, "a bunch of our young fellows went to a whorehouse one night and smashed up the furniture in the place." The damage cost the cowmen three hundred dollars for repairs. The district attorney became quite agitated over the affair. They had been quartered in the opera house since the soldiers turned them over to the civil authorities. So, the district attorney established limitations on the group. They were prohibited from going into saloons and brothels and restricted to certain sections of the town.

One day shortly after that, Tucker and two other men went down by the railroad tracks to a "blind pig" to have a few beers.[19] Basically, the establishment sold alcohol beverages illegally. They stayed there long enough to have more than a few and got about half-tight. They left the establishment and started up through town. In the door of the Oriental Hotel, the district attorney was standing, engaged in conversation with one of the so-called rustler leaders. When the district attorney saw the trio, he motioned for them to come over to him. They went. He invited them in for a drink, and they all had several rounds of drinks. The judge got word of it the next day and stormed and swore that he would disqualify the attorney for what he had done. The regulators' lawyer interceded on behalf of the prosecutor and the judge finally let him off with no more than a severe reprimand.

They finally agreed to offer bail and set the bond at $30,000 for each man. The ranchers had no trouble in raising the money for the bonds. Tucker wrote, "We Texans returned home until August, when the trial was called. The outcome was a foregone conclusion. The ranchers had all the money and the political influence. Under those conditions, we could not have been convicted. Of course, we demanded a jury trial. They couldn't find a jury in the whole state that would have been nonpartisan. Finally, in desperation, the judge impaneled a jury from those in the courtroom. We were all acquitted. I never knew whether the judge was or was not handpicked but I always suspected was the case." Tucker was in error concerning the trial. Those gunmen were not returned or tried for their alleged crimes.[20]

One incident that took place in Cheyenne revealed the real connection between the ranchers and the high political officials. They threw a big dinner for the gunmen. Each rancher took two of the men to the dinner. Charlie Campbell took Jeff Mynett and George Tucker. "I'd never drank champagne before," said Tucker. "I had been used to drinking whiskey and could do a pretty good job of it. I started out taking the champagne in gulps. I expected a breathing spell, but every time I emptied my glass, some flunky would fill it up again. Pretty soon things began to go round. I remember Charlie Campbell saying that everything goes tonight boys, except the top of the house."

That's when both Jeff Mynatt and George took their six-guns out and were going to start shooting at the top of the house but their guns were taken away before they could fire. The cattlemen treated the gunmen well for they had fought their war for them. Governor Amos Barber was at the dinner and during the meal, he came around to Jeff and pinned a bouquet on him. "Everybody there knew that the Governor was merely thanking Jeff for having killed Champion," said Tucker. "So, you can see, with a Governor openly approving out actions, there was little chance of our being convicted in the trial."[21]

Tucker reported that he would always remember that Cheyenne dinner, not for the champagne alone, but for the general hilarity of the occasion. He said that Major Egbert got so far along that he fell out of his chair. The cattlemen were mostly intelligent and well educated and some were native Englishmen and Scotchmen. They were all gentlemen in the grand manner. Among them, besides Major Whitcomb and Major Wolcott, were the two Tisdales, Bob and Jack, who were Englishmen; Colonel Parker, Mike Shoney, F. D. B. DeBiller and Teschemacher, partners of the Teschemacher and DeBillier Cattle Company, Joe Elliott, and Billy Irwin.

The Texans in the party were not all gunmen, as had been generally assumed. Some were mere saloon bullies, who did the group more harm than good in Wyoming. "Tom Smith was a fearless, courageous, and good officer," said Tucker;

> *But I never could explain why he chose so many fellows who knew nothing at all of gun fighting. The two Barlows, Jim Dudley, Alex Lowden, Cliff Shultz, and John Benson were of this character. They were more dangerous than helpful. Men in their own companies were in about as much danger as those at whom they thought they were shooting and besides they were brawly, always getting into arguments and personal altercations. If one of them could get to a man with his fist, he would give a good account of himself. But we were not mixing in that sort of trouble. We would have been much better off if those fellows had been left in Texas.*[22]

Tucker remembered an incident during their stay at Fort Russell, soon after they were brought there by the military. Fort Russell was a few miles west of Cheyenne. Buck Garrett and Cliff Shultz got into a problem with some soldiers at the military canteen. It was unclear exactly what started the difficulty. "Buck Garrett put the fireworks into play when he slammed a brickbat up side of a soldier's head, knocking him to the floor," wrote Tucker. Shultz ended the argument by getting one of the soldier's bayonets jabbed through his shoulder. A newspaper article supported Tucker's claim but he failed to mention the fact that the fight included a lot more of the Texans besides Garrett and Shultz.

On May 12, 1892, it was noted that the weather had been bad for several days and the Texans had been confined rather closely to their quarters. That afternoon, a couple of them began sparring, trying to knock off each other's hats with their open hands. One accidentally struck the other in the face and they began to fist fight. Others joined in and before it was over nearly every Texan was involved in the row.

When the sentry appeared, he was obliged to used his bayonet vigorously before he could put an end to the trouble. One Texas received two painful gashes in the neck from a Bowie knife and was taken to the post hospital for treatment. The Texas Kid, who, allegedly killed Nick Ray at the K. C. Ranch, emerged from the fight with two black eyes and others were more or less battered and bruised.

The officer of the day ordered all prisoners searched so that weapons could be removed. The feeling between the stockmen and the Texans was not becoming very pleasant as the days went by. The constant difficulties of the Texans having liberties allowed to them and the stockmen were not happy about it.[23]

The news article supported Tucker's version but with his failure to include the additional Texans. Also, while the Texas Kid is mentioned in the news article and in other news accounts, his alias was never linked to his true name. Historians have speculated by claiming the Texas Kid was Dave Booker, who was too old to be nicknamed a kid. Then they decided Buck Garrett was the kid because he was in his early twenties. The real Texas Kid was overlooked and he was Starling Tucker.

Some have claimed that the Texas Kid was hanged in New Mexico for horse theft, while another claims he was lynched after killing his wife. Seems they were all wrong. Actually, some of his relatives killed him in a gunfight. The details are mentioned later. The real Texas Kid was, indeed, Starling S. Tucker.

Buck Garrett and Shultz were just kids when they were in Wyoming and they thought they were tough guys. They were according to Tucker;

The pair would fight anyone, under any odds; especially was the case with Buck. He was a hell-diver with his fists. The first time

I ever saw him was in the jail at Paris. He'd been thrown in jail for beating up some fellow in a brothel. He loved to fight in those days. Later, when he got over most of the foolishness of his youth, he became a good, dependable officer. And he never lost his courage but, contrary to the usual estimate of him, he was never a gunman in any sense of the term. Bud Blue did most of his killing for him when Buck was sheriff of Carter County, Oklahoma, in later years.[24]

Tucker was not happy with the problem of Starl Tucker. Although he was Tucker's own brother, or half-brother, he considered him a wildcat. After he shot the first rustler out at the K. C. Ranch, he was pegged as the Texas Kid by newspaper reporters. He was put on a pedestal in Tucker's eyes and it made a fool of him, making him wilder and wilder. "He was damnably dangerous, for he never knew what fear was. He had no respect for anybody," said Tucker.

The officers at Fort Russell took a liking to Starl. They would take him out with them almost every night on their sprees. They evidently enjoyed his antics when he was drunk. He was also very cocky according to Tucker. One night, he went out with some of the soldiers and they all got drunk. Showing off, Starl picked up a little fragile elderly man and threw him down a stairway. The poor man died from his injuries. But Starl went back to the quarters that night all proud of himself.

He and George Tucker were sleeping near each other. He awakened George to tell him about the fun. "He bragged about how funny the fellow looked going down those stairs," said Tucker. He couldn't do anything much to calm him down and he wouldn't listen to George, but let the others make him even wilder. George said, "It was the undoing of him. He never quieted down after that. He was later killed by one of his cousins. The latter had to kill him. Starl was unreasonable. I have always believed that Starl got what was coming to him—any man ought to know better than to fight with his kin folks."

Starling S. Tucker was born in Franklin County, Arkansas, in the fall or winter of 1869. He was twenty-two or twenty-three-years of age when he was allegedly killed in a gunfight on Mud Creek, at the town of Atlee, in Chickasaw Nation. It was in the same year that he committed his evil deeds in Wyoming.

Starl had an uncle, Frank M. Tucker, nicknamed "Butcher Knife," and the town of Atlee was often referred to as Butcher's Knife. The nickname came from Frank using a butcher knife to cut corn on his farm. He wore the knife in his belt, not only for cutting corn, but for self protection.

The Daily Ardmoreite, the newspaper in Ardmore, Oklahoma, ran an article in 1903 stating that F. M. Tucker (aka Butcher Knife Tucker), who lives six miles southeast of Ardmore, was here this morning with a stalk of corn measuring fifteen-feet high with substantial evidence of a bountiful crop.

Newspaper accounts were found giving some details about Starling Tucker's demise. The *Dallas Morning News*, reported on December 1, 1892, that on November 30, 1892, news was received from Gainesville, Texas, that a triangular shooting took place the previous day in the Chickasaw Nation, just across the Red River from Spanish Fort. The participants were two brothers named Tucker and their nephew, a young man whose name could not be learned. One of the Tuckers was seriously shot in the shoulder and the other two were badly wounded. The fight was the result of a family feud.

Then, the next day, December 2, 1892, the *Galveston Daily News* received word of the shooting scrape at Butcher's Knife near Ardmore, on November 30. News had been received of a shooting scrape at a dance on Mud Creek at Butcher's Knife. Star Tucker, one of the participants, is seriously if not mortally wounded. The names of the others injured and who were in the affray is unknown. Officers left Paris, Texas, with warrants for the scene of the trouble.

On December 8, the *Denton County News* reported the event was a cotton picker's dance and Starl Tucker did not pick enough cotton to secure at ticket. They were opposed to Tucker dancing.

Another article, from December 6, the *Fort Worth Gazette*, reported that deputy marshal Tucker was in Gainesville, on the 5th with two men in custody; L. B. Tucker and B. P. Tucker, en route to Ardmore, where they will be given an examining trial on a charge of murder. These men were two of the participants in the shooting affray which occurred near Spanish Fort. The other participants were S. S. [Starling] and Pug Tucker, cousins of the prisoners, and

Will Shy. Instead of being a family feud, as was first reported, the shooting was the outcome of a quarrel at a dance given [not at Butcher Knife] at the house of Bone Reynolds, twenty miles north of Spanish Fort. A man named Joe Means was killed in the gunfight. S. S. Tucker was the worst sufferer, having his arm badly wounded above the elbow, necessitating amputation at the shoulder joint. Pug Tucker and Will Shy were shot in the hip, but not dangerously wounded.

According to Tucker, Starling was killed, so it is likely he died from the shock of amputation. The two Tucker men were released from custody without being charged. Joe Means was probably John Means. He was the same man in the party accused of hanging those horse thieves in the Woodworth [*sic*] Lynching. Means was also known as a cattle rustler and horse thief.

Newspaper reporters were notorious in those days of listing names incorrectly and it seems the farther away from the scene the worse they reported on names and details of events. Tucker failed to say specifically how he was related to Pug and L. B. Tucker. They may have been the son's of George's cousin Frank "Butcher Knife" Tucker.

Tucker finalized his version of the Wyoming affair by stating;

> *I have tried to tell the story of the Johnson County cattle war as I saw it. I could have made it much longer, but that would have served little purpose. A Mr. David has already written it up in his book entitled Malcolm Campbell, Sheriff.*[25] *That is a true account, generally speaking. The cattlemen were not quite so innocent, nor were the rustlers as bad as he pictured them. The trouble as I saw it was a fight between the big ranchers and the small farmers. There undoubtedly were some rustlers among the latter group. But they could not have all been rustlers, for there would not have been enough cattle to go around.*[26]

They were in Wyoming as paid assassins of the big ranchers. They were brought there to kill men. "Let no one mislead you by saying that we had the law on our side," wrote Tucker. "We had the politics and the money, but not the law. We were not convicted of our crimes because we had the politics and the money with us."

Tucker had read Frank Canton's account of the war.[27] He didn't purchase the book but someone sent him a copy. "I gave it away, for I wouldn't be caught with it," said Tucker. "It was all about Canton being the big 'me' and the little 'you' with him. He was always seeking publicity."

Tucker recalled one little incident of Frank Canton's when they were in Cheyenne. Canton got drunk and was out on the street flourishing his gun. As he waved it around he accidentally dropped it and it went off. The bullet took him in the leg, going through the fleshy part of his leg and missing the bones. They carried him into the court house on a stretcher.

"The veteran deputies cracked many a joke about the tough fellow who shot himself accidentally," said Tucker. "If Frank had been two hundred miles west when his accident occurred, he probably never would have lived to write a book, for blood poisoning sets in quickly up there in the high altitudes. Two of our boys died up there from wounds that would not have been considered serious down in Texas."

It is unknown who those two men were as Tucker did not provide their names. Today, medical professionals agree with George. High altitude reduces the oxygen supply and flesh wounds would suffer with slow healing at best.

There were other episodes about the Wyoming affair that Tucker knew of but did not consider them important and some "were trivial," he said. When they left Casper, Wyoming, they had a Doctor Penrose with them and he was a brother of Boise Penrose, a senator from Pennsylvania. They took Doctor Penrose along to take care of wounds but he left the regulators after one or two days.

Tucker concluded his remembrance of the Wyoming affair as being taken up there under false pretenses. He doubted that many would have gone had they known the real purpose of the expedition. However, once they were up there, it would have been difficult to try and turn back. They went stuck with a bad bargain, knowing it to be just that. But the cattlemen were not stingy with their money. They gave the regulators the best that money could buy, especially weapons. They paid for all of the transportation, equipment, living expenses, bails and court expenses. One in particular, Billy Irwin, bought the men anything they wanted. "We could not have asked for nicer treatment in this respect than we got from them," wrote Tucker.[28]

Deputy Marshal C. L. Hart talked with a reporter in Ardmore on April 21, 1892, as he was on his way home from Paris, Texas. Hart stated that the people of Paris were quite uneasy about the men who went from Paris to Wyoming to fight the rustlers. He gave the following names of deputy marshals who went: Jeff Mynatt, George Tucker, Booker [Dave], and Tom Smith. The report titled the article *Parisians In Trouble* and concluded that it appeared those men were hired by the cattlemen to go, and were not sent by the

Cylinder from Tucker's boot gun. The cylinder shows that one bullet remained in the pistol and remained in the chamber though the years. Perhaps Tucker believed in the old adage "save the last round for yourself." *Photo courtesy of Justin Barnes.*

government authorities. Marshal Dickinson has discharged those deputies who went on the expedition. Tucker's claim of those dep-

This Ivory gripped pistol belonged to George R. Tucker and was handed down to a Mr. Barnes, along with a book about the Wyoming range war. Both had belonged to Tucker. *Photo courtesy of Justin Barnes.*

uties being fired prior to boarding that train is inconclusive.[29]

Tucker mentioned a number of books about the Wyoming range war and claimed he did read Frank Canton's book. However, when he died he left a six-gun, now in the hands of a collector. He also had a .32 caliber pistol, called a boot or hideout gun along with a copy of the book, *War On Powder River*. Those two items were handed down to a descendant named Justin Barnes.

The pistol is chambered for six rounds making it a .32 S&W caliber, not a .32 S&W Long, and is a black powder only model. There were five variations of the weapon. The barrel lengths of 2½ (rare), 3¼ (standard), 4, 5 & 6 inches were manufactured. Tucker's weapon falls into the fifth variation which had five patent dates; Oct-4-87, May 14 & Aug-6-89, April-2-95, April-7-96 and sold from 1897-1904. Tucker's pistol falls into this category. It is probable that he carried the pistol while a deputy marshal in the late 1890s.

Mr. Barnes and brother Travis are sons of William Lee Nash of Leavenworth, Kansas. For personal reasons, they changed their surname from Nash to Barnes. William Lee's father was James Lee Spruill Nash. James Lee was son of Gladys Tucker Spurill, and she was a daughter of George Redman Tucker.[30]

Chapter Twenty-Three

Chasing Outlaws & Tom Smith's Murder

When some of the hired gunman returned to Paris they went back to work as deputy U. S. marshals. Tucker claimed he had not been fired nor did he resign, as he had two criminals in his custody when he turned them over to another officer after his friend Tom Smith encouraged him to board the train for Wyoming.

Tucker was back to his old job as deputy marshal as though he had never left for the Wyoming affair. Dave Booker, Tom Smith, Jeff Mynatt, and Bill Little were rehired as deputy marshals. Buck Garrett, who had been a posseman, became a deputy marshal. All of the deputies out of the Paris office served their warrants and made arrests in their district which included Indian Territory. There was a change, however. Instead of making the arrests and bringing them back to Paris, they began the custom of taking the prisoners to Ardmore, in the territory. There the accused were given preliminary hearings and if charged, they were then taken to Paris for trial.

By 1892, the Territory had become much more orderly than it had been. People were coming in large numbers. The outlaw element still existed, but it had become far less important than it had been. Local communities were preventing a great deal of the crimes. The deputies' work, after that time, was mostly routine. But Tucker did report a number of important cases over the next nine years, after which, in 1901, he turned in his deputy marshal badge. He wrote about a few of those cases.

The Don Wilson case occurred in late 1892, after Deputy Marshal George Tucker, Jeff Mynett, Tom Smith, and Jim Chancellor had returned to Paris from Wyoming. All four deputies were carrying warrants for various arrests. Tucker was to go after Don Wilson, who was wanted on a charge of hog-stealing. The other deputies decided to go along with Tucker.

They located and arrested Wilson without difficulty near Marlow, in Indian Territory. They decided to take him to Anadarko for his preliminary hearing and started for that town, traveling in two buggies. One night, when camped at a place named Turkey Springs, they decided to try and kill a deer. According to Tucker, it was merely a desire to get a good meal, for the fare they carried with them on trips got pretty old if they were out for very long periods of time.

Accordingly, early the next morning, Jim Chancellor and Tucker hitched up to their buggy and started out to find a deer. While they were driving out through the brush, the other deputies with the prisoner in tow, got out ahead of them. Tucker and Chancellor thought Smith and Mynett were still back in camp with the prisoner.[1]

Tom Smith and Jeff Mynett, with the prisoner between them on the buggy seat, were driving out through the brush. The top of the buggy was down and there were brownish colored blankets showing up over the back of the buggy seat. Tucker caught a glimpse of those blankets through the brush and thought it was a deer. Jim stopped their rig and Tucker opened fire with his Winchester. He was shooting a high-powered rifle that he claimed he had brought back from Wyoming. He must have obtained the weapon following the confiscation of all weapons from the invaders. A moment after he shot, he realized that he had made a terrible mistake. He saw it was not a deer, but was the other buggy with Smith, Mynett, and Wilson, the prisoner.

They then hurried over to them. The bullet had hit one of the buggy bows in the top and had gone on through hitting the prisoner, knocking him over the dashboard. Mynett and Smith both thought that he was dead. They stripped off his shirt before Tucker and Chandler got to them. Tucker mistook his red underwear for blood.

"I thought that I had surely killed him," said Tucker. "However, when we examined him more closely, we found that the bullet had only barked him. Anyone can imagine the difficulty I had in convincing Smith and Mynett that I had not originally intended killing the prisoner, said Tucker. "I would not have shot him on purpose, and I did my best to make them believe it. I was never sure that I convinced either of them."[2]

They took Wilson on to Anadarko for the hearing and from there to Paris. Tucker went immediately to Marshal Dickerson and told him the whole story. "His first reaction was unfavorable," said Tucker.

"If you were brought before a jury, they would never believe that story," said Dickerson. "And he was probably right," said Tucker. "Even though the story was as true as anything I ever said."

Marshal Dickerson immediately called in the three deputies who had been with Tucker on the Wilson arrest and they gave him the details exactly in the same frank and straightforward manner that Tucker had reported. Apparently, they convinced Dickerson that the whole thing was an accident as no further action was taken and Wilson recovered from his slight wound without difficulty. Tucker said, "It was only a minor one, though it might easily have been otherwise. In the latter event, I would certainly have been tried for murder. But my good luck persisted." The time frame for the incident was late 1892 according to Tucker, however, the event would have occurred before November 1892.[3]

* * * * *

November of 1892 would be a time to remember. First off, the *Muskogee Phoenix* reported three historic events on the same day, On November 10, President Benjamin Harrison commuted the sentence of Merideth Crow, a black man, who killed John Courtney, at Courtney Flats, Choctaw Nation, in 1888. Crow was convicted in the federal court at Fort Smith and sentenced to hang. His sentence was afterwards commuted to life imprisonment.

Secondly, a full-blood Indian lived up to the belief that he was the original blood thirsty savage of the "Western Wilds." His name was Ned Christie. The remains of the noted desperado, together with his adopted son, Charley Hare, were brought in Sunday morning from Fayetteville. The corpse was placed on the front entrance of the U. S. jail and the public were allowed to see the disfigured body so recently occupied by a more contorted soul. Several photographs of the corpse were taken for souvenirs. The body was shipped to Fort Gibson, on the 4 o'clock train, where the father of Ned Christie took charge of it.

Lastly, the *Muskogee Phoenix* reported the death of Deputy U.S. Marshal Tom Smith, a deputy of the Paris court, killed on the Santa Fe train near Thackerville, by an unknown black man who was immediately after killed by Deputy Marshal Tucker.

The deputies were passing through the compartment of the car reserved for black people, when the black man began abusing them, saying that if black people could not ride with white folks, the whites should not ride with the blacks. Smith replied very angrily to the abuse, when the black man drew a revolver and fired, killing Smith instantly. Tucker then shot the black man through the neck, from which he died in a short time.

Smith's body was put off at Ardmore, where it was prepared for burial. It should be noted that there were many newspapers reporting Deputy Smith's demise and the *Muskogee Phoenix* was the only paper claiming Deputy Tucker was the deputy who killed the unnamed black man.[4]

A number of newspapers reported the killing of Smith with varying accounts. Tucker claimed that he and Smith were good friends in his memoirs and indicated Smith "was killed by a Negro on the train." If they were good friends and if Tucker had been on that train that fatal day, it seems he would have mentioned it. He did not. He was believed to be in Paris on the day Smith was killed.

Tom Smith was residing in Taylor, Texas, with his wife Sallie and children at the time of the incident. Sallie received a brief telegram on November 4, 1892, from Deputy Marshal J. M. Chancellor which read: "Tom Smith was killed tonight by a Negro. What shall we do with the body?" U. S. Marshal James J. Dickerson sent a second wire to Sallie saying: "I will bring the body of Tom."[5]

Several deputies were mentioned as being with Smith on the train. Booker was mentioned most consistently. The *Hesperian* of Gainesville, Texas, on November 5, reported deputies Booker and Ingram as being with Smith. The *Lexington Leader* of Oklahoma Territory, on November 12 reported deputies Booker and Armstrong as being with Smith. The *Muskogee Phoenix* of November 16, was the only newspaper to mention Tucker.

Like all other incidents, the newspaper reports telling of the shooting varied widely in the details. Some had it happening in the car for African Americans, some at the depot in Thackerville. There was also a dispute as to why the officers were in the African American car as some said they were checking on a man they thought was peddling whiskey. One report claimed that the black man matched the description of Commodore Miller, a convicted criminal who had escaped from a Louisiana prison after killing a guard and was wanted in Dallas for killing a police officer during December 1892. Commodore Miller was not the black man on the train as he was lynched in Bardwell, Kentucky, in July 1893, after being accused of rape. The only positive identification of the black man who killed Tom Smith was that he was an older man from Guthrie.[6]

After Tucker wrote about the hunting accident he never mentioned Tom Smith again. Had he been on that train with Smith, he would surely have written about it. In his memoirs, he went from the hunting accident to writing about the opening of the Cherokee Strip for settlement.

* * * * *

When the government decided to open the strip, it faced a ticklish problem of granting to everyone equality in the run. Several deputy marshals were sent by new U. S. Marshal Shelby Williams, who succeeded Marshal Dickerson during President Grover Cleveland's second administration.[7] The deputies were ordered to aid U. S. Marshal E. D. Nix[8] and to report to him at Hennessey, in Kingfisher County, Indian Territory.

The Chicago, Rock Island and Pacific Railroad reached Hennessey on October 1889, and the deputy marshals were assigned the task of keeping people off the boxcars before the starting signal was given. The train was going to make the run, furnishing transportation to those who had no other means of transportation.

At the appointed time, the official starter was to fire his gun. Long before the "zero hour" people began to sneak up into the cars. The deputies would drive them out. They kept sneaking in and being driven back. Finally, they teamed up and came in a rush. Tucker pulled his gun and said, "I'll shoot every damned one of you."

The people didn't believe him and called his bluff, knowing a lawman wouldn't shot down an unarmed man. Therefore, they poured in to the cars like a flood of water. Tucker and the other deputies did their best to enforce Marshal Nix's orders, but the odds were against them, and there was nothing to be gained by killing anyone.

Tucker was of the opinion that those people were land crazy. He had never seen a crowd of people act more like a herd of stampeding Texas longhorns. Their greed seemed to result in all of that crowd having lost all sense of decency and social friendship.[9]

The train filled rapidly and every place of vantage was taken before the run began. At the signal, things began to happen. The train slowly started but never gained much speed as it ran slowly down the tracks. From time to time, men would drop over the sides and rush off on foot across the prairie to stake their claims.

Those not on the train, made the run with all sorts of contraptions. Some were on horseback, some in buggies, some in wagons, and some in carts. Tucker remembered distinctly one case that will show how really excited people were in these runs. Setting on the front edge of his buggy seat, a man was whipping a skinny, old horse. The horse was doing pretty well under the circumstances. Evidently the man felt that it was too slow, for he jumped to the ground and ran ahead of his rig and started trying to put some distance between himself and his rig. But, just about the time he was running neck and neck with the head of his horse, he stumbled and fell. He wasn't far enough to the right or left and when he fell the buggy ran over him. That ended one man's quest of free land.

Tucker's assessment of the run was summed up with, "Unless one witnessed these runs, he may never imagine how dumb, how stupid, those people really can become under conditions that are favorable to personal advantage. I've seen desperate criminals who never tried nearly so hard to escape arrest as these people did to get title to a piece of land that they couldn't make a living on, even during rainy seasons."[10]

* * * * *

A man named McKinney was murdered up in Indian Territory and Tucker was sent to Ardmore to arrest three men who were accused of killing him. Two of those men, Morris and Nunn, owned a store in Ardmore. McKinney had been in the store and had gone to the toilet in the rear of the building. As he came out, somebody waylaid and killed him. Ollie Nunn was supposed to have shot him. Tucker did not remember what the motive was for the killing.

In addition to Morris and Nunn, Bob Bridgman was also alleged to have been a party to the crime. Tucker had a warrant for his arrest as well as the other two. Tucker went up to Ardmore and had no trouble finding and arresting the three. As he was going south with his prisoners they stopped at Sherman and Tucker had the trio placed in jail.

They decided to sue out [file] a writ of *habeas corpus* against the arrest but Judge Bryant refused to issue the writ. However, he did grant them to try and make bail. According to Tucker, murder was not a bailable crime, and Tucker failed to understand why the Judge granted it. But, Tucker removed them from Sherman and took them on to Paris before they could make their bonds.

It was late in the administration of Shelby Williams as United States marshal. Tucker was very displeased with Marshal Williams. According to him, Williams helped them make their bonds. "He knew every criminal in the country and was almost one himself, but he would do everything he could to capture them. His knowledge of them was really an asset to him and to us," said Tucker.

They made bond and Tucker received his fees for the arrest and bringing the trio into custody. Tucker claimed he received two dollars and fifty cents for each arrest and ten cents per mile for himself and ten cents for each guard and prisoner. According to the National Park Service in Fort Smith, Arkansas, an arrest earned two dollars. Mileage rates were six cents per mile for traveling to the arrest and ten cents per mile each for the deputy and the prisoner while returning. Serving a subpoena garnered fifty cents and six cents per mile to the place of service but nothing for the return trip. The U.S. marshal collected twenty-five percent of these fees before paying his deputies. Those guards assisting Tucker in taking those prisoners to Paris were S. E. McElmore and Joe Hellums.

Ironically, the final trial at Paris, set the three men free. They were acquitted. The prosecutor did not have much evidence against them, only circumstantial.[11]

* * * * *

Dave Little and a man named Johnson, near Oklanda, in the Chickasaw Nation, had been feuding for a long time and on September 30, 1891, Dave Little took his Winchester rifle and shot Johnson in the chest. The bullet entered below his left nipple and passed through his body. He turned and ran about sixty steps, then fell to the ground dead. Both men had large families.[12]

Deputy Tucker was handed a warrant by the marshal for

the arrest of Dave Little, for the killing of Johnson. Little lived at Mannsville, about fifteen miles due east of Ardmore.[13] The charge listed on the warrant was assault to murder.

Tucker started out after him. Before Tucker arrived on the scene, Dave Little had killed yet another man. This one went by the name of Smith. Dave Little was known as a very mean and tough hombre. He met Smith in the road and shot him down in cold blood. When Tucker learned of the second murder he wondered if Little might have been crazy. "At least, he was flighty," said Tucker. " Nothing made him so angry as criticism. He couldn't stand it at all."

When Deputy Tucker arrived at his house, Little was gone. So, Tucker decided to wait there at his house for him. He knew him quite well. Dave Little finally came home during the night and Tucker was there and awake. When he heard Little enter his house, he pulled his six-gun and told Little he was under arrest. Little put his hands up and was taken into custody without a problem.

When daylight came, Tucker mounted up with his prisoner and started riding toward Ardmore. They met a man whom Tucker knew but did not mention by name. He began to clown around in the presence of Tucker and his prisoner. The man was making faces and cutting up in general. While he was going through his antics, he backed into a clothes line, which knocked him off his feet. A normal person would have laughed but not Dave Little. It made him angry. He thought the man was making fun of him for some unknown reason. He broke loose from Tucker and started after the man but Tucker caught him in time to prevent damage.

"If Dave Little had a gun, he would have killed a third man right there," said Tucker. "I've heard lots of tough men try out their swearing ability but I never saw anyone who could equal Little. How he burnt up that fellow. He was almost a raving maniac. There is small wonder that he would kill people when in such a state of mind."[14]

Deputy Tucker took him on to Ardmore. It took some time before he got him calmed down. After his preliminary hearing, Tucker took him on to Paris, where he was incarcerated without bail. At his trial he was convicted and sent to the penitentiary, but Tucker did not remember how long a rap he took. Anyway, said Tucker, "I always felt as though he ought to have been put in the penitentiary or some other institution permanently. He was too dangerous to live outside."[15]

Another report discredits Deputy Tucker's arrest and transport of Dave Little to Ardmore. The report stated that Dave Little did kill Jim Johnson at Sam Little's ranch near Oakland, a correct spelling of the town of Oklanda, twenty miles east of Ardmore. The shooting was the result of an old feud, and both parties had it in for each other for some time past, and always went armed with the expectation of meeting each other.

Last Christmas they met by chance and exchanged several shots without effect. This time their gun-play resulted more seriously, and Johnson was dead with a .44 caliber Winchester bullet in his left breast. After the killing, Little turned himself in and was confined in the Ardmore jail for safe keeping until he could be taken to Paris.

Johnson had a wife and two children and Little was also married with family.[16] Up at Marlow, in Indian Territory, lived a man by the name of John Johnson. He was either a bachelor or a widower; Tucker wasn't sure. Anyway, he hired a lady named Mrs. White to do his cooking and housework. She worked for him quite a while, and then decided that she didn't want anything more to do with her husband. They had some trouble and she left Mr. White and went to live with Johnson.[17]

One morning, Mrs. White's husband came over to the Johnson house, presumably to quarrel or to try and reason with his wife, but he never fulfilled his mission. John Johnson happened to be watching the approaches to the house and spotted White coming up the lane. He grabbed his rifle and jacked a round into the chamber, took aim, and fired. He saw White fall to the ground and saw no movement. He killed the husband before he could get to the house to confront his wife.

Tucker was ordered there immediately. He didn't have far to go for upon reaching the Johnson place, he observed White's body still lying in the lane. Tucker stopped and dismounted. He picked up the body and laid him across the back of his horse and went on up to the house. He went to the shed and left White's body there next to the house. He then approached Johnson carefully and told him to drop his weapons and raise his hands. Johnson gave him no trouble. Tucker believed Johnson was a nice and likeable man but still a killer.

He took Johnson to Ardmore for the preliminary hearing and then on to Paris, where he was tried sometime later. According to Tucker, "He came clear. He belonged to a family that didn't draw convictions in the courts."[18]

* * * * *

Another case related by Tucker involved Cal Suggs, a big rancher in Indian Territory. Tucker believed the year was 1894, but according to news reports the event occurred in late 1889. Apparently, time and memory had faded for Tucker to be five years off of the correct year.

Tucker was sent to arrest Cal Suggs for the murder of George Canterbury. Cal Suggs was the biggest rancher in that entire section of the country. It seems that Deputy Tucker believed justice to be blind when it came to citizens such as the Suggs who had enough money and power to influence the court system in their favor. The news article portrayed the killings as a feud. The following accounts are from Tucker as well as news reports.

The Suggs' ranch house was situated about thirty miles from the railroad and telegraph lines and he had cattle all over that country. Canterbury was one of Suggs' hired men. After a while, he had married Cal Suggs' niece. Suggs didn't think that Canterbury treated her right. There may have been something to it, or Cal probably would not have killed him. But Cal was professed to be a headstrong old fellow, who was a cattle king and figured his word was law and whatever he wanted was the order of the day.

Tucker arrived on the day after the killing. Someone had disposed of the body but Tucker saw where he had been killed. They hadn't taken the trouble to mop up the blood just yet. "After all, a killing was just a killing out in the cattle country," said Tucker.

Tucker spoke of justice being blind, however, he himself was a contributor to that blind justice by showing undue favoritism toward Cal Suggs. When he received the warrant back at the federal building in Paris, the court clerk told him that if Cal Suggs was not ready to come down, that he should wait until he was ready.

That didn't sit right with Tucker at the time and in later years, after thinking it over, it still set a sour note with him. But, what he did was dead wrong. If Suggs had been an average run of the mill person or some poor devil against whom a warrant had been issued, they would not have taken the trouble to await his convenience. But that is exactly what Tucker did for Cal Suggs and Tucker openly admitted to the mistake.

When he rode up to the ranch house, Cal Suggs was there waiting, evidently expecting a deputy marshal to show up. They talked a while. He said to Tucker, "I won't be ready to go with you for a few days." Tucker told him that was all right.[19]

He made arrangements for Tucker to enjoy himself in the meantime. He provided a gun and his dogs to Tucker and Tucker hunted quail for three or four days and enjoyed himself. It wasn't hard to pass the time while waiting on a fugitive to decide when to give himself up.

Finally, Suggs told Deputy Tucker that he would be ready to go with him the next morning. If Suggs had not decided to go, Tucker would probably have been out there until his welcome turned sour. Only one man would have had his hands full, and then some, trying to take Cal Suggs off his ranch against his will. He had a regular army of cowboys and work hands about the place. So, Cal decided to submit to the warrant and he and Deputy Tucker rode out for Paris.

"I can't say that I brought him in, for he came as near bringing me in as that," said Tucker. It was not one of Tucker's proudest arrests.

In the meantime, Judge Boarman got a little scared because Deputy Tucker had not returned. He asked Williams why he hadn't reported. The marshal explained that it was a long way over there and that it would take some time to make the trip. When Tucker reached Paris with Cal Suggs, Williams took Suggs into the court for Tucker, as he was afraid that the judge would jump Tucker for staying out so long.

However, Judge Boarman never mentioned the case to Tucker, "So I suppose he either forgot it or came to understand the situation, or both," said Tucker.

Marshal Williams put Suggs in his private office. None of the Suggs went to jail. They were different from other people. On the first night after their arrival in Paris, Tucker saw Marshal Williams and Cal Suggs playing billiards in the biggest hotel in Paris. It appeared as though Cal was on a visit to Paris.

University of Oklahoma Professor Alley, who edited George

Tucker's manuscript, confirmed that Tucker's story on the Suggs family being immune to convictions by judges in that section of the country to be accurate. He further stated that judges allowed this immunity from imprisonment based upon the influence of the Suggs as well as strong and influential personalities.

However, a news report indicated Judge Boarman gave instructions for Suggs to be locked up in jail. Bond was set at $20,000 and while the judge was out of town, Deputy Marshal Latherman allowed Suggs to be released on bond illegally, as the judge had not approved the bond. Upon return, the judge instructed the marshal to send a deputy back to Suggs' ranch to arrest him and said, "Do not return without him."[20]

Of course, Cal Suggs was returned and made bond legally but he beat the case when it came up. He reportedly had friends all over the country and was one of the biggest cattlemen in the southwest. The cattlemen were important people in that country during those days. According to Tucker, everyone who knew Suggs respected the stern old fellow. By sheer grit, he had put his authority over a large scope of country. Everything else around him was outlaw territory.

"In fact, Cal had the only place in that whole section where a deputy marshal could really stay in anything like personal safety," said Tucker.

With those facts, it is easy to see why he would not be convicted for one of his killings. In forging his ranch kingdom, he had killed, or had been the cause of numerous killings. The law enforcement officials really looked upon him as an ally in the suppression of the outlaw element.[21]

But, the situation was not yet over. Colonel E. C. "Cal" Suggs, was tried in federal court at Paris, Texas, for the killing of George W. Canterbury. He was acquitted. The principle witness for the government was R. P. Short.

While his testimony wasn't strong enough to convict Suggs, it did create bitter feeling against him by Cal Suggs. The bitter feelings were shared by the brothers of both men and on December 20, 1889, Cal's brother, I. D. "Ike" Suggs, retaliated against Mr. Short, solely because of his testifying against his brother. R. P. "Bob" Short and his brother, Jeff Short, were fired upon from ambush and they immediately returned fire. A desperate gun battle took place. When it was over and the smoke cleared, Jeff Short had taken a bullet and was killed and his brother Bob was seriously wounded. The Short brothers had fired at Ike Suggs three times, wounding him slightly in his side and shoulder.[22]

According to Deputy Tucker, he and Deputy Mynett were then called upon to arrest I. D. "Ike" Suggs. Ike had killed Jeff Short and Bob Swindell, but not Bob Short, as stated in the news report. Both men were killed with one shot from a shotgun according to Tucker.

Jeff Short was an Indian who lived with his brother, Bob Short. The latter had a little farm close to the Suggs' ranch. I. D. and Short had some trouble over a pasture but Tucker was not aware of the details. Swindell was staying with the Short brothers. I. D. decided to ride over to the Short place but he and Jeff Short got into an argument near the Short house.

Of Course, both men were armed. I. D. Suggs was packing a shotgun and Jeff Short carried a Winchester. I. D. got behind a tree that was barely large enough to protect him. Short cut loose with his rifle and kept shooting into the tree and his bullets tore into the tree, carving it up badly.

"I saw it afterward," said Tucker. "I suppose he intended to shoot it down and then kill I. D. If that was his intention, he didn't get it done, for I. D. saw his chance and took a shot at Short. Just as he shot, Swindell ran across the line of fire. The shot killed Jeff Short dead, and wounded

Jeff Mynett served in various capacities as a lawman and was close friends with George Tucker. Later in life, Jeff took his own life. *Photo From group photo. Courtesy Jim Gatchell Historical Museum.*

Swindell, but he wasn't hit that hard."

When Tucker and Mynett got there, Swindell was still alive. "He was crying out terribly, just the same as if somebody were cutting him with a knife," said Tucker. He had been shot in the leg.

Tucker told Jeff Mynett, "I don't think there is a damn thing wrong with him except that he's scared to death."

Jeff believed Swindell would die in spite of everything they could do for him. He said, "He'll have lockjaw as sure as sin." And Jeff was right about his dying, for before they got back to Paris a telegraph reported that he had died, lockjaw or otherwise.

After killing Jeff Short and wounding Bob Swindell, I. D. left the country. Tucker and Mynett tracked him for a mile or two by the blood that came from a wound in his shoulder, one of Short's compliments from his Winchester. They were only going through the motion because they weren't really trying to find him. The two deputies could not have taken him off his ranch against his will anyway. And they were sure that he would turn up some time and surrender. Tucker saw him as "a good fellow."

Sure enough, a month later he telegraphed from Belcher that he was back home now and ready for the law to come up and get him. Tucker was sent up alone to serve the warrant and bring him in. By then, I. D. had fully recovered from his wound. Tucker escorted him back to Paris and reported having a nice, pleasant trip. Tucker didn't see I. D. Suggs as being worried in the least over the killings, nor was Tucker.

I. D., like his brother Cal, was not put in jail. The Suggs family received better treatment than the average person. Mr. Daugherty came over from Gainesville and made his bond. At the trial later, naturally, as expected, he was acquitted.

"They had better have saved the money that was spent on the trial, for, so long as Williams was marshal, there was no chance of convicting one of those big cattlemen," said Tucker. "They had juries picked that would not convict such a man. And I suppose the juries were picked with that end in view. At least, we never convicted the cattlemen."[23]

Tucker recalled Cal Suggs telling him and other marshals how the outlaws would try to establish their camps on his ranch, or near it. "He said that he would go out and run the damned buggers off, and if they wouldn't go, he would kill them."

Cal Suggs was the type of man who wouldn't send his cow-boys out to do his work for him, at least not that kind of work. He did it himself. He always drank quite a lot but didn't become mean while intoxicated according to Tucker. " He never struck me as a fellow who just hungered to kill people," said Tucker. "If he killed a fellow, he had to have a pretty good reason for it."

In those early days on the frontier, range law was about all that was administered. Tucker saw him as a most respectable man—that is, he was respectable according to the standards of that range law. Of course, Tucker did not mean to imply that Cal would have been overly friendly to settlers, however honest they might have been. "The ranchers and the settlers had viewpoints that just didn't beget friendliness between them," said Tucker.

Deputies Tucker and Jeff Mynett were once sent to guard a lot of money which Cal Suggs was taking to Anadarko. He was going to pay the Indians for the leases on their lands which he had been using for cattle grazing. There were several other ranchers in the party. Daugherty, the Gainesville banker, was also among the party. They all camped together.

Tucker said, "Of course, there was plenty of whiskey in the chuck wagons and saddle bags. Old Cal got awfully drunk on the way up. And did he have a good time, joshing everybody in the party." [24]

A small troop of fourteen soldiers, under the command of Lieutenant Rivers came out as far as Cold Springs to meet them and provided an escort to Anadarko. They were being pretty care-ful with the lease money, for there was no end of danger from ban-dits. As they got up in the neighborhood of Anadarko, the Indians came out to meet them. Nearer the city, they lined the road.

"They would yell at Cal," said Tucker. "They liked him."

"Hello! Yahoo Chief!" they would yell at old Cal.

"Go to hell, you old son-of-a-bitch!" Cal would return.

"It was that way for quite a while. Cal was having a perfect-ly good time and the Indians didn't seem to care about what Cal said," wrote Tucker.

Banker Daugherty said to Cal, "Shut up, Cal, you may want to lease their lands."

"Oh, hell, Daugherty," Cal replied. "Those ignorant sons-of-bitches don't know anything. They don't even know the meaning of the term."

Cal Suggs may or may not have been right in his opinions concerning the Indians. At least, they never openly objected to his swearing to them. It is doubtful if they understood it, and more doubtful that they would have resented it even if they had understood. They were too canny for that. Many people regarded the Indians as stupid, "but those same people usually came off second-best when they had dealings with their stupid Indians," said Tucker.[25]

Upon reaching the Indian agency, the whiskey held out and the party got livelier. All the paymasters got drunk. Guthrie, a government official, got so drunk that he decided to get generous with Uncle Sam's supplies. So, he began to hand out government army blankets to everybody.

"Maybe he was so drunk that he couldn't tell Jeff and me from Red Indians. Anyway, he gave us one each with his and the government's compliments," said Tucker. "Either Guthrie or someone higher up in the government, or both, changed their minds about being so generous, some days after the pay-off had passed."

As a result, both deputies received messages to the effect that it would simplify matters if they would send back two army blankets that they were supposed to have fetched with them from Anadarko. Guthrie must have gotten into considerable trouble over the affair. Tucker and Mynett sent the gifted blankets back as requested. They appreciated the spirit, or possibly the spirits, that moved Guthrie to be so generous, but what stuck in Tucker's mind over the years concerning that trip was the fact that after returning from the Indian reservation, they started itching and discovered they were literally covered up with lice.

"When those little lice decided to changed locations, none of them seemed quiet as large as ants," reported Tucker.[26]

* * * * *

Tucker recalled that he believed the year was 1894 when Tom Westmilam [*sic*] killed Ed Green over in Indian country at the town of Courtney Flat. They had a difference of opinions over a blacksmith shop. But it wasn't a gunfight. Westmilam had poisoned Green by fixing up some whiskey for him.

Tucker took a posseman by the name of Williams with him to make the arrest. They slipped up to the house without being seen.

When they sneaked inside the house to make the arrest, they saw that Westmilam was asleep. Tucker had one of the handcuffs on him before he awakened. He didn't give them any trouble and they took him back to jail in Paris.

Two days later, Tucker was sent back to Courtney Flat. Tucker admitted to being sent after many tough hombres and sent to obtain many objects when it came to evidence but this was the first time Tucker had ever been sent to obtain a stomach; this one being that of the deceased, Mr. Green.

"That was the first time I'd ever been ordered to bring in so harmless a captive as a dead man's stomach," said Tucker.

It seems there was a so called quack doctor there at Courtney Flat who practiced his skills on the innocent people of the Flat. Tucker got him to get the object that he was ordered to bring after digging up the body. The doctor had no problem getting the stomach out but he wanted to do the job so well and neat that he washed the stomach out nice and clean.

"It was as white as a piece of chicken when he gave it to me," said Tucker. Tucker didn't know anything about poison cases then but he was soon to learn something. When he took the nice white stomach to the doctor in Paris who was going to make the test for poison, he was not very happy with Tucker. As a matter of fact, he was somewhat bitter that anyone would bring a washed-out stomach to him to be tested for poison.

The Paris doctor blurted out, "You'd just as well brought me the lower end of the big intestine."

"I knew then that my second trip to the Flat had not been completely successful," stated Tucker.[27]

Even though the stomach could not be used as evidence, Westmilam was convicted. He was sentenced to hang, however, the sentence was not carried out.

An unusual situation involving Westmilam occurred, according to Tucker. The condemned man had a $10,000 life insurance policy. If he were hanged, the insurance company would have to pay the beneficiaries. So, as Tucker understood at the time, the company felt very sorry for Westmilam. They enlisted Frank Lee to go to Washington and beseech the President not to carry out so harsh a sentence against so nice a fellow as its policy holder. The company's wish was finally granted and the sentence was commuted to life imprisonment.

"We heard at the time that Lee, who died only a year or so ago, received $1,000 from the insurance company for his service," said Tucker.[28]

Tucker served under Marshal Williams during those years. He was referred to as Colonel James Shelby Williams, born in Clinton County, Kentucky, and came to Texas with his father in 1857. He was then six-years of age. In his younger years, he was a successful traveling salesman in the state of Texas. His first public appointment came in 1892, when President Grover Cleveland appointed him United States marshal of the Eastern Texas District.

The years of his incumbency covered the Cleveland and part of the McKinley administrations, forty-eight violent law breakers met death at the hands of his deputies, an even dozen were hanged, five met death under death sentences, and 815 were imprisoned. It was because of the record he had made during the Cleveland administration that the late President McKinley reappointed him without solicitation to the work for another term. Williams died in 1920.[29]

Chapter Twenty-Four

A Transfer to Ardmore

In 1897, when President William McKinley took office, Dr. John Grant, from Sherman, was appointed U. S. marshal for the Eastern District of Texas. None of the Paris deputy marshals liked him. Tucker reported that all of the deputies quit and went up in the Territory to Ardmore, being the Southern District of Oklahoma had just been organized. They took commissions under U. S. Marshal John S. Hammer.[1]

Provision was made in the *Act of 1895* creating the Southern District Court of Indian Territory, for the offices of presiding judge, district attorney, clerk, marshal and deputies, as well as commissioners. One of the unique features of the Ardmore District Court was that a large number of men who served as marshals or commissioners in the Southern District were Chickasaw by birth or marriage.

Charles B. Stewart, who had served as a Pontotoc County constable under Sheriff James Frazier, was appointed as the first judge of the new Southern District Court. John A. McClure and Lucius L. Stowe were the first U. S. marshals appointed. Captain Stowe also acted as prosecuting attorney in the early stages of the new court.

Marshal Stowe was born in North Carolina in 1852 and moved to Sherman, Texas, in 1866. In 1879, Stowe moved the Indian Territory where he was a store manager at Fort Arbuckle and White Bead Hill. Marshal J. J. McAlester appointed Stowe chief division deputy for the 3rd Division of Indian Territory.

When judicial redistricting occurred Stowe won appointment from President Grover Cleveland as marshal for the Southern District at Ardmore. After his appointment, Stowe was a frequent visitor to the Middle Washita communities, mixing business and pleasure during his trips. Following Stowe's death in 1895, he was replaced by his brother, Charles L. Stowe, who, after two years, was in turn replaced by A. H. Law. Captain John S. Hammer replaced Law, and was himself replaced by Benjamin H. Colbert, who served until 1902.

According to the editor of the *Ada Evening News*, John Hammer was a former Rough Rider, the best cook in the regiment, and a scrapper from way back. Ben Colbert, too, was a former Rough Rider and served under Teddy Roosevelt in the Spanish-American War. Colbert was selected as one of the twenty-nine members of the Rough Riders to act as a bodyguard escort of President Roosevelt on inauguration day.

The last U. S. marshal, before statehood, was Grosvenor A. Porter who served between 1902 and 1907. "Grove" Porter was born in 1876 in Frederick County, Maryland, and when ten-years-old was placed by his parents in the St. Paul Military School, at Garden City, Long Island, from which he ran away to become a cowboy. Porter went to Cheyenne, Wyoming, where he secured employment and rode the range for six years. Later, Porter was appointed deputy marshal and served during the hottest period ever known in that state. Not long afterward he was commissioned a deputy sheriff in Laramie County, where he served for four years.

To ensure fairness of trial, particularly in jury selection, offenders within the Southern District were tried in courts away from their home turf. For instance, those arrested in Pauls Valley were tried in Purcell or Ardmore which were the courts closest by rail, the primary means of transportation, and if there was a change in venue approved, the case usually went to Paris, Texas, or McAlester, in the Choctaw Nation, for trial. Later, venue cases were transferred to courts at Ada, Chickasha, Purcell and Ardmore.[2]

Tucker believed Marshal Hammer came from Illinois. At least, he knew he was not a native of that part of the country and he didn't think he knew very much about it or the problems which faced him. But, to his credit, he was less politician and more marshal than most. Few of the old deputies liked him as much as they did marshals Reagan, Dickerson or Williams.[3]

Actually, John Hammer was a native of Oklahoma Indian Territory, being born there in 1873. His father was of Kentucky stock and his mother was from Missouri. He was a private in Troop A, 6th Regiment, Company B, U. S. Calvary out of Texas, was a Rough Rider serving in the Spanish-American War. John became disabled and awarded a pension from the government in 1912.

He was living with his brother George S. Hammer in 1930,

Choctaw Nation. John was listed as being three years younger than George. They are both buried in Newkirk Cemetery, Kay County, Oklahoma. George was born on March 21, 1870, and John's headstone states he was born only two months prior on January 4, 1870. It is very likely he was born in

The birth date of Mr. John S. Hammer is likely in error. His brother George was born in March, 1870 and John was not born until 1873. *Photo from author's collection.*

1873. John's brother George Sutton Hammer was christened on April 28, 1870, at Saint John's Episcopal, Fort Smith, Arkansas. His date of birth was recorded as March 21, 1870. Their parents were John S. and Belle Sutton Hammer.[4]

"Hammer said that he wanted men who would enforce the law," explained Tucker. "We would do that alright, for we had been in the habit of doing it for a good long while."

Tucker saw himself and other deputies as being seasoned lawmen and saw their boss, Marshal Hammer, as a political appointee with little or no experience in dealing with the criminal element. George, along with deputies D. E. "Dave" Booker, Jim Chancellor, Seldom Lindsay, Hillary Lindsay, Wilburn Reynolds, and George Stewart, were the men who turned in their badges at Paris and took commissions at Ardmore.

Buck Garrett was chief of police at Ardmore by that time. He was reelected several times as sheriff of Carter County and became the most famous, if not the most glamorous, sheriff in the history of Oklahoma.[5] According to a news report, Buck Garrett opted out his chief of police job and had once again received a commission as deputy marshal under Marshal Hammer and was listed as being present and accounted for when Hammer stepped down for his political replacement, Marshal Ben H. Colbert.[6]

There was only one important incident that Tucker could recall during the administration of Marshal Hammer. It was the Bob Terrell case. The office telephoned Tucker one day and told him to go after Henry Mashore. They thought that he was a member of the Al Jennings Gang that had only a short time before robbed a train up near Chickasha.[7]

Tucker went out looking for Mashore and found him over near Atlee. He figured he knew where he might be and found Mashore at Bob Terrell's place just at dusk. Mashore was standing in the yard and when he saw Deputy Tucker coming, he ran around the house with a Winchester in his hands.

Tucker opened fire on him and thought Mashore fell but he was mistaken. About that time Tucker saw Terrell who was also in the yard and he raised his rifle and fired at Tucker. The bullet came close but missed. Tucker drew and fired, his bullet taking Terrell squarely in the chest. He was out of the fight and never spoke again after Tucker plugged him. In the meantime, Mashore got away.

Tucker couldn't understand how Terrell missed him when he fired. He was using a Winchester and when Tucker stepped it off, Terrell was only nineteen steps away. Tucker didn't see Mashore again for two years. By then, he was in prison over at McAllister where Tucker had a short visit with him. They talked about his escape and the fact that Mashore could have stayed and mixed in the mettle being he was armed. Tucker had expected him to get to cover and open up on him.[8]

The Terrell killing proved to be somewhat sentimental. Some of his neighbors and friends didn't like it very much so they brought charges before the grand jury. Two women brought damaging testimony. One testified that she saw Deputy Tucker shoot Terrell after he went down.

"It was all a lie," said Tucker.

A reporter from the local newspaper in Ardmore interviewed Deputy Tucker when he came into town from Mud Creek in March, 1898. The report;

> Robert Terrell, a notorious character, opens a duel in which his is killed by deputy Tucker near Orr. It seems that the country out there is infested by a horde of horse thieves, and a man by the name of Bateman a few days ago received a note from J. A. Cline asking him to communicate the fact to Deputy Tucker that the woods was full of them, alluding to the horse thieves. The deputy, with a posse, started for their haunts on last Saturday, and the appearance of the officers scattered the gang.
>
> On Tuesday last, while going over the ground again, Robert Terrell, who has been making some terrible threats about

the officers and the peaceable settlers, appeared close by, and with a pistol, [not a Winchester as Tucker stated] began shooting at Deputy Tucker. He shot twice [not once] and, the officer, not relishing the idea of being made a target of, began pumping his Winchester [not one shot as Tucker wrote] at Terrell. He fired four shots and Terrell was a dead man. The deceased was considered tough, and only a very short time ago was released from the Ardmore jail, where he was held on a charge of horse theft. His pedigree also shows that he served a term in the penitentiary in Texas for cattle theft. No blame seems attachable to the officer, he had to shoot in self defense.[9]

Tucker was indicted and tried for the killing. A woman testified for the prosecution against Tucker. Tucker said, "The woman whose eyesight was so good didn't help the prosecution very well in the trial. It was proven that she couldn't see a covered wagon at the distance that she thought she saw me pumping lead into Terrell. But even if it had not been false evidence they could not have convicted me with the jury that I had. To say the least, it was not unfavorable to me. Colonel Russell of Dallas, defended me and I was acquitted in short order."

One of the deputies had seventeen warrants for Terrell when Tucker killed him. But Tucker was not carrying a warrant for his arrest when he approached the house. "I didn't need it for he was trying to kill me when I shot him. That is the best warrant that any officer can have; the right to protect his life." said Tucker. The outstanding warrants on Terrell were for cow stealing while some were for other offenses. Tucker summarized it with, "Terrell was just a rough, ignorant, country boy, who was awfully sure that nobody was going to run over him. And they didn't---he ran over himself."[10]

Chapter Twenty-Five

End of the Ride

When Theodore Roosevelt became president upon the assassination of President William McKinley, Deputy Marshal George Redman Tucker's commission with the United States law enforcement machinery stopped. The new president selected Ben Colbert to succeed Marshal Hammer.

Colbert was Native American and had been one of the Rough Riders who fought in Cuba. He may have been a good enough Rough Rider but Tucker didn't think much of him as a United States marshal. Deputy Marshal Tucker refused to take a commission under him. Tucker had been a lawman continuously since 1878 and though the job still had a certain hold on him, he had to admit that he was getting burned out with law enforcement. Tucker saw that the general character of the work had changed completely since the old days. One was now a process server and no longer a man hunter.[1]

Tucker turned in his badge and drifted about for a time, even trying to farm for a while down on the rich bottom land near Courtney Flat. It was hard for Tucker to get away from the old stomping grounds and in 1908, he was elected chief of police of Waurika, Oklahoma. He remained in that position for four years. There was only one Waurika case that deserved attention according to Tucker, even though there were many cases worked. This particular case involved the scriptures, fists, knives, and crazy fanatics, and apoplexy.[2]

It happened this way. Two unnamed brothers got off of the midnight train in Waurika and took lodging at the DeLong Hotel. Actually, Mary D. DeLong, a widow, kept a boarding house.[3] They were headed to a Bible debate at Duncan the next day. Their enthusiasm for their mission was evidently unbounded for they became engaged in a heated argument over some philosophical question. The argument lead to a fist fight and they knocked each other all over the room and fought their way out into the hallway.

At that point one of the brothers pulled a knife and cut the other's throat down to the neck bone, almost beheading him. Of course the victim bled to death immediately.

Mrs. DeLong, telephoned Chief Tucker and asked him to come immediately, Tucker hurried over to the hotel and upon entering he saw the victim lying on the floor with his brother kneeling over him mumbling to himself. Tucker stepped to the door and blew his whistle to summons his police officers on duty that night. Two policemen came running to the scene and Tucker instructed them to take the surviving brother to the jail and lock him up but alsokeep an eye on him.[3]

In talking with Mrs. DeLong, Tucker learned the name of the two boys and their address from the register. Tucker called the father on the telephone and told him about what had happened. The boy's father told Tucker he would depart immediately and be there as quickly as possible. He showed up right away.

Pat Hammons, the prosecuting attorney and Tucker had a talk and agreed that it was all just crazy business and that the best thing they could do was to turn the murderer over to his father along with his deceased son and let him take them home and deal with the problem. The father started out with them by wagon to Palestine but when he arrived at Gainesville, the father dropped dead from apoplexy.

"It was one of the most mixed up cases I had ever seen," said Tucker. "I do not know what became of the survivor or how he succeeded in getting the two dead family members out of Gainesville, if he ever did."[4]

While Tucker's story may very well be true, no newspaper reports could be located to support his claim. It is logical that the Widow DeLong would not want the murder to be publicized as it would harm her boarding house business. In 1910, she had three daughters, two sons, and eight lodgers living in her boarding house. For a widow to support five children, she didn't need negative press to drive away her only source of income. With the father dropping dead at Gainesville should have sparked a reporter's interest, but again, no record could be located concerning the incident.

George Tucker did not speak of his family in his memoirs and little can be proven of his family. However, in 1900, Federal

Census records indicate Tucker was living at Orr, Indian Territory; Chickasaw Nation. Then, in 1910, Tucker was living at Waurika, Jefferson County, Oklahoma, and by 1920, in Carter County, Oklahoma, where he owned a rooming house with twenty-five boarders. He was listed as a laborer, possibly oil field worker.

Records indicate he was married three times. His first wife was believed to be Martha Chapman and they married in Hill County, Texas, before Tucker became the marshal of Spanish Fort. They had three children. The oldest was Bert Oliver Tucker, born October 19, 1880, either at Spanish Fort or Indian Territory. Then Brooks Tucker was born January 1888, then Ruth was born in May of 1890.

After Martha died George married a woman named Belle who died in 1898 in Ardmore. She is buried at Rose Hill Cemetery in Ardmore. Then George married Mrs. Anna Ellen Johnson, born in Kansas. She had been previously married and had a son, or stepson named William Johnson who was born in Kansas during 1880.

She indicated in federal census that her father was from Pennsylvania and her mother from New Jersey. The Dawes Roll showed Tucker to be intermarried to a woman with Indian blood. By 1910 he is widowed again and not remarried but has William Johnson in his household as adopted. By 1920 he is married once again to Annie, born in Arkansas.

The 1910 Federal Census record revealed that George Tucker had adopted William Johnson, Siney and another Homma child. The Homma children were full-blood Choctaw Indian. Tucker was responsible for registering the children with the U.S. government. Siney's mother was Ceely or Celia. Her father was named Paul.

They became ill and Ceely died on October 25, 1900, and Tucker adopted the young children. Their father Paul died in 1916. Siney married George Booker Knox, a nephew of George Tucker, and they had ten children. She lived a full-life and is buried in Memorial Park Cemetery, Tulsa, Oklahoma, near many other Knox family members. She lived in the suburb of "Red Fork" all her years from childbearing age to her death. Her headstone indicates her name was Sina N. "Siney" Homma Knox, born March 16, 1895, at Antlers, Oklahoma. and died on March 28, 1987 in Tulsa, Oklahoma.

In 1912, Tucker moved back to Ardmore and became assistant

chief of police under D. N. "Dave" Booker, the man who killed the elderly black man who murdered Tom Smith, and one of his old deputy companions from Paris days and one of the Wyoming regulators. Tucker served in that capacity for three years and then went out to the one and only infamous Ragtown as a law officer. That was another story in itself according to Tucker but he did not write anything further about the oilfield tent city called Ragtown.[5]

Tucker suffered a stroke causing some paralysis and that ended his career as a active peace officer, although he went on to serve as meat inspector under both Whitehurst and Cordell, presidents of the State Board of Agriculture. Tucker also held two commissions as a game warden but considered it to be puny work as he did practically nothing.[6]

Tucker's close friend and fellow Deputy Marshal Jeff Mynatt, also known as Mynatt, turned in his badge and was elected sheriff of Woodward County in 1899, for a two-year term. He and his wife Ella lived in Judkins. Jeff's wife died in 1910 and he had moved back to his roots in Anderson County, Texas.

Jeff appears on the 1920 federal census as a widower, living with his sister and her son. Kurt House, gun collector, historian and author, reported that sometime after that, Jeff sold and promised his pistol to a conductor of the Santa Fe Railroad but still had the gun in his possession when he walked into the parlor of a Palestine funeral home. There in the parlor, on the July 18, 1927, Jeff Mynatt drew the pistol from his holster, raised it to his head, and squeezed the trigger. Hot lead exploded his brain as he fell dead to the floor.

According to House, a note was found in Mynatt's pocket saying he had sold the pistol to the conductor and requested it be sent to him. A newspaper stated that the note found on Mynatt said: "It is my own act. I blame no one." His reasoning for taking his own life is unknown.

That same pistol was recently purchased by House who made the discovery concerning Mynatt's death and this was confirmed by a newspaper report. According to House, Jefferson D. Mynatt was buried next to his wife in the Old City Cemetery in Palestine. While Tucker and Mynatt were very good friends, they apparently did not stay in touch as Tucker never mentioned his demise in his memoirs.[7]

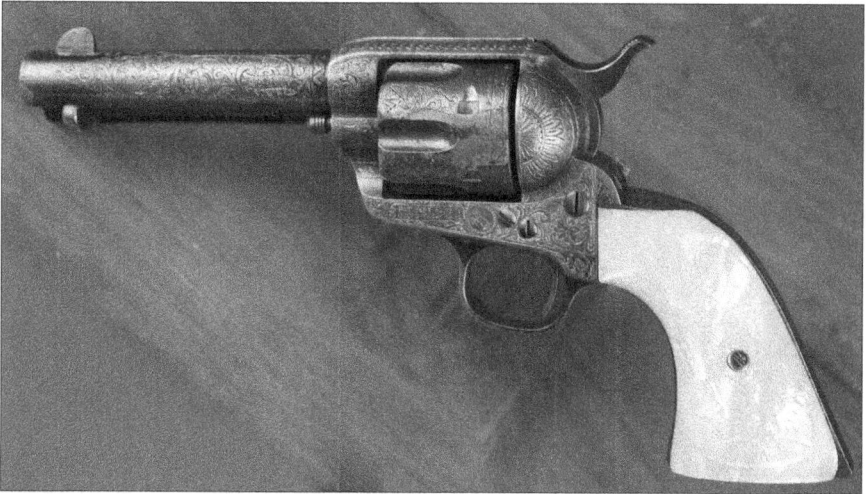

This was the .45 caliber colt pistol used by Jeff Mynatt to take his own life. *Photo courtesy of Kurt House who recently purchased the pistol.*

When the fierce-looking, lean old frontier lawman died in 1945, hundreds of people came from miles around to pay their last respects. These days, the name George Redman Tucker doesn't mean much. It's not inscribed on an ostentatious monument or sung in a ballad. There are no books, movies, or organizations dedicated to idolizing his memory as there are for some of his contemporaries. But in his day, he stood in the shadow of no man.

"He scared the Hell out of me," said great grandson Tommy Tucker, remembering him in the early 1940s when he and his parents visited Tucker at the Confederate Home in Ardmore, Okla. "But I didn't know much about him," said Tommy.

Few people do, save a vague memory recalling he was part of the infamous Johnson County, Wyo., range war. A shame, because in his unpublished manuscript Tucker had a lot to tell of that event; experiences which both clarify and refute prevailing theories. Moreover, for over fifty years he represented the lawful government and its parent civilization in a time and place where neither was wanted; the border counties between Texas and Indian Territory and later, to become the state of Oklahoma.

He, along with the other early-day peace officers, were the most fearless of deputy United States marshals, who did their part in trying to bring law and order to the Indian Territory. It was on a Thursday afternoon on a cold day in late January of

The Confederate Home in Ardmore, Okla., was built in 1912 and George Tucker spent his final years in the old soldiers' home. *Photo from author's collection.*

1945 when more than twenty peace officers, cattlemen, friends, and relatives gathered around the grave to honor, the very last one of the early day deputy United States marshals who worked the Indian Territory. When his headstone was erected it read: George R. Tucker, born August 29, 1855, died January 21, 1945. He served more than fifty years as deputy U. S. marshal and in other law enforcement capacities in Oklahoma before statehood and afterwards.[8]

As an eighty-nine-year-old pioneer, he was fondly called "Uncle George" and a son-in-law jokingly called him "Piss Whiskers," because of perpetual tobacco stains on his beard which turned his whiskers yellow.[9] He was preceded in death by three wives and one child. His body was buried but not his memory. He was the George Redman Tucker; one of the last of a rare breed of lawmen; a man hunter in Indian Country.[10]

Tucker's death was not big news in the major newspapers but Oklahoma's *Healdton Herald* gave him a full page obituary. World War II was still raging and Franklin D. Roosevelt was president until he died a few months later. The Manhattan Project would test the first atomic bomb at Alamogordo, New Mexico. on July 16. A

George Redman Tucker was laid to rest beside his wife Belle in the Rose Hill Cemetery, Ardmore, Okla. *Photo from author's collection.*

U. S. military B-25 bomber flew into the Empire State Building on
July 28, damaging the 78th and 79th floors, killing thirteen people.
A first class postage stamp was three cents and unemployment
was around 1.9 percent.

That was the big news but George Redman Tucker wasn't
around to read about it or be concerned over it. Only his
unpublished memoirs, news clippings, a few documents, a family
Bible, family stories, a few photographs, a .32 caliber boot gun,
and a copy of *The Banditti of the Plains* remain.

Tucked away in a drawer at a library was a typed but
unpublished manuscript that Tucker wrote around 1934. It is most
likely that George Redman Tucker wanted Major Alley to complete
the edit of his manuscript and have it published as a book. It would
likely have been titled *I Played the Law Game and Won*. During all of
his years a a lawman, he was never wounded by any of the Indian
Country outlaws that he tracked down. Tucker never mentioned
if he was a gambler but it was never necessary because being a
lawman made the biggest gamble of all, his life!

George Tucker was not politically correct when he wrote about
his law enforcement life. He had little use for Frank Canton, but
Oklahoma, at the time, had a lot of use for Canton. They held him
in high esteem. George saw him as a braggart who made himself
a hero with false claims and grandeur. George knew that his half

-brother, Starling S. Tucker, was the "Texas kid" and wrote about it, but his story about his brother, his character, and demise, was never brought to light until now.

A photograph of George Redmon [*sic*] Tucker was recently located in the National Cowboy Museum, Oklahoma City, Okla., by historian and author Chuck Parsons. His middle name was listed by the museum incorrectly and upon request, it was changed to Redman.

George Redman Tucker, spent half a century enforcing the law. He saw himself as a man hunter, to which he surely was, and he summed it up nicely by saying "I played the law game for fifty years." He won.[11]

Appendix A

George Redman Tucker Obituary

From *The Healdton Herald*
Healdton, Okla. Thursday, January 25, 1945.

Funeral Held Tuesday for George R. Tucker

Funeral services were held at the First Baptist Church at 2:00 p.m. for George Redman Tucker, the last one of the early day Deputy United States Marshals, who passed away at the Confederate Home in Ardmore Sunday, following a month's illness from a stroke.

Emphasizing the important part played by the early day fearless peace officers, Rev. O. Hamblen, pastor of the church, conducted the services, assisted by Rev. R. M. Catlett, pastor of the Assembly of God church in Wilson. A beautiful tribute was paid to the memory of the deceased by Rev. Hamblen.

Special songs sung by Mr. Clifford Watson and Mrs. J. L. Harder were 'Abide with Me' and 'Nearer My God to Thee.'

Burial was in the Rose Hill cemetery, Ardmore, with Collier Brothers Funeral Home in charge of the arrangements. Active pallbearers were Dan Blackburn, Bill Ratliff, and Joe Lewis, of Healdton, Floyd Randolph, Barney Ross, and Horace Kendall, of Ardmore, long time friends of the deceased and his family.

Honorary pallbearers were Steve Pike, R. Reynolds, J. E. McClanahan, J. K. Pipkin, Bob Adams, Dad Featherstone, Tom and Bryant Ballew and Slim Thompson.

George R. Tucker was born Aug. 29, 1855 and died at the Confederate Home in Ardmore, Jan. 21, 1945. He served over 50 years as Deputy U. S. Marshal and in either law enforcement capacities in Oklahoma before statehood and afterwards.

He was preceded in death by his wife and one child. Among friends here for the funeral was more than two score early day cattlemen and peace officers with whom he had closely associated in the past and who valued his friendship. Many expressions as a peace officer were heard. 'Uncle George,' as he was better known, never met a stranger, and his death is regretted by many friends.

Survivors include one son Bert Tucker, Healdton city constable, two daughters Mrs. Ruth Riggs, [of] Wilson and Mrs. Gladys Nash, [of] Oklahoma City, a number of grand-children and great grandchildren.

Appendix B

Family Matters

Ruth Tucker, daughter of George Redman Tucker, married John Overstreet Gilliam and they were in the household with her father in 1910, where he was Chief of Police in Waurika, Jefferson County, Oklahoma. John Gilliam was listed as age twenty-five, born in Oklahoma and his parents were of Missouri stock. Ruth was born in May of 1890, but was listed as age eighteen in 1910. Ruth died before 1920 and John Gilliam moved to Clarendon, Donley County, Texas to his sister Lula Maude and her husband Doctor J. W. Webb. George Tucker was listed as widowed.

Bert Oliver Tucker was the first born of George Redman Tuck-er and his mother was probably Martha A. Chapman. He was related through marriage to the Pruitts. They were said to be a bad bunch. George Tucker's son Bert O. Tucker died in 1948. His wife was Sophia Parker Tucker and they had six children: Bert Jr., Tommy, Mrs. Harley Hurt, Mrs. Doris Jo Clark, Mrs. Mittie Giles, and Mrs. Fred Blockinger.

Appendix C

George Redman Tucker Death Certificate

A photostatic reproduction of a Standard Certificate of Death, State of Oklahoma, No. 125, for George Redman Tucker. The form shows place of death as Carter County, Ardmore; usual residence Oklahoma, Carter County, Ardmore; date of death January 21st, 1945; born August 19, 1855; age 89 years 5 months 2 days; birthplace unknown, Arkansas; usual occupation Peace Officer; sex male, race white. Cause of death noted as "Hemiplegia" of 17 days duration. Burial at Ardmore, Okla.

Endnotes

Chapter One

1. Angelina Tucker, Family lore told to her granddaughter.

2. Federal Census record, Franklin County, AR, 1860; Tucker family bible.

3. Federal military archives; Tucker family bible; Stories told by Angie Tucker.

4. Headstone marker displaying the names Burk and Tucker and states double burial in Ballinger Cemetery, Madison County, Arkansas.

5. J. D. Little, Historian, handwritten report, 1973, Madison County, Arkansas.

Chapter Two

1. Most counties have only one county seat. However, some counties in Alabama, Arkansas, Georgia, Iowa, Kentucky, Massachusetts, Mississippi, Missouri, New Hampshire, and Vermont have two or more county seats, usually located on opposite sides of the county. There are thirty-six counties with multiple county seats in eleven states.

2. Carlile, B. interview, August, 2014, on Tucker family history. Carlile's grandmother Angie Tucker, was closely related to George Redman Tucker and his family; family Bible of Angie Tucker provided names, dates, marriages, and deaths of the Tucker clan. They were of Cherokee, French, and Irish blood.

3. Federal U. S. Census, 1850, Boston township, Franklin County, Arkansas, lists Bartly J. Welton, age 24, born in Illinois, and son of Bartly Sr., age 65 from Virginia and Nancy Welton, age 49 from Kentucky. Three children of this family were born in Illinois and two in Arkansas. The family came to Arkansas around 1839.

4. Tucker, George R., unpublished autobiography. 3

5. *Ibid.*

6. Russell, Joy, *The Huntsville Massacre*, Huntsville, Ark., Madison County Record, January 31, 1908.

7. Tucker unpublished autobiography. 4

8. *Ibid.*

9. *Ibid, 5*

10. *Ibid.*

11. *Ibid.* The marriage record is on file at the courthouse in Ozark. Obituary from *The Waurika News-Democrat*, Waurika, Oklahoma, Aug 2, 1946.

Chapter Three

1. Tucker, George Redman, unpublished autobiography, circa 1936, 6.

2. *Ibid.*

3. *Ibid, 7.*

4. *Ibid;* Texas death record of James A. Faulkner; Ron Griffin, personal interview. Mr. Griffin is a descendant of James Faulkner. James Faulkner's mother was a McMichael and the McMichael and Faulkner families settled in Texas. There were many men named Hill in the area during that time and it was impossible to determine exactly which Hill was involved in the incident.

5. *Ibid.*

6. *Ibid.*

7. *Ibid.*

8. *Ibid.*

9. *Ibid.*

10. *Ibid, 7-8.*

11. *Ibid, 8.*

Chapter Four

1. Tucker unpublished autobiography, 9.

2. From Elizabeth Ann Harper's thesis on the Taovayas Indians in the trading relations on the Oklahoma and the Texas frontiers (1719 to 1835) for the M. A. degree in the History Department of the University of Oklahoma, in 1951. The article appeared in *The Chronicles of Oklahoma*.

3. *Ibid.*

4. Alley, John, editor of Tucker manuscript. His footnote gave a history of Burlington, Spanish Fort, and noted that it had become a ghost town.

5. *Ibid,* handwritten footnotes.

6. Tucker unpublished autobiography, 10.

7. *Ibid.*

8. *Ibid.*

9. Federal Census records, 1900, lists William H. Bagwill, widower and father of two sons with occupation as bartender in a local saloon of Spanish Fort.

10. Tucker unpublished autobiography, 10.

Chapter Five

1. Tucker unpublished autobiography, 10.

2. *Ibid,* 10-11.

3. *Ibid,* 11.

4. *Ibid.*

5. Tucker, Tommy, telephone interview, May 14, 2012. George Tucker was his grandfather and his father took him to the Confederate home in Carter County, Oklahoma to visit George. He was just a boy but he recalled some of the event. He stated a photograph was taken and believed a cousin had a copy but he was unable to obtain; Email interview with Mr. Justin Barnes, June 10, 2017. Justin owns the .44 bulldog boot gun that belonged to George Tucker. He knew nothing about him, only that he was related and had been gifted the pistol and a book about the Wyoming range war.

6. Little is known about Melton. No records have been found to determine exactly who he was.

7. Author's assessment from prior experiences of interviewing convicted criminals and death row inmates for the Governor of Texas.

8. Tucker unpublished autobiography, 12.

9. *Ibid.*

10. *Ibid,* 13.

11. *Ibid,* 14.

12. *Fort Worth Daily Gazette,* Fort Worth, TX, March 28, 1885; *Cheyenne Transporter,* Darlington, I. T., April 15, 1885. Darlington was a community located on the southern Cheyenne Reservation and no longer exists but was near present El Reno, Oklahoma.

13. Tucker unpublished autobiography, 13.

14. *Ibid.*

15. *Ibid,* 13-14.

16. *Fort Worth Gazette,* Fort Worth, TX, January 23, 1886.

17. Tucker unpublished autobiography, 14.

18. *Ibid*; Tower, Mike, email correspondence of documented court records of the Watson gang.

19. *Ibid*; History of Agent Owen at Wikipedia https://en.wikipedia.org/wiki/Indian_agent.

20. *Ibid.*

21. Interview with Mike Tower, authority on Indian Territory law enforcement., 2015.

22. *Ibid.*

23. *Ibid.*

24. Bob Murray was Robert L. Murray and he came into Indian Territory in 1857 and settled north of Colbert in Panola County. He married Louie Collins, daughter of Dan Collins. He was sheriff of Panola County, served in the Chickasaw Senate and later became a United States Indian policeman. However, court papers of G. R. Tucker listed the Indian policeman as H. F. Murray, probably in error.

25. Texas State Historical Association: At the Philadelphia Centennial Exposition in 1876, Col. A. H. Belo from Texas, became interested in an exhibit by Alexander Graham Bell of his new invention-the telephone. Belo, publisher of the *Galveston News* and later founder of the *Dallas Morning News*, on March 18, 1878, had a line installed between his newspaper office and his Galveston home. This telephone, according to some sources, was the first installed in Texas. The first Texas telephone exchange opened for business on August 21, 1879. George Washington Brackenridge of San Antonio installed the first telephone believed to be in 1877. It is also possible that he was using a talking system by 1877. The first exchanges were built by the Western Union Telegraph Company under patents awarded to Thomas A. Edison. The Southwestern Telegraph and Telephone Company, organized in 1881 to operate exchanges in Arkansas and Texas.

26. Tower, Mike; unpublished Tucker autobiography, 14.

27. Tucker unpublished autobiography, 15.

Chapter Six

1. Watson, William, Larceny, October 30, 1879, Jacket number 198, *Defendant Jacket Files for U. S. District Court Western Division of Arkansas, Fort Smith Division, 1866-1900*. Records of District Courts of the United states, 1685-2004, ARC ID: 201532, Record Group Number 21, The National Archives, Fort Worth, Texas.

2. Courtney Flat was named after Henry Courtney who settle there around 1878 and operated a ferry and farm. The town was first named Watkins.

3. Watson, Larceny, March 15, 1881.

4. *Ibid.*

5. *Ibid*; Bearss, Edwin C., Research Historian report, *Law Enforcement at Fort Smith, 1871-1899*, National Park Service Library, Denver, CO, January, 1964.

6. *Ibid.*

7. *Fort Smith Elevator*, Fort Smith, AR, February 22, 1882. Deputy J. T. Ayers Dies.

8. *Galveston Daily News*, Galveston, TX, December 25, 1886. Deputy U S marshal Tyson sent a dispatch to the U S marshal at Fort Smith. He reported

from Muskogee, Creek Nation, that Captain Sam Sixkiller, of the Indian police, had been assassinated on the night of the 24th by an unknown party at the time.

9. Bearss' research report.

10. Tucker unpublished autobiography, 17.

11. *Fort Worth Daily Gazette*, Fort Worth, TX, March 26, 1886.

12. Tucker unpublished autobiography, 17.

13. *Ibid*; Tower, Mike, Interview.

14. *Ibid*.

15. *Ibid*, 18.

16. *Ibid*.

17. *Ibid*.

18. *Ibid*.

Chapter Seven

1. Lyon, Owen, The Trail of the Quapaw, *Arkansas Historical Quarterly*, Arkansas Historical Association, Autumn 1950, 206; Cash, Marie, Arkansas Achieves Statehood, *Arkansas Historical Quarterly*. Arkansas Historical Association. December, 1943, 2.

2. Bearss, Edwin C., Research Historian Report, *Law Enforcement at Fort Smith, 1871-1899*, National Park Service Library, Denver, CO, January, 1964. 1.

3. *Ibid*.

4. *Ibid*, i-ii

5. *The Seattle Star*, Seattle, WA, September 16, 1899; *Bryan Morning Eagle*, Bryan, TX, June 13, 1899.

6. Bearss, Research Historian Report, 173

7. *Chicago Daily Tribune*, Chicago, Illinois, September 25, 1887; George Maledon's memory of fifty-two executions and the first six condemned by Judge Parker.

8. *Ibid*.

9. *Ibid*.

10. Bearss, *Research Historian Report*, 173

11. *Ibid*.

12. True bill, warrants, and other documents from the National Archives.

13. Tucker unpublished autobiography, 18-19.

14. *Ibid*, 19.

15. *Ibid*.

16. *Ibid*, 19-19a.

17. *Ibid*, 19a.

18. *Ibid*.

19. Cravens Family Papers, 1886-1982, Repository: University of Arkansas at Little Rock.

20. In 1875, Congress passed a civil rights act granting equal rights in public accommodations and jury duty. It did not mention gender.

21. Tucker unpublished autobiography, 19b.

22. Fort Smith, Arkansas, Criminal Cases 1866-1900, the National archives, Fort Worth, Texas.

23. *Ibid*.

24. *Ibid*.

25. Tucker unpublished autobiography, 19b.

26. *Ibid*, 19b-20.

27. Galonska, Juliet, National Park Services, Fort Smith, AR.

28. Tucker unpublished autobiography, 20.

29, Records of District Courts of the United States, The National Archives, Fort Worth, TX.

30, *Ibid*.

31. *Dallas Morning News*, Dallas, TX, June 24,1887. U. S. Marshal Hector Thomas left Gainesville, Texas, on June 23 for Fort Smith with Bill Watson, charged with a murder six-years ago in the Indian Territory.

32. *Dallas Morning News*, Dallas, TX, June 24,1887.

Chapter Eight
1. Tucker unpublished autobiography, 20-21.

2. *Ibid*, 21.

3. *Ibid*.

4. *Ibid*.

5. *Ibid*, 22-23.

6. *Ibid*.

7. *Our Brother In Red*, Muskogee, I. T., December 21 and 26, 1889.

Chapter Nine
1. George Redman Tucker, unpublished autobiography, circa 1934, 33-36; Harrell McCullough, *Selden Lindsey, U. S. Deputy Marshal*. Diamond Bar, CA, Paragon Publishing, 1993, 39. McCullough told the same story and gave his source as the Oklahoma Pioneer papers, which was actually from Tucker's

autobiography.

2. *Hamilton Daily Democrat*, A Lynching Party, Hamilton, OH, February 17, 1887;   From a search of the Ft. Smith Records at the Forth Worth Federal Archives, John Means and Lewis Brewer had a case for murder dating 1885 under Jacket Number 9.

3. *Fort Smith Elevator*, A Triple Lynching Near Healdton In Chickasaw Nation, Fort Smith, AR, April 20, 1888. The report erroneously named the victims as Tom Sanford, Abe Morgan, and a third part whose name was not given; all suspected of horse stealing. The stealing of horses and cattle in that vicinity was becoming so common that the people took the law into their own hands.

4. Mike Tower, historian and author, interview via email, October 20, 2016.

5. *Records of District Courts of the United States, 1685 - 2004*, Record Group Number 21, Jacket #9, The National Archives at Fort Worth, Fort Worth, Texas.

6. *Ibid.*

7. *Ibid.*

8. *Ibid.*

9. *Ibid.*

Chapter Ten

1. Tucker unpublished autobiography, 26.

2. Bob Reams was probably George R. Reames, born 16 Mar 1857, died September 26, 1884, buried at the old Spanish Fort cemetery.

3. Tucker unpublished autobiography, 27.

4. *Ibid.*

5. *Ibid*, 28.

6. *Ibid*, 28a.

7. *The Guthrie Daily Leader*, Indian Territory, June 7, 1896, reported Julia Moore, living near Courtney, Chickasaw Nation, is in jail at Paris, Texas, on a charge of murdering her illegitimate child. The baby was born May 4, and its mutilated corpse was found four days later after being dragged from its place of concealment and partially devoured by hogs.

8. *The Daily Ardmoreite*, Ardmore, Indian Territory, June 14, 1896.

9. Cemetery survey of Crow Cemetery, Orr, Oklahoma.

10. Tucker unpublished autobiography, 28b.

11. Hunnewell was founded in 1880. It was named for Boston financier and railway owner H. H. Hunnewell. In its heyday, Hunnewell was serving as a shipping point for Texas cattle, and was a prosperous cattle town during the 1880s. The Leavenworth, Lawrence and Galveston Railroad provided quick

access to the Kansas City, Kansas, stockyards, and the town had one hotel, two general stores, one barber shop, two dance halls, and eight saloons. Violence was common. There were no local lawmen to speak of during the 1880s and cattle rustling and other crimes were dealt with by the ranchers. The Hunnewell, Kan. gunfight occurred on October 5, 1884, between two drunken cowboys and lawmen traveling through the area. The lawmen lost. A post office was opened in 1880, and remained in operation until 1960.

12. Tucker unpublished autobiography, 28b.

13. Federal Census records, 1880, Cooke County, Texas, enumerated on May 26, 1880.

14. When Governor Wolf wrote about the intruders within Indian Territory, he listed a Butch Gardenhire as one of sixty intruders. It is highly probable that this was the same man. Jacob Gardenhire and wife Susan had nine children and lived near Spanish Fort in 1880, just over the line in Cooke County. One of those nine children was twenty-two-year-old Milton Gardenhire. Jacob died in 1886 in Spanish Fort. The gravesite where Milton Gardenhire is buried is the Ozias Cemetery in Kaufman County, Texas. While highly suspect, no solid proof was found to link Milton Gardenhire to the Bully fugitive Tucker wrote about.

15. Tucker unpublished autobiography, 29.

16. *Galveston Daily News*, Galveston, TX, December 25, 1886.

17. Tucker unpublished autobiography, 29.

18. *Ibid*; Saint Jo is near the Cooke County line fifteen miles east of Montague in extreme east central Montague County.

19. *Ibid*, 30.

20. *Ibid*.

21. Houston Fleetwood was born May 30, 1848 at Sycamore, Delaware County, Okla.. He died from his wounds on May 18, 1888 at Terral, in Jefferson County Okla.. He was buried in the Fleetwood Cemetery near Terral. The Fleetwood Cemetery is a private burial location said to be named for a pioneer of south Jefferson County. Over time, nature has removed the names of many in this final resting place. The only known names buried there are Houston F. Fleetwood, born 30 July, 1847 and died on 18 May, 1888. Beside him is Emily Fleetwood, born 16 August, 1830 and died 29 November, 1930. The relationship is unknown.. The only others identified are David W. Colbert, Nov 19, 1888-May 4, 1889; Houston Colbert, Feb 25, 1894-May 30, 1894; and Ella May Coffey, Feb 15, 1870, and died Jan 5, 1892.

22. Her first name is unknown. The transport of Mr. Trout was in 1888. After Trout was released from prison he married again based on Tishomingo County records as follows: John M. Trout married Ida J. Stelwell on October 26, 1895, by Judge B.F. Harris.

23. Tucker unpublished autobiography, 31-32

24. Fort Smith Elevator, Fort Smith, Ark., November 2, 1888; Fort Smith Historical list.

Chapter Eleven

1. Tucker unpublished autobiography 32.

2. *Ibid.*

3. *Ibid*, 33.

4.Tower, Mike, Oklahoma author and historian, email communications.

5. *Ibid.*

6. *Ibid.*

7. Tucker unpublished autobiography, 34.

8. *Fort Worth Daily Gazette*, Fort Worth, TX June 27, 1887; *Sherman Daily Register*, Sherman, TX, April 14, 1887.

9. *Ibid.*

10. *Sherman Daily Register*, Sherman, TX, April 14, 1887.

11. *Gainesville Daily Hesperian*, Gainesville, TX, August 20, 1889.

12. *Daily Globe*, St. Paul, MI, December 25, 1888; *Gainesville Daily Hesperian*, Gainesville, TX, January 29, 1888; *Fort Worth Daily Gazette*, Fort Worth, TX, June 27, 1887.

Chapter Twelve

1. Tucker unpublished autobiography, 34.

2. Harman, S. W., *Hell on the Border*, original copyright 1898; first printing by Bison Books: Lincoln, NE, 1992, 54.

3. Boarman, Alexander (Aleck), a Representative from Louisiana; born in Yazoo City, MS, December 10, 1839; lost his parents in infancy and raised by relatives in Shreveport, LA; attended common schools of Shreveport and Kentucky Military Institute at Frankfort; graduated from the University of Kentucky in 1860; enlisted in Confederate Army and served as lieutenant of the Caddo Rifles; promoted to captain; studied law; admitted to the bar in 1866 and commenced practice in Shreveport, mayor of Shreveport from May 7, 1866, to August 8, 1867; city attorney of Shreveport 1868-1872; unsuccessful candidate for election as secretary of state in 1872; elected as a Liberal Republican to the Forty-second Congress and served from December 3, 1872, to March 3, 1873; resumed the practice of law in Shreveport, judge of the tenth judicial district court, Caddo Parish, 1877-1880; appointed United States judge for the western district of Louisiana by President Garfield on May 18, 1881, and served until his death at Loon Lake, NY, August 30, 1916; interment in Oakland Cemetery, Shreveport. According to the New York Times, February 25, 1891, Boarman, a bachelor, was ousted from office

because he got caught up in a sex sting, twice, which nearly became the subject of a congressional investigation.

4. *Galveston Daily News*, Wednesday, March 27, 1889.

5. *Dallas Morning News*, Dallas, TX, May 16, 1889. Charged with Horse Theft. Montague, Tex., May 15 - W. L. Purcell of this place, formerly of Abilene, was arrested by Deputy Marshal G. R. Tucker and carried to Paris. He is charged with the theft of horses in the Indian territory.

6. Tucker unpublished autobiography, 35; Editor Major John Alley made many corrections/changes to Tucker's manuscript but it was never published in book form but remained in the hands of Alley. Apparently, the manuscript was still in his possession when he died. Federal field worker Selfridge omitted the Wyoming range war because Tucker held one of Oklahoma's hero's as a criminal under false colors.

7. *Ibid*, 36.

8. U. S. Marshal Richard B. Reagan was a Democrat, selected by President Cleveland to succeed Marshal James G. Tracy. The latter was a Republican. He was suspended when the Democratic administration came into power. Reagan was officially nominated on December 21, 1885 and confirmed on May 21, 1886. See *Congressional Record, 49th Congress*, 1st session, Vol. 17, Part 1, page 361 (Dec. 21, 1885) and Part 5, Page 4776 (May 21, 1886). He served until July 20, 1889. Therefore, George R. Tucker's appoint was prior to July 20, 1889.

9. Parsons, Chuck & Brown, Norman Wayne, *A Lawless Breed, John Wesley Hardin, Texas Reconstruction, and Violence in the Wild West*, University of North Texas Press, Denton, TX, 2013. 124.

11. Tucker unpublished autobiography, 37.

12. *Ibid*.

13. *Ibid*.

14. *A Lawless Breed*, 125.

15. Tucker unpublished autobiography, 38.

16. Mike Tower, Oklahoma historian; Wikipedia at https://en.wikipedia.org/wiki/Susie Peters.

17. Tucker unpublished autobiography, 38

18. Mike Tower, Oklahoma historian and author, email interview, 2015.

Chapter Thirteen

1. *Ibid*.

2. Tucker unpublished autobiography, 39.

3. *Ibid*, 40.

4. *Ibid*.

5. *Ibid*, 40.

6. *Ibid*.

Chapter Fourteen

1. William H. "Bill" Carr was a deputy U. S. marshal commissioned in the Western District Court at Fort Smith, Arkansas, in 1887. He was later commissioned in the Southern District of Indian Territory at Paris, Texas, and in the Kansas District Court at Wichita. He developed a reputation and was called "King of the Chickasaws" by the *New York Times*. They ran a feature article on his deeds of daring in April, 1895. He was also referred to as "Fighting Bill."

2. C. L. Hart became a deputy U. S. marshal and served for eleven years. He was credited with killing Bill Dalton in 1894. Hart arrived in Indian Territory around 1879. He had smallpox in 1897 but survived. He farmed and at one time had a blacksmith shop at Burneyville, Indian Territory, just north of the Red River.

3. Tucker unpublished autobiography, 41.

4. *Ibid*, 42.

5. *Ibid*, 43; *Dallas Morning News*, Dallas, TX, October 10, 1889. The article tells Tucker's story somewhat differently by stating that Terry and Hart remained at the house while Tucker departed to get help and while he was gone Terry shot and killed Bowie. The article gave Bowie's age as nineteen while Tucker said he was just seventeen.

6. *Ibid*.

7. James J. Dickerson succeeded Reagan as United States marshal for the Eastern District on July 20, 1889. The former was a Republican supported by President Harrison. He was officially nominated on December 16, 1889, and confirmed on February 11, 1890. See *Cong. Record, 51ˢᵗ Cong., 1ˢᵗ session.*, vol. 21, pt. 1, p1 99 (Dec, 16, 1889) and pt. 2, p 1205, (Feb 11, 1890), Dickerson served throughout the Harrison administration. [Note of editor Alley]; Belcher, Texas, is south of Gainesville, Texas and just north of Denton.

8. Tucker unpublished autobiography, 44.

9. Tucker unpublished autobiography, 45.

10. *Ibid*.

Chapter Fifteen

1. Tucker unpublished autobiography, 46.

2. *Ibid*.

3. *Ibid*.

4. *Ibid*, 47.

5. Name Index to Leavenworth Federal Penitentiary Inmate Case Files, 1895-

1931. National Archives, Kansas City, Missouri.

Chapter Sixteen

1. Tucker unpublished autobiography, 70.

2. *Waurika News-Democrat*, Waurika, OK, August 2, 1946.

3. *Sugden Leader*, Chickasaw Nation, Indian Territory, September 17, 1904.

4, Tucker unpublished autobiography, 71.

5. *The Lancet*, Norman, OK, July 26, 1904.

6. Tucker unpublished autobiography, 71.

7. Tower, Mike, interview, 2016.

8. Tucker unpublished autobiography, 70-71

9. Douglas, C. L., *Famous Texas Feuds*, Dallas: Turner, 1936.

10. Wikipedia, The Free Encyclopedia, Jaybird-Woodpecker War.

11. Fricke, Paul, was selected as U. S. Marshal on March 27, 1889.

12. Tucker unpublished autobiography, 54-55

13. *Ibid*.

Chapter Seventeen

1. Tucker unpublished autobiography, 56-59.

2. *Ibid*.

3. *Ibid*.

4. *Ibid*.

5. *The Telephone*, Tahlequah, Indian Territory, March 1, 1895; *The Indian Chieftain*, Vinita, Indian Territory, January 9, 1896.

6. Robert Ernst, *Deadly Affrays, The Violent Deaths of the US Marshals*, Scarlet-Mask Enterprises, United States, 2006. 259-262

7. Tucker unpublished autobiography, 59.

8. *Stevens Point Daily Journal*, Stevens Point, Wisconsin, February 10, 1913, Interview with Horace Speed, the first United States attorney for Oklahoma Territory stated: "The most bloodthirsty man that ever came under my observation was Bert Casey, one of the last outlaw leaders in the Southwest;" Ken Butler, *Oklahoma Renegades: Their Deeds and Misdeeds*, Pelican Publishing, New Orleans, LA, 1997. 231-2.

9. Robert Ernst, written communication on February 15, 2017 regarding the Hughes gang, Jud or Judd South with many aliases, and associates.

Chapter Eighteen

1. Tucker unpublished autobiography, 61-63.

2. *Ibid*.

3. *Brenham Daily Banner*, Brenham, TX, April 19, 1889, Federal court has opened at Paris with Judge Bowman [sic] of the Western District of Louisiana presiding;　United States District Court for the Western District of Louisiana records, Wikipedia online.

4. *Indian Chieftain*, Vinita, I. T., November 21, 1889.

5. Tucker unpublished autobiography, 61

6. *Ibid.*

7. *Gainesville Daily Hesperian*, Gainesville, TX, November 2, 1889.

8. Tucker unpublished autobiography, 60.

9. *Ibid.*

10. *Ibid.*

11. *Ibid*, 64-70.

12. *Ibid.*

13. *Ibid*; She was Ella Foster, b. circa 1859 in Texas and was daughter of Wm. and Clarinda Foster. The family migrated from Tennessee to Anderson Co., TX in the 1850's.

14. *Ibid.*

15. *Ibid*; *Galveston Daily News*, Galveston, TX, May 18, 1890. 1, 4.

16. *Ibid.*

17. *Ibid.*

Chapter Nineteen

1. He was George A. Knight and was a United States marshal from April 9, 1889 to January 27, 1890, Northern District, Dallas, Texas.

2. Tucker unpublished autobiography, 47-50.

3. *Ibid.*

4. *Ibid*; According to editor, Alley who edited Tucker's manuscript made the following footnote: "Croxton had the reputation of being a model saloon-keeper. He is said to have been a teetotaler and to have refused to sell liquor in violation of law."

5. *Ibid.*

6. *Ibid.*

7. *Ibid.*

8. Kelly, Charles Jr.. an article, Fort Smith, AR, 1966; Tower, Mike, email correspondence concerning the pay of deputy marshals.

9. Tucker unpublished autobiography, 50.

Chapter Twenty

1. Tucker unpublished autobiography. 72-86.

2. *Ibid.* 73

3. *Ibid.* 74; *Lampasas Dispatch*, May 10, 1877; The *Denison Daily News*, February 5, 1875, September 16, 1875 and April 25, 1877.

4. *Ibid.*

5. *Ibid*, 75.

6. *Ibid*, 76; United States Federal Census Record, Douglas, WY, 1900 and 1910. Communication with historian and author P. H. Schroeder.

Chapter Twenty-One

1. Tucker unpublished autobiography, 72-86

Chapter Twenty-Two

1. Tucker unpublished autobiography, 72-86

2. *Ibid*; U. S. Federal Census Records of Franklin County, AR, 1870 and 1880; Tucker family bible lists Starling S. Tucker, born 1869 and son of William Tucker and his second wife Jane.

3. Tucker unpublished autobiography,74

4. *Ibid.*

5. *Fort Worth Gazette*, Fort Worth, TX, March 30, 1892.

6. Tucker unpublished autobiography, 73.

7. Federal Census Records, Franklin County, AR, 1870 and 1880.

8. Starling Tucker was born in Franklin Co., AR, to William Tucker and his second wife Jane. Starling and his brother George had the same father.

9. Tucker unpublished autobiography, 74

10. *Ibid.*

11. *Ibid*, 75.

12. *Ibid*, 75-76.

13. *Ibid*, 76.

14. *Ibid*, 77.

15. *Ibid*, 78.

16. *Ibid.*

17. *Ibid*, 79.

18. *Ibid*, 80.

19. The term blind pig (or blind tiger) originated in the United States in the nineteenth century; it was applied to establishments that sold alcoholic beverages illegally. The operator of an establishment (such as a saloon or bar)

would charge customers to see an attraction (such as an animal) and then serve a "complimentary" alcoholic beverage, thus circumventing the law.

20. Tucker unpublished autobiography, 81.

21. *Ibid.*

22. *Ibid,* 84

23. *Sundance News*, Cheyenne, Wyoming, May 12, 1892, Special report, "Cowboy Prisoners fight."

24. Tucker unpublished autobiography, 83-84.

25. Tucker refers to R. B. David, author of *Malcolm Campbell, Sheriff, Casper, Wyoming;* Wyomingana Publishing Co., 1932.

26. Tucker unpublished unpublished autobiography, 85.

27. Tucker refers to Frank Canton, *Frontier Trails* by Dr. E. E. Dale, Houghton, Mifflin Co., 1930.

28. Tucker unpublished autobiography, 85.

29. The *Daily Hesperian*, Ardmore, I. T., April 21, 1892.

30. Email communication with Mr. Justin Barnes numerous times during 2016. Mr. Barnes was interested in learning of George Tucker's possible Indian heritage.

Chapter Twenty-Three

1. Tucker unpublished autobiography, 87.

2. *Ibid,* 87.

3. *Ibid,* 87a.

4. *Ibid.*

5. The *Muskogee Phoenix*, Muskogee, I. T., November 10, 1892.

6. Ernst, Robert R. and Stumpf, George R., *Deadly Affrays, The Violent Deaths of the U.S. Marshals*, Scarlet Mask Enterprises, 2006.

7. *Honey Grove Signal*, Honey Grove, TX, July 14, 1893. On July 12, a photo was received by officials in Bardwell, KY from Dallas, Texas. They claimed the picture sent from Dallas of Commodore Miller was him, beyond doubt. He was hanged in early July, 1893.

8. J. Shelby Williams succeeded Dickerson during Cleveland's second administration. Of course, he was a Democrat. For his nomination and confirmation, see *Cong. Record, 53rd Cong.*, 2nd Sess., Vol. 26, pt. 1, p. 524 (Jan. 8, 1894 and p. 820 (Jan. 15, 1894). Williams served throughout Cleveland's second administration.

9. E. D. Nix was appointed U. S. marshal over the Oklahoma Territory by President Grover Cleveland and Nix supervised over 150 deputy marshals, including the famous *Three Guardsmen*. His autobiography *Oklahombres* was

published in 1929 and republished in 1993.

10. Tucker unpublished autobiography, 87b.

11. *Ibid*, 87c.

12. *Ibid*, 88.

13. *Dallas Morning News*, Dallas, TX, October 1, 1891.

14. Mannsville is a town in Johnston County, Okla. The population was 587 at the 2000 census.

15. Tucker unpublished autobiography, 89.

16. *Ibid*.

17. *Temple Weekly Times*. Temple, TX, October 9, 1891.

18. Tucker unpublished autobiography, 89-90.

19. *Ibid*, 90.

20. *Ibid*, 90-91.

21. *Gainesville Hesperian*, Gainesville, TX, November 3, 1889.

22. Tucker unpublished autobiography, 92.

23. *Territorial Topic*, Purcell, I. T., December 26, 1889. [added Purcell, I. T.]

24. Tucker unpublished autobiography, 92.

25. *Ibid*, 93.

26. *Ibid*, 94.

27. *Ibid*.

28. *Ibid*, 97.

29. *Ibid*.

30. *Paris News*, February 29, 1920.

Chapter Twenty-Four

1. John S. Hammer became United States marshal for the Southern district of Oklahoma Territory in 1897. He succeeded Charles L. Stowe, a Democrat. For Hammer's nomination and confirmation , see *Cong. Record, 55ᵗʰ Cong., 2d sess., vol. 31*, pt. 1, p. 293 (Dec. 18, 1897) and p. 479 (Jan. 10, 1898).

2. Mike Tower, historian, Interview April 30, 2014.

3. Tucker unpublished autobiography, 98.

4. *Federal Census Records of Oklahoma* 1930; Christening record from Fort Smith, AR.

5. Tucker unpublished autobiography.

6. *The Daily Ardmoreite*, Ardmore, Carter County, Oklahoma Territory I. T., January 16, 1902.

7. Tucker's unpublished autobiography, 99.

8. *Ibid.*

9. *The Daily Ardmoreite*, Ardmore, I. T., March 24, 1898.

10. Tucker unpublished autobiography, 100. pg 211 Tucker's close friend and fellow Deputy Marshal Jeff Mynatt, also known as Mynatt,?

Chapter Twenty-Five

1. Tucker unpublished autobiography, 101.

2. *Ibid.*

3. 1910 Federal Census Record, Waurika, Jefferson County, Okla., lists Mary D. DeLong, keeper of a boarding house.

4. Tucker unpublished autobiography, 101.

5. *Ibid.* 102.

6. *Ibid.*

7. *Ibid.*

8. *Breckenridge Daily American*, Breckenridge, TX, July 18, 1927. The pistol Jeff Mynatt used to end his life was recently purchased by collector and historian Kurt House.

9. The *Healdton Herald*, Healdton, OK, January 25, 1945.

10. Phyllis Z. Knox-Housouer, descendant of an Indian girl adopted by G. R. Tucker, story from her grandfather.

11. The <u>*Healdton Herald*</u>, Healdton, Oklahoma, January 25, 1945.

12. Tucker unpublished autobiography, 1.

Bibliography
Books

Abbott, E. C. and Helen Huntington Smith, *We Pointed Them North*, Norman; university of Oklahoma press, 1955.

Adams, Ramon F., *Six-Guns and Saddle Leather*, Norman: University of Oklahoma Press, 1969.

Bearss, Edwin C., *Research Historian report, Law Enforcement at Fort Smith, 1871-1899*, National Park Service Library, Denver, Colorado, January, 1964. Butler, Ken, *Oklahoma Renegades: Their Deeds and Misdeeds*, Pelican Publishing, New Orleans, LA, 1997.

Canton, Frank M., *Frontier Trails*, Boston and New York, Houghton Mifflin Co., 1930; *Frontier Trails, The Autobiography of Frank M. Canton*, (Reprint) Norman: University of Oklahoma Press, 1966.

Canton, Frank M., *Frontier Trails*, Houghton Mifflin Co., Boston and New York, 1930.

David, R. B., *Malcolm Campbell, Sheriff, Casper, Wyoming*, Wyomingana Inc., Casper, *Wyoming*, 1933.

Davis, John W., *Wyoming Range War: The Infamous Invasion of Johnson County*. Norman: University of Oklahoma Press, 2010.

DeArment, Robert K., *Alias Frank Canton*, Norman; University of Oklahoma Press, 1996.

Drago, Harry Sinclair, *The Great Range Wars, Violence on the Grasslands*, Lincoln: University of Nebraska Press, 1970.

Ernst, Robert R. and Stumpf, George R., *Deadly Affrays, The Violent Deaths of the US Marshals*, ScarletMask Enterprises, United States, 2006.

Flagg, Oscar H., *A Review of the Cattle Business in Johnson County, Wyoming, since 1882, and the Causes That Led to the Recent Invasion.* New York, Arno Press and the New York Times, 1969.

Gage, Jack R., *The Johnson County War; Is a Pack of Lies/Ain't a Pack of Lies*, Cheynee, Wyoming, Flintlock Publishing Co., 1969.

Gard, Wayne, *Frontier Justice*, Norman; University of Oklahoma Press, 1949.

Hall, Ted Byron, *Oklahoma Indian Territory*, unknown Publisher, 1971.

Harper, Elizabeth Ann, Chronicles of Oklahoma, thesis, *the Taovayas Indians in the trading relations on the Oklahoma and the Texas frontiers 1719 to 1835*, for M. A. degree in the History, University of Oklahoma, 1951.

Hufsmith, George W., *The Wyoming Lynching of Cattle Kate, 1889*, Glendo, Wyoming; Hight Plains Press, 1993.

King, Robert, *The Marshal's Force : Biographies of Oklahoma & Indian Territory Marshals & Deputies*, self published, Seiling, Ok, 1990.

Mason, Henry F., *County Seat Controversies in Southwestern Kansas*; Kansas Historical Quarterly, February, 1933(Vol. 2, No. 1)

McCullough, Harrell, *Selden Lindsey, U. S. Deputy Marshal.* Paragon Publishing, Diamond Bar, CA, 1993.

Mercer, A. S., *The Banditti of the Plains*, Norman; University of Oklahoma Press, 1954.

Nix, Evett Dumas and Gordon Hines, *Oklahombres, Particularly the Wilder Ones*, Omaha, NE, University of Nebraska Press, 1993.

O'Neal, Bill, *The Johnson County War*, Eakin Press, Austin, TX, 2004.

Parsons, Chuck, Brown, Norman Wayne, *A Lawless Breed, John Wesley Hardin, Texas Reconstruction, and Violence in the Wild West*, Denton: University of North Texas Press, 2013.

Penrose, Charles Bingham, *The Rustler Business*, Douglas, Wyoming; Douglas Budget, 1959.

Shirley, Glenn, *West of Hell's Fringe; Crime, Criminals, and the Federal Peace Officers in Oklahoma Territory; 1889-1907*, Norman; University of Oklahoma Press, 1978.

Smith, Helena Huntington, *The War on Powder River: The History of an Insurrection*, McGraw-Hill, NY, 1966;

Smith, Robert Barr, article in *Wild West*, June, 2003,

Records of District Courts of the United states, 1685-2004, The National Archives, Fort Worth, Texas.

Russell, Joy, *The Huntsville Massacre*, Huntsville, AR, Madison County Record, 1908.

Tucker, George Redman, unpublished autobiography, *Life of a Lawman*, from the John Alley Collection: Box M-8: Folder 7-15, Western History Library, Norman: University of Oklahoma, circa 1936.

Letters

Cravens Family Papers, 1886-1982, Repository: University of Arkansas at Little Rock

Governor Wolf, Chickasaw Nation, letter of intrusions within I. T., 1884.

Federal Census Records

Arkansas

Franklin County, Boston Township, 1850

Franklin County, 1860

Franklin County, 1870

Oklahoma

Anderson County, 1920

Carter County, 1910, 1920, 1930, 1940

Jefferson County, 1910, 1920

Anderson County, 1910, 1920, 1930

Woodward County, 1900.

Texas

Cooke County, 1880

Hill County, 1870, 1880

Donley County, 1920

Lamar County, 1900

Montague County, 1880, 1900

Wyoming

Douglas, 1900. 1920

Interviews

Carlile-Brown, Bettie: stories remembered from her Cherokee grandmother Angeline Tucker, whose tribal name was Hokie, a niece of George R. Tucker, August, 2014.

Galonska, Juliet, National Park Service, Fort Smith, AR, April 25, 2014.

Griffin, Ron, family history of the Faulkner family.
Selfridge, Jennie, Federal Field Worker, interview of George Tucker, February 17, 1937..

Tower, Mike, Oklahoma historian and author; April 30, 2014, June 10, 2015, October 20, 2016, and other dates concerning laws, regulations, and the functioning of the U.S. marshals and deputies during the 1800s.

Tucker, Tommy, telephone interview, May 14, 2012. He is a grandson of George Tucker.

Personal Correspondence

Barnes, Travis, email correspondence September 10, 2017.

Barnes, Justin, email correspondence, September, 2017 and January, 2018.

Ernst, Robert, written communication on February 15, 2017.

House, Kurt, email correspondence, June 10, 2018, with report on Mynatt's death.

Knox-Housouer, Phyllis Z, written communication. She is a descendant of the Indian girl adopted by G. R. Tucker; a story from her grandfather.

Little, J. D., Madison County, Arkansas Historian, handwritten report, 1973.

Parsons, Chuck, author, numerous emails and phone conversations.

Schroeder, P. H., Historian and author. December, 2016.

Tower, Mike, email correspondence of court records of the Watson gang.

Newspapers

Brenham Daily Banner, Brenham, TX, April 19, 1889.

Breckenridge Daily American, Breckenridge, TX, July 18, 1927.

Bryan Morning Eagle, Bryan, TX, June 13, 1899.

Cheyenne Transporter, Darlington, I. T., April 15, 1885.

Chicago Daily Tribune, Chicago, IL, September 25, 1887.

Daily Globe, St. Paul, MI, December 25, 1888.

Denton County News, Denton, TX, December 8, 1892.

Dallas Morning News, Dallas, TX, June 24,1887.

Dallas Morning News, Dallas, TX, May 16, 1889.

Dallas Morning News, Dallas, TX, October 10, 1889.

Dallas Morning News, Dallas, TX, October 1, 1891.

Dallas Morning News, Dallas, TX, December 1, 1892.

Fort Smith Elevator, Fort Smith, AR, February 22, 1882.

Fort Smith Elevator, Fort Smith, AR, April 20, 1888.

Fort Smith Elevator, Fort Smith, AR, November 2, 1888.

Fort Worth Daily Gazette, Fort Worth, TX, March 28, 1885.

Fort Worth Daily Gazette, Fort Worth, TX, January 23, 1886.

Fort Worth Daily Gazette, Fort Worth, TX June 27, 1887.

Fort Worth Daily Gazette, Fort Worth, TX, March 30, 1892.

Galveston Daily News, Galveston, TX, December 25, 1886.

Galveston Daily News, Galveston, TX, May 18, 1890.

Gainesville Daily Hesperian, Gainesville, TX, January 29, 1888.

Gainesville Daily Hesperian, Gainesville, TX, August 20, 1889.

Gainesville Daily Hesperian, Gainesville, TX, November 2, 1889.

Gainesville Daily Hesperian, Gainesville, TX, November 3, 1889.

Hamilton Daily Democrat, Hamilton, OH, February 17, 1887.

Honey Grove Signal, Honey Grove, TX, July 14, 1893

Indian Chieftain, Vinita, I. T., November 21, 1889.

Madison County Record, Huntsville, AR, January 31, 1908.

Our Brother In Red, Muskogee, I. T., December 21, 1889.

Our Brother In Red, Muskogee, I. T., December 26, 1889.

Stevens Point Daily Journal, Stevens Point, WI, February 10, 1913.

Sugden Leader, Chickasaw Nation, I. T., September 17, 1904.

Sundance News, Cheyenne, Wyoming, May 12, 1892.

Temple Weekly Times. Temple, TX, October 9, 1891.

Territorial Topic, Purcell, I. T., November 28, 1889.

Territorial Topic, Purcell, I. T., December 26, 1889.

Territorial Topic, Purcell, I. T., April 23, 1891.

Territorial Topic, Purcell, I. T., November 5, 1891

The Daily Ardmoreite, Ardmore, I. T., June 14, 1896.

The Daily Ardmoreite, Ardmore, I. T., March 24, 1898.

The Daily Ardmoreite, Ardmore, I. T., January 16, 1902.

The Daily Hesperian, Ardmore, I. T., April 21, 1892.

The Guthrie Daily Leader, I. T., June 7, 1896.

The Healdton Herald, Healdton, OK, January 25, 1945.

The Indian Chieftain, Vinita, I.T., January 9, 1896

The Lancet, Norman, OK, July 26, 1904.

The Muskogee Phoenix, Muskogee, I. T., November 10, 1892.

The Paris News, February 29, 1920.

The Seattle star, Seattle, WA, September 16, 1899.

The Sherman Daily Register, Sherman, TX, April 14, 1887.

The Telephone, Tahlequah, I. T., March 1, 1895.

Waurika News-Democrat, Waurika, OK, Aug 2, 1946.

Historical Markers
Headstone marker, considered historic, displaying the names Burk and Tucker and states double burial in Ballinger cemetery, Madison County, Arkansas.

Articles
Cash, Marie, "Arkansas Achieves Statehood," *Arkansas Historical Quarterly*. Arkansas Historical Association. December, 1943.

Douglas, C. L., *Famous Texas Feuds*, Turner Publications, Dallas, TX, 1936.

Kelly, Charles Jr., Article: *Deputy Marshal pay*, Fort Smith, AR, 1966.

Lyon, Owen, "The Trail of the Quapaw," *Arkansas Historical Quarterly*, Arkansas Historical Association, Autumn 1950.

Other

Congressional Record, 49th Congress, 1st session, Vol. 17, Part 1, page 361 (Dec. 21, 1885) and Part 5, Page 4776 (May 21, 1886).

Congressional Record, 51st Cong., 1st session., vol. 21, pt. 1, p199 (Dec, 16, 1889) and pt. 2, p1205, (Feb 11, 1890),

Congressional Record, 53rd Cong., 2nd Sess., Vol. 26, pt. 1, p. 524 (Jan. 8, 1894 and p. 820 (Jan. 15, 1894).

Congressional Record, 55th cong., 2d sess., vol. 31, pt. 1, p. 293 (Dec. 18, 1897) and p. 479 (Jan. 10, 1898).

Criminal Cases, Defendant Jacket Files for U. S. District Court Western Division of Arkansas, Fort Smith Division, 1866-1900. The National Archives, Fort Worth, Texas.

History of Agent Owen at Wikipedia https://en.wikipedia.org/wiki/ Indian_agent.

Index to Leavenworth Federal Penitentiary Inmate Case Files, 1895-1931; National Archives, Kansas City, Missouri.

Texas death certificate on James Faulkner.

Texas State Historical Association; Col. A. H. Belo is believed to be the first person in Texas to use the telephone. On March 18, 1878, he had a line installed between his newspaper office and his Galveston home.

Index

Symbols

8th Missouri Calvary 7

A

Abilene, Texas 100
Abner, John 56
Abney, John 38
Act of 1895 198
Ada Evening News (newspaper) 199
Adams, Ramon F. 155
Alabama (state of) 13, 69, 214
Alamogordo, New Mexico 208
Alexander Boarman 138
Al Jennings Gang 200
Alley, John 10, 161
Alley, Major 100, 209
Allison Gang 80-82
Allison, Jim 80-81
Anadarko, Okla. 32, 106, 180-181, 194-195
Anderson County, Texas 206
Angelina County, Texas 88
Antlers, Oklahoma 205
Arapaho (tribe) 18, 108
Arbuckle Mountains 70, 74, 93
Arkansas River 1, 5, 8
Arkansas (state of) 1-5, 7,-10, 13-16,
        41-44, 46, 48-52, 55-56, 58, 61,
        63-64, 66, 76-77, 90, 99, 121, 123,
        141, 162, 174, 186, 200
Armstrong, William 159
Arthur, Pres. Chester A. 99
Atlee, Oklahoma 123-124, 174-175, 201
Avis, Frank 56
Avis, James 56
Ayers, Jacob T. "Jake" 41-42, 217

B

Bagwell, William H. (Bagwill) 22, 56
Bagwill, Angelina 23
Bagwill, Joseph 23

Bagwill, William H. (Bagwell) 22, 23, 38
Baker, Sam 133
Banditti of the Plains (book) 27, 154,
        209
Barber, Gov. Amos 171
Bardwell, Bob 115
Bardwell, Kentucky 184
Barling, Bob 159-160
Barling, Jerry 159
Barlin, J. 159
Barlin, Robert 160
Barlow Gang 81
Barlow, John 81
Barnes, Justin 178-179
Barnes, Mr. 27, 178-179
Barrett, Judge 147
Beard, William L. 64, 66
Beavers, Gid 69
Beck, Ellen (Lynch) 63
Beech Grove, Arkansas 6, 9
Beenblossom, Zeno 136
Belcher, Texas 113
Bellvue, Texas 133
Benbrook, Texas 133
Berry, Dick 14
Berry, Howard K. 115
B. F. Melton & Company 87
Bill Tucker 123
Birmingham, Bud 113
Bitter Creek, Oklahoma 31
Black, William 38, 56
Blevins, Captain 4
Blue, Bud 174
Bollinger Cemetery (Madison County
        Ark.) 3
Booker, Dave 6, 9, 152, 158-161, 173, 180
Boone, Thomas 60
Boston Mountains 1
Boston Township, Arkansas 8
Bounds, Jim 95
Bowie, Charley 4, 109-112

Author Bio

Norman Wayne Brown is coauthor of *A Lawless Breed, John Wesley Hardin, Texas Reconstruction, and Violence in the Wild West.* Norman has written six books and numerous magazine articles. He writes for *True West* magazine, *Tombstone Epitaph*, and *Journal of Wild West History Association.* He is retired from the Air Force and is a disabled veteran. His second career was with the Texas state parole board and upon retirement he started writing about Texas and the old west. He resides near Justiceburg, Texas, with his wife Bettie and pets.